Power, Patronage, and
Political Violence

Power, Patronage, and Political Violence

State Building on a
Brazilian Frontier, 1822-1889

JUDY BIEBER

University of Nebraska Press
Lincoln and London

Library of Congress Cataloging-in-Publication Data
Bieber, Judy.
Power, patronage, and political violence: state building
on a Brazilian frontier, 1822–1889 / Judy Bieber.
p.   cm.
Includes bibliographical references (p.   ) and index.
ISBN 0-8032-1297-6 (cloth: alk. paper)
1. Minas Gerais (Brazil)—Politics and government—19th century.
2. Patronage, Political—Brazil—Minas Gerais—History—19th century.
3. Power (Social sciences)—Brazil—Minas Gerais—History—19th century.
4. Municipal government—Brazil—Mineas Gerais—History—19th century.
5. Political corruption—Brazil—Minas Gerais—History—19th century.
6. Political violence—Brazil—Minas Gerais—History—19th century.
I. Title.
F2581.B55   1999
306.2'0981'5109034—dc21
99-22581   CIP

Contents

Illustrations

Acknowledgments

I owe thanks to the many individuals and institutions that helped make the completion of this book possible. The Fulbright Commission funded field research in Minas Gerais, Brazil, in 1991–92. I also received financial assistance from the Jacob Javits Foundation, from the Teagle Foundation, and from the History Department of the Johns Hopkins University for additional fieldwork and writing up. A Title VI Foreign Language Area Studies grant allowed me to participate in an intensive Portuguese program at the University of Wisconsin, Madison. The Research Allocations Committee of the University of New Mexico funded follow-up research during the summer of 1995.

A number of individuals deserve special mention. Philip D. Curtin and A. J. R. Russell-Wood of the Johns Hopkins University guided this project from its inception. They also trained me in the fundamentals of Brazilian, African, and world comparative history. Franklin Knight guided me through the intricacies of Spanish American historiography and provided many insightful suggestions and comments. My colleagues Bill Storey, Helen Wheatley, Tamara Giles-Vernick, Michelle Johnson, Kim Butler, and Sarah Hautzinger lent solidarity and moral and intellectual support throughout my graduate studies at the Johns Hopkins University.

At the University of New Mexico, Howard Rabinowitz challenged me to think more critically about the meaning of language and political rhetoric. Betsy Jameson, Linda Hall, Betsy Kiddy, and Barbara Sommer provided support and friendship. Suzanne Schadl deserves special thanks for pushing me to read more theory. She has shown me that graduate advising can be a two-way street and has contributed to my intellectual development and the genesis of this project. I received valuable criticism in the final stages of writing from John Tutino, John Chasteen, and Jeffrey Needell. Input from the three reviewers who read the manuscript for the University of Nebraska Press was invaluable. I would also like to thank the staff at the University of Nebraska Press for their guidance and encouragement.

Severino Albuquerque and Mary Shils of the University of Wisconsin at Madison deserve credit as diligent and engaging instructors in the Portuguese language. I owe a great debt to Luiz Figueiredo and Janaina Amado for their friendship, for intellectual insights, and for enduring many hours of conversation in halting Portuguese in 1990–91, while Janaina was a visiting scholar at the Wilson Center and the Johns Hopkins University.

In Minas Gerais, Douglas Cole Libby ably served as my on-site adviser, providing practical information about the ins and outs of coping with the Brazilian economy and bureaucracy as well as providing orientation to local archives and libraries. The hospitality and friendship of Flávio Saliba Cunha, Jane Saliba Cunha, João Baptista Chagas, and Eliane F. C. Ferreira contributed to a relatively smooth cultural adaptation. In Belo Horizonte, I benefited from two separate courses in quantitative methods taught by Herbert Klein and Laird Bergad at the Federal University of Minas Gerais. The staff at the Arquivo Nacional, the Biblioteca Nacional, and the Instituto Histórico e Geográfico Brasileiro in Rio de Janeiro and the Arquivo do Museu Imperial in Petropolis graciously assisted me in locating key documents. The late Professor Hélio Gravatá of the Arquivo Público Mineiro provided valuable bibliographic suggestions. The staff of the Arquivo Público Mineiro were extraordinarily helpful in locating documentation pertinent to my study. Thanks go to my research assistants, Reinaldo Nunes Ribeiro and Natalia Além, who ably transcribed data from the parochial land registers and other sources.

Fellow students of history, Marcelo Magalhães Godoy, Anny Ribeiro, Josanne Guerra Simões, Marcelo Mafra Sanchez, and Vanessa Caravelli, provided many hours of intellectual discussion and companionship. Special gratitude goes to my colleague Tarcísio Rodrigues Botelho and his family. Tarcísio introduced me to local archives throughout the region that was once the *comarca* of Rio São Francisco. His family offered me the hospitality of their home in Brasília de Minas (Contendas) on many occasions.

Final thanks go to my family. My husband, Bill Stanley, provided intellectual insight, constructive criticism, editorial skills, innumerable discussions on the nature of state building, and above all the emotional support necessary to help turn a dissertation into a book. In short, he read drafts. My sisters, Diane Bieber and Nancy Bieber Savage, attempted to understand what they consider to be arcane intellectual pursuits and peculiar travel itineraries. My grandmother, Solveig Johnson, was a faithful correspondent when I was abroad and at home provided me with a steady supply of Norwegian cookies. My father, Herman—the "other Dr. Bieber"—provided emotional and occasional financial support throughout, despite the fact that he would have preferred that I become a chemical engineer. My mother, Doris, continually supported my intellectual aspirations and taught me that my gender should give me strength and not hold me back. This book is dedicated to her memory and to my father.

A Note on Orthography and Units of Currency

Written Portuguese has changed substantially in its standard orthography. In this book, I have chosen to use modern spellings, except when citing bibliographic sources and proper names. Even the spelling of proper names can be inconsistent within the primary documents, so, when in doubt, I have used the most common form. All translations of quoted material are my own unless otherwise noted.

During the nineteenth century, the basic unit of currency was the *milréis*, written as 1$000. A *conto de réis*, or one thousand milréis, appears as 1:000$000. At midcentury in the São Francisco region, the annual salary of an artisan was about 200$000, and a horse or a head of cattle could be purchased for 10$000. The milréis was worth about U.S.$0.50 or twenty-five British pence in the 1840s. Thereafter, it fluctuated, beginning a steady downward trend in the late 1880s.

Power, Patronage, and
Political Violence

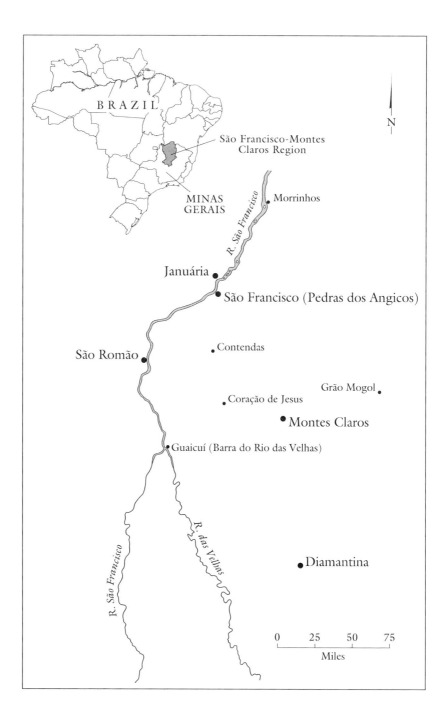

The São Francisco–Montes Claros Region of Minas Gerais

Introduction

Party spirit has killed public spirit; the merchant, the landowner, the police delegate, the block inspector, find themselves seriously regimented in one of the belligerent parties; the law is to obey the inspirations of one's party and its leaders. . . .

The most pernicious war, however, is waged in the administration of justice. Any criminal, if not a miserable unknown, has an entire party as defense and another as prosecutor; the arrest is labeled despotism, the accused is innocent, persecuted because he belongs to the party in opposition to the one that wields the despotic authority. . . .

A statistical study of our district and municipal judges, police delegates, and subdelegates arrested during our political struggles would be a curious thing. We hear that, in the city of Paracatú in 1849, the only criminal brought before the jury was the district judge of the comarca, accused of the crime of sedition; we read in the provincial president's report that, in that same year in Paracatú, eighty homicides were perpetrated. This fact proves that justice is impossible in a country divided by party hatred. —O Bom Senso, 26 July 1855

The epigraph to this chapter illustrates a key dynamic of nineteenth-century politics in the Brazilian interior: that political patronage and corruption of the justice system were intimately intertwined. According to this commentator, party loyalty was the ultimate arbiter, used to convict or acquit in courts of law. Constitutional procedures yielded before the will of local authorities, who used the policing and judicial apparatus to protect their political allies and punish their enemies. Within three decades after Brazilian independence in 1822, legal precepts and liberal institutions that had been introduced in the 1820s and 1830s had been distorted and co-opted in the interests of electoral politics.

Local corruption and violence were not products of rural isolationism but stemmed from regional integration into a system of national electoral politics that encouraged and even institutionalized such abuses. The Brazilian state centralized its control over municipal administration by midcentury and traded official positions for particular electoral outcomes. For the state, run alternately by one of the two national parties, the Liberals and Conservatives, the economic and social costs of patronage were low. The ruling party strategically allocated official positions in the police, municipal judicial system, and National Guard to municipal allies, who received little or no remuneration for their services. If these officials subsequently abused their authority, resulting in violence, upheaval, or injustice, the ramifications tended to remain localized and represented little threat to the stability of the state.

The existence of widespread violence and corruption at the municipal level calls into question the enduring scholarly interpretation of Brazilian exceptionalism. Brazil has long been highlighted for its so-called peaceful transition to independence under a constitutional monarchy. In stark contrast to the protracted struggles experienced by the former Spanish colonies turned republics, Brazil was seen as a model of political stability. Regent Dom Pedro I's dramatic call for independence on 7 September 1822 met only nominal resistance either in Brazil or abroad.[1] Although marked by personalism, a certain degree of autocratic arbitrariness, and some localized dissent, Dom Pedro I's reign (1822–31) ended with only minor upheaval when he voluntarily abdicated the throne in favor of his five-year-old son, Pedro II. The transition to a regency (1831–40) proceeded relatively smoothly. At the urging of a political faction, Dom Pedro II unconstitutionally assumed the throne in 1840 at age fifteen, three years before attaining his majority. His premature ascent ushered in nearly a half century of relative political stability, which ended with a bloodless military coup in 1889, the year after the monarchy abolished slavery.

Between 1822 and 1850, the nation pursued a course toward state centralization. That process did not occur in a smooth and linear fashion. During the regency of the 1830s, Brazil adopted a political system that decentralized power and in practice tended toward a monarchical republic of confederated provinces. Provincial strongmen seldom challenged the central state, although, in the 1830s and 1840s, a series of regional revolts did erupt. The social and political significance of these revolts is currently being reconsidered by scholars, who are challenging the benign nineteenth-century portrait of peaceful transitions and political order.[2] At the time they occurred, the uprisings served as cautionary warnings of the dangers of decentralized authority and contributed to a national political reorientation toward increased federal control and curtailment of local autonomy.

The Brazilian state strengthened itself with respect to both provincial and municipal government by establishing a system of machine politics using political patronage to distribute bureaucratic positions and financial subsidies among local elites. Crucial to this evolution were changes made in the structure and function of municipal government. During the colonial period, municipal councils had enjoyed broad discretionary powers, especially those corporations located in Brazil's interior, far removed from effective crown control. Imperial legislation passed in 1828 and 1834 curtailed the legislative powers of municipalities, requiring provincial oversight of nearly all municipal decisions.

Municipal autonomy came under further attack as central appointment replaced local election as the basis for holding most local offices. In so doing, the state gained control over the municipal police, judiciary, and National Guard. Municipal officials who secured their positions through patronage then had an interest in seeing the administration or party that brought them to power stay in power at both the provincial and the national levels. They enjoyed a structural advantage over political rivals outside the system because they controlled the formal policing mechanisms in their communities and could use those powers to influence voters and alter election results. Elite members of the opposition party, in turn, drew on their personal authority as landowners to mount private armies and overturn electoral proceedings through force.

Municipal politics, therefore, served as the linchpin of the liberal constitutional monarchy that superseded Portuguese colonial rule in 1822. The structural role of the municipality within the political system was crucial to Brazil's ability to maintain territorial and political unity within a constitutional monarchical framework. Yet contemporary historical analyses of political centralization and decentralization tend to deal only with the central and provincial governments and have underestimated the role played by municipalities. The process of administrative centralization and the creation of a national political machine displaced political violence to the level of the municipality, where it posed no great threat to the state. However, the social costs exacted at the municipal level in the violation of basic civil and juridical rights, the arbitrary use of public and private power, and the excessive use of violence would be high.

This study of the interrelation of state centralization and municipal politics in imperial Minas Gerais provides an empirical basis on which to reconstruct the nineteenth-century origins of *coronelismo*, a form of clientelist machine politics that linked rural power and patronage at the municipal level to state and federal politics.[3] Under this system, members of the rural elite, identified by the use of the National Guard title *coronel* (pl. *coronéis*), ensured victory at the polls for a particular party or candidate. In exchange, they received the power to distribute bureaucratic and administrative positions at the local level to their friends, allies, and kin. Coronelismo is most commonly associated with the structural decentralization that occurred during the era of the First Republic (1889–1930), which weakened the federal government and strengthened the prerogatives enjoyed by the states.[4] I maintain that coronelismo has its roots, not in the decentralization of the republic, but rather in the centralization of the empire. Moreover, it continued despite the relative strengthening of state power after 1889, not because of it. By 1850, all the elements of coronelismo were in place, consolidated, not uncoincidentally, at the same time that provincial challenges to the Brazilian nation ceased.

Centering the Municipality

Placing my study at the margins of the state rather than the center not only represents a theoretically and methodologically strategic choice but also reflects the centrality of municipality as expressed by politicians and intellectuals at the time.[5] In the words of the historian Thomas Flory:

> *Brazilian political liberalism of the post-independence period derived equally from a philosophic commitment to localism and a reinforcing strategic commitment to decentralization. Brazilian liberalism was thus strong and well founded, but it was also parochial in every sense. In Mexico and Argentina contemporary politicians argued over federalist reforms to guarantee or diminish the autonomy of provinces. In Brazil they debated the autonomy of the parish, and they did so because the dimensions of this smallest administrative unit coincided most closely with their social and political thinking. Morally the parish was the family slightly enlarged; politically it was the state in remote and extreme miniature.[6]*

In her sensitive and thought-provoking analysis of rural clientelism during the First Republic, Maria Isaura Pereira de Queiroz concurs, calling for an inversion of historical bias that emphasizes the role of statesmen in Rio de Janeiro. She maintains: "The importance of family solidarity and the role of municipal conflicts in our politics indicate the necessity to begin research starting from the municipality. Historians must break with the myth that a group of imposing figures at the court or in the federal capital commanded party conflicts, pulling the distant strings that moved the *coronéis* of the interior."[7]

Placing the municipality at the center produces a portrait of the "peaceful" empire characterized by a corrupt justice system, fraudulent election disputes, and violence. Changes introduced in Rio de Janeiro required profound adaptations at the local level. As municipal institutions lost autonomy, local leaders had to forge links with higher levels of government. This transition required a modernizing, ideological adaptation from kin-based, personalized politics to more formal bureaucratic and partisan alliances. The historiography of Brazilian state formation has failed to address this process adequately because it has focused on the goals of the center rather than on the responses of the periphery. Centralization efforts purportedly designed to promote national order and stability instead resulted in increasing levels of disorder, corruption, and instability at the municipal level.

State and Sertão

This study departs even further from traditional approaches to imperial political history in selecting as its focus a case study, the *comarca* of Rio São Francisco, located in northern Minas Gerais. The *comarca* was an administrative unit consisting of three municipalities, Montes Claros, São Romão, and Januária. It was originally settled in the early eighteenth century and served as a conduit for provisions and contraband between the gold mines of central Minas and coastal Bahia.[8] The area was, and is, a relatively isolated semiarid region with a mixed agricultural and ranching economy oriented toward production for regional markets. It was sparsely populated, geographically isolated, and generally poor and possessed few slaves. It is not an area well known to ordinary Brazilians, much less to scholars of Brazil. Why, then, choose it?

My interest in this frontier region grew out of a debate concerning the nature of slavery in the nonexport economy of nineteenth-century Minas Gerais.[9] While exploring police documentation in search of information on slavery at the Arquivo Público Mineiro, I uncovered an incredible wealth of material about the functioning of the petty bureaucracy of imperial Brazil.[10] These documents not only yielded information about the array of crimes perpetrated in rural Minas Gerais but also provided insight into the *mentalité* and preoccupations of local authorities. Sources left by other municipal authorities, including town councils, the judiciary, the National Guard, and electoral colleges, proved extremely rich. By revealing the dynamics of local government and administration, they enable the reconstruction of a social history of petty bureaucrats and political life on the municipal level.

My choice to analyze the dynamics of a rural periphery poses a challenge to much of Brazilian historiography, which tends to be "export-led," that is, driven largely by economic trends. Within this framework, coastal sugar-producing areas receive most emphasis for the sixteenth and seventeenth centuries, gold mining for the eighteenth century, the coffee sector for the nineteenth century, and industrialized, urban areas for the twentieth century.[11] To a certain extent, these scholarly patterns may be pragmatic; dynamic sectors and regions produced more abundant documentation, which remains more readily accessible to the researcher. The end result, however, contributes to the assumption that the sector that is most economically productive is also the most representative and most important in historical terms. According to an "export-led" approach, studies based in Salvador da Bahia, Rio de Janeiro, or São Paulo have more validity because these areas produced more, consumed more, and attracted more human resources.

In sharp contrast, the semiarid interior or *sertão* has been conceptualized as the very antithesis of the civilized coast. The term *sertão* originally signified unexplored or undeveloped lands and was used by the Portuguese on the European continent, in West Central Africa, and in Brazil. In Brazil, it came to be associated with semiarid, sparsely populated cattle range and to be known as a place of personal danger, economic risk, and possible mineral resources. Those who penetrated the interior could encounter either sudden wealth or sudden death at the hands of Indians, other explorers, or like-minded renegades.

The Brazilian sertão covers fully one-quarter of Brazil's land area.[12] Vulnerable to drought, the sertão suffered fifty-one years of total crop failure between 1692 and 1970. As a general rule, in only three of every five years does enough rain fall to support subsistence agriculture.[13] Because of these environmental constraints, few Portuguese cared to settle in the sertão during the first two centuries of colonial occupation. The only profitable means of exploiting the land was to raise cattle. The discovery of substantial alluvial gold deposits in Minas Gerais at the turn of the eighteenth century spurred the development of extensive ranching and intensified trade throughout the northeast to provision the miners.[14]

Coastal and urban dwellers believed that the unpredictability of the sertão environment exerted a deleterious effect on its inhabitants. The colonial historian A. J. R. Russell-Wood has aptly described the sertão as a psychological frontier that embodied the idea of limitless, unexplored space. It represented a potentially hostile territory inhabited by marginal types, including Indians, *bandeirantes* (*mestiço* frontiersmen and adventurers), cowboys, criminals, fugitives, deserters, and *poderosos do sertão* (quasi-feudal lords). The center viewed it as confusing, threatening, violent, and unorthodox. Russell-Wood writes: "It was barbarous, chaotic, unchristian, uncivilized, and hostile to those values and tenets—justice, Christianity, orderliness, stability, good governance—which the Portuguese held dear. It was a region forsaken by God and unknown to civilized man. In short, civilization and orthodoxy stopped where the sertão began. The concept was essentially ethnocentric, the conceit of colonial administrators, Catholic missionaries, and colonists who prided themselves as representatives of civilization as understood by the Portuguese."[15]

Although the sertão represented opportunity, it did not function as a democratizing frontier that mitigated class and race hierarchies, as demonstrated by Alida Metcalf and Billy Jaymes Chandler in their studies of the Paulista and Cearense sertões, respectively.[16] Those who arrived with capital and connections to the metropolis secured royal land grants and prospered. Individuals without influence, free but often poor and racially mixed, squatted or attached themselves to large landowners, hoping eventually to win customary rights to the land that they cultivated. For slaves, be they of Amerindian or African descent, the only opportunity that the sertão represented was the hope of escape from bondage. Both sertões allowed for some social mobility to and from the middling strata of small landowners and cowboys.

For coastal inhabitants, prejudice against the sertão survived intact the transition from colony to empire and acquired additional layers to conform to a Europeanizing rhetoric of modernization.[17] Imperial statesmen in Rio de Janeiro conceptualized the interior as a colonial hinterland in social, political, and economic terms.[18] The elite enjoyed greater access to Lisbon than to the sertão, and this was not merely a question of intellectual proximity. In 1850, it took only fifty days to sail from Rio de Janeiro to Europe but over three months to travel overland to the interior capital of Goiás. Coastal urbanity and export agriculture were valued; unproductive rusticity was not.

The Brazilian empire adopted constitutional monarchy as its system of government, setting out guidelines for broadly based suffrage and the election of municipal, provincial, and national legislative bodies. The constitution of 1824 borrowed extensively yet selectively from the French Rights of Man, promulgating certain individual freedoms while simultaneously retaining a slave regime intact. Imperial statesmen not only excluded slaves from the benefits of these new liberal institutions but also quickly came to question the ability of the retrograde *sertanejos* (inhabitants of the sertão) to participate in the new political system in any meaningful way. Consider the words of the Brazilian minister of justice from an annual report written in 1841: "That population does not participate in the meager benefits of our nascent civilization; they are lacking in moral and religious instruction because there exists nobody to provide it. Imbued with dangerous ideas of a poorly understood liberty, ignorant of the law, they laugh at the weakness of the authorities every time they come up against the whims of the people. It [the sertão] thus constitutes a part of society separate from our coast and many of our districts and villages and is characterized principally by barbaric customs, ferocious acts, and horrible crimes."[19]

The perceived laziness, irresponsibility, ignorance, and criminality of the sertanejo permeates the vast documentation generated by Brazilian bureaucrats, politicians, and administrators. Foreign travelers acculturated to a capitalist ethos similarly portrayed the sertanejo in unflattering terms.[20] The harsh environment supposedly engendered both personal vices and economic mismanagement. Lazy, shiftless, imprudent, and spendthrift, mired in *rotina* (careless agricultural methods), preferring the idle pleasures of fishing and hunting to the plow, frittering away meager earnings on drink, women, and gambling rather than accumulating capital, the sertanejo embodied all ills that retarded economic growth and progress. People of the interior tended to be of mixed racial descent, and this fact was frequently invoked to explain frontier backwardness. Such attitudes persisted during the First Republic, finding articulate and forceful expression in Euclides da Cunha's epic account *Os sertões.*[21]

The sertão was not considered a topic worthy of historical study until the late nineteenth century, when the historian João Capistrano de Abreu highlighted the positive role that northeastern transportation and trade networks had played in Brazil's national unification and integration. He even argued that the real Brazil lay in the interior and that the coastal cities represented mere European outposts.[22] In the 1930s, the economist Roberto Simonsen also recognized the important role of cattle ranching as a generator of independent capital and stimulus for interior settlement.[23] Vicente Licínio Cardoso, a prominent First Republic essayist, also emphasized the importance of the São Francisco as a counterbalance to the centrifugal forces of regionalism.[24] In the twentieth century, the sertão came to be loosely identified with the "frontier" and was incorporated into myths of national identity in a way similar, but not identical, to the way in which the frontier experience has been treated in U.S. historiography.[25]

Historians of imperial politics, however, still tend to accept at face value the biases about the interior inherent in the primary documentation produced by the center. Consequently, little scholarship addresses the political history of the Brazilian sertão. This poses a significant challenge to the researcher. Even the basic narrative of many interior regions remains to be written, and the São Francisco area is no exception. Back in 1916, Urbino de Sousa Vianna lamented that the "scarcity of books that deal with the sertão leaves us abandoned in an intricate labyrinth of doubt: we penetrate, without a guide, the interior of Brazil."[26] Regrettably, Vianna's observation still holds true some eighty years later. Only a handful of books written by local historians have been published since, most having little value for the detailed reconstruction of imperial politics in the São Francisco region.[27]

Like Vianna, I found myself lost in "an intricate labyrinth of doubt" as I worked my way through the manuscript collections of the Arquivo Público Mineiro. Lacking reliable and detailed secondary sources, my understanding of the political dynamics of the region grew one document at a time. Letters to provincial authorities that were written by town councilmen, municipal police delegates, members of the National Guard, justices of the peace, and magistrates provided valuable insights about how local elites defined themselves and their integration into larger networks of power and patronage. Gradually, through the discovery of more evidence, the dynamics of municipal politics came into clearer focus. The subtleties revealed by this local documentation caused me fundamentally to rethink the meaning of imperial politics and the relation between center and sertão.

Relocating the Center

This study also reevaluates much of the scholarship of the imperial era by challenging the Rio-centrism that has contributed to long-standing assumptions that interior populations were either politically inert or purely self-serving in their political objectives. Such stereotypes did apply to certain individuals and groups, but, on further investigation, the remote São Francisco region showed itself to be far more connected politically, ideologically, and intellectually to the center than I had anticipated. My sources contradicted assumptions voiced by nineteenth-century commentators and contemporary scholars alike, that the rural elite of the sertão adopted liberalism purely out of convenience or strategic interests rather than ideological commitment.

Conventional wisdom held that the uncivilized sertão was incapable of meaningful political participation. Because the remote comarca of Rio São Francisco presumably existed beyond the reach of the central government, statesmen argued that it was the site of some of the most violent political contests witnessed during the empire. On the surface, this region appeared to be one of the least likely places to be affected by state centralization. Local realities, however, contradicted provincial and national expectations. A strategic commitment to examine the "everyday forms of state formation" allows this alternative experience to become visible and significant.[28] Although existing scholarship effectively documents the violent nature of imperial and First Republic rural politics, its largely centrist orientation has caused it to emphasize certain explanatory factors to the exclusion of others. Analysis of the dialectical nature of the relation between center and periphery from the municipal perspective demonstrates that geographic isolation did not insulate the sertão from the effects of centralizing political change. In fact, this book will demonstrate that the level of violence that the sertão experienced *illustrates* how closely bound the region was to the central government and national political parties. Considerable variation did exist within the sertão mineiro, however, and each community on which this study focuses displayed differing degrees of political complexity, sophistication, and integration with or resistance to external networks of patronage. The political diversity expressed within the São Francisco region challenges the geographic determinism and blanket stereotypes that still shape studies of the Brazilian interior.

My methodological repositioning of center and periphery represents a deliberate and conscious choice, inspired by poststructuralist theory and the subaltern studies group founded by Ranajit Guha. Subalternity has been applied to anyone who is subordinated "in terms of class, caste, age, gender and office or in any other way."[29] Yet the term *subaltern* should not be invoked simply as the latest catchphrase to signify the oppressed or manifestations of resistance. Nor should we romantically impose subaltern solidarity on contentious historical actors located within a hierarchical continuum who simultaneously may dominate or be dominated, depending on context.[30] Rather, subalternity should be adopted as a tool to explore the dialectic that links the privileged and the marginalized and to uncover the strategies invoked by subalterns to resist, rework, and redefine elite opinion and ideology.[31] Although the term *subaltern* has typically been applied in the Latin American context to peasants, bandits, women, and the politics of resistance, it may also be fruitfully employed to analyze municipal bureaucrats, who are simultaneously marginal within the political system yet dominant within their local communities.[32] By exploring how these players participated in the process of state building, and by shifting our focus from the center to the periphery, interpretations of the relative strength or weakness of the state and its national political elite may be transformed.

Some critics of postmodern studies have contended that to focus on text over historical context often results in research that is empirically empty and burdened by impenetrable literary jargon. I hope to demonstrate that this need not be the case. Rather than freeing the historian from the rigors of the archive, the study of the subaltern demands intensive and innovative archival research. As the historian Florencia Mallon has pointed out, even Gramsci declared that the study of the subaltern "can only be dealt with monographically, and each monograph requires an immense quantity of material which is often hard to collect."[33] The challenge lies in the critical interrogation of documentary sources to rethink their significance. This commitment is reflected in the following eloquent statement by Mallon:

> The contradictory attempt to "know" the past, to become acquainted with the human beings who made it, leads us through archival sources that refuse to yield clear pictures. But because the archives provide unique clues about power relations, and about the human, moral, and philosophical quandaries faced by the people who produced them and by the people whose shadows inhabit them, we cannot afford to do without them. In my experience, it is the process itself that keeps us honest: getting one's hands dirty in the archival dust, one's shoes encrusted in the mud of fieldwork; confronting the surprises, ambivalences, and unfair choices of daily life, both our own and those of our "subjects." However poignantly our search is conditioned by the understanding that we will never know for sure, occasionally, just for a moment, someone comes out of the shadows and walks next to us. When, in a flash of interactive dialogue, something is revealed; when for a brief span, the curtain parts, and I am allowed a partial view of protagonists' motiva-

*tions and internal conflicts—for me, those are the moments that make the
quest worthwhile.*[34]

Not only is this study grounded in extensive archival research and historical events, but it also highlights the importance of language and narrative.
Both the content and the style of the language invoked by municipal bureaucrats provide important clues about how their understanding of political culture changed over time. Two years of archival immersion in the world
of rural petty bureaucrats enabled me to document changes over time in the
discursive style of political rhetoric in both private correspondence and
public forums. The meaning of such changes remained elusive for some
time. Most scholarship on nineteenth-century Brazilian politics assumes
that urban centers monopolized political culture and that interior towns
vegetated in rustic ignorance. Why, then, did many municipal bureaucrats
come to adopt the rhetorical forms of the center? How did they come by the
1850s to compartmentalize politics and administration as realms of endeavor
that were distinct and separate from their private lives, something that they
did not do a generation before? Why did some of them embrace the logic of
nineteenth-century economic liberalism, of order and progress, of thrift and
industry, and of European culture? Finally, as municipal politicians began to
contribute to the provincial press, how did they come to defend their political and personal honor in the form of histrionic, partisan character defama-
tions, a form of public discourse that dominated political life in Brazil's core
cities?

Such linguistic clues reinforced my contention that the rural periphery actively participated in the construction of political discourse at the provincial
and national levels, albeit from a marginalized, subaltern position. The urban center did not unilaterally impose a hegemonic system on an inert interior. Municipal bureaucrats and politicians did not idly squat back on their
haunches as politicians from Rio de Janeiro and the provincial capital, Ouro
Preto, issued legislation from above. Some members of the municipal elite
actively sought to participate, strategically adopting the political language
of the center to enhance their legitimacy.

This process should not be romanticized; interior communities negotiated from a position of relative weakness, and frequently they lost.[35] Nonetheless, the strategic invocation of certain forms of political rhetoric could
and did have political consequences. Adopting the appropriate language in
and of itself was not sufficient for success, but, in combination with integration into provincial and national networks of political patronage, it could
potentially yield returns in the form of funding and influence within re-

gional hierarchies. Over time, as the Brazilian state centralized, the space in which the municipal political elite could operate narrowed. Communities that chose isolation over integration, either actively or through disinterest, became increasingly marginalized over time, and this had practical consequences for growth and infrastructure.

By 1850, a political machine based on patronage integrated nation, province, and municipality. Imperial political parties tapped into preexisting patronage networks based on the principles of kinship, both real and fictive, and class differentiation. Some scholars have assumed that the substitution of the underlying logic of party for kinship and class wrought little ideological change among the rural elite in their understanding of patronage. If they adopted the political language and the concepts of the center, they did so for purely instrumental reasons, and as such that adoption represented a superficial veneer adopted for self-interest rather than a "true" transformation. Such formulations are overly simplistic. The nature and meaning of patronage did change over time in subtle ways. Moreover, as historians, we cannot ever discern "the truth" but, rather, interpret documents to reveal one of many possible truths. Documents do not "speak for themselves," but we make them speak in ways that are shaped by our own experience, training, and identity.

Municipal bureaucrats adopted a form of self-righteous, enlightened, and moral prose to describe their participation in a system of electoral politics that was characterized by increasing levels of violence and corruption at the municipal level. The tension between the ideal and the real lies at the heart of this analysis. Although political narratives cannot be taken entirely at face value, the ways in which their authors construct them serve as reasonably reliable indicators of actual strategies and partisan dynamics. Political factions in power accused their enemies of resorting to extralegal means to win elections and to escape justice. Those on the "outs," in turn, accused their enemies of manipulating their control of the municipal police and justice system to harass political rivals. Probably both sides were guilty of what their respective accusers claimed, and neither could afford to take the high moral ground. What is important for this analysis is not whether individual accounts are entirely "true" but that municipal narratives reveal the strategies used by those in power and those who sought to usurp them.

The structural underpinnings that upheld the unholy alliance between electoral violence and judicial impunity in imperial Brazil demand interpretation. Although I cannot claim that the dynamics revealed in the case of the comarca of Rio São Francisco are representative of all Brazil, I suspect that the three communities may provide a more accurate reflection of the lived experience of the majority of rural Brazilians rather than the minority who lived in coastal cities or provincial capitals. Clearly, additional local studies are needed. It is hoped that this research will stimulate interest not only among specialists in Brazilian history but also among a growing body of scholars dealing with the problem of local government throughout the Americas.[36] Although Brazil represented a unique example of a relatively stable constitutional monarchy, in comparison to its more chaotic Spanish republican neighbors, conflicts concerning political centralization and decentralization were common throughout South America in the nineteenth century. This study offers new causal factors to explain Brazil's uniqueness and opens up possibilities for comparative research.

Organization

This book is organized thematically and chronologically around the pivot of state centralization, a process that had been largely achieved by 1850. I use this date as a convenient, but by no means rigid, marker to analyze political change in the arena of municipal politics. Not only were institutional and legislative changes that centralized politics and administration in effect by midcentury, but also a new political generation acculturated to imperial political norms had begun to come of age. The book divides chronologically into two parts. The first five chapters deal primarily with events leading up to 1850, and the last three focus on the latter half of the empire, although some overlap exists throughout.

Chapter 1 sets the stage by documenting the ecological, geographic, and demographic challenges faced by the region from the colonial period to the late nineteenth century. It provides the answer to one of the puzzles that the remainder of the book will piece together: Why did Montes Claros forge ahead to become a regional political and economic center, leaving the river ports of Januária and São Romão behind? Chapters 2 and 3 put some of the pieces in place. As the empire stripped municipal corporations of most of their prerogatives, local elites could no longer operate autonomously but had to work through political connections with members of the provincial assembly, the main site of funding decisions.

Success involved two components. The first was the adoption of a civic identity consistent with the new tenets of liberal government. A comparison of the role played by municipal councils in Montes Claros and Januária demonstrates that the former adapted to new norms more quickly and completely than did the latter. The second component was the formation of local political societies and parties that could make connections to provincial and national party directorates. Forging patron-client relationships became essential in order to receive patronage in the form of funding and bureaucratic jobs in the post-1850 era.

Strikingly, widespread violence became a feature of electoral contests at midcentury. Previously, political violence had been comparatively rare in the São Francisco region, a fact surprising in itself given that violence was socially sanctioned in many areas of the Brazilian interior. Lack of political upheaval suggests either disinterest or that, in the decades immediately following independence, rural peoples considered state authority to be legitimate. Subsequently, statesmen in Rio de Janeiro created and consolidated dependent institutions of social control by midcentury, institutions that were used to manipulate electoral outcomes. As the central government became increasingly intrusive and top-down pressures to force particular outcomes grew, social unrest associated with elections increased.

The institutional and legislative development of centralized administration and electoral machinery is analyzed in chapter 4. Between 1822 and 1850, the imperial state gradually centralized the appointment of all municipal officeholders in the police, judiciary, and National Guard, thereby transforming them into benefits to be bestowed to loyal municipal clients. By making patronage the underlying logic of local administration and requiring officials to use their positions to deliver votes, corruption and violence became institutionalized. The central government, however, was unable or unwilling to see where the responsibility lay for electoral unrest and responded by attempting to curtail suffrage. Rather than blame the system, statesmen targeted the vulnerable voters, who were locked into economic relationships of dependence with local patrons.

Together, chapters 5 and 6 show how institutions of social control formulated by the empire worked in practice. The state expressed lofty ideas when it created a network of police delegates and subdelegates, a hierarchy of judges, and a civilian national guard but failed to back these officials with the resources they needed to do their jobs effectively. Moreover, many members of the elite used their public positions to protect allies, to get even with enemies, and to act with virtual impunity. Abuse of power was hardly a new phenomenon in Brazilian society, but partisan appointees were virtually impossible to dislodge, barring entry of a new administration at the national level. After midcentury, the medium of favoritism began to shift from kinship to party. Chapter 6 discusses some of the consequences associated with a corrupt judicial and policing system, namely, a generalized increase in corruption and violent crime, especially associated with electoral politics.

The implementation of a centralized political system yielded mixed outcomes, addressed in chapters 7 and 8. Chapter 7 examines how municipal actors experienced partisan politics, both in terms of their own political identity and in terms of their attempts to set appropriate boundaries of patronage and to define meanings of political honor. Regional bureaucrats and politicians were not merely strategic and hypocritical in their actions and choice of party. They came to adopt liberalism as a moral yardstick of acceptable behavior and began to make subtle ideological and ethical distinctions between the two parties.

The benefits of patronage politics are explored in chapter 8. Attempting to recast the image of the uncivilized sertão according to the political rhetoric of order and progress yielded only modest rewards. More crucial was the ability to get municipal representatives elected to the provincial assembly or the national Chamber of Deputies. Montes Claros excelled in this regard, electing at least one local son to every mineiro assembly from 1846 to 1889. In comparison, São Romão and Januária elected their own representatives to the provincial legislature only in the 1880s, when an electoral reform guaranteed the election of one candidate per ward. The difference in terms of infrastructural funding received by the three municipalities is striking. Montes Claros even came to challenge the supremacy of other regional centers like Diamantina.

In the conclusion, I summarize the social costs of adaptation and resistance to the political system that emerged in imperial Brazil. I argue that material rewards were modest compared to the high costs exacted in the form of politicized violence. The patterns that developed in the later decades of the empire were perpetuated into the First Republic despite the shift from a tripartite to a single party system. Factionalism, patronage politics, electoral fraud, and violence continued to characterize regional politics for decades.

Part 1

CHAPTER 1

The Development of Minas Gerais

In a short story entitled "Visions," published in the *Correio do norte* on 15 April 1888, the Conservative politician and journalist Antonio Augusto Velloso projected a rosy future for Montes Claros, then still considered an isolated municipality deep in the sertão mineiro. In the story, on waking from a fifty-year sleep, the narrator is confronted by a rich and bustling city, the *capital* of the *new province* of Northern Minas Gerais. After observing a number of thriving and modern industries, railroads, independent rural banks, and schools offering both technical training and the liberal arts, our protagonist exclaims, "What a marvelous utopia! Montes Claros, the capital! Northern Minas! Railroads, factories, churches, daily papers, so many things!"

These visions turned out to be plausible predictions, not just the fanciful musings of a puffed-up local politician. Although the province of Northern Minas Gerais never did come to pass, various proposals had been discussed in Velloso's day to create a new province called *São Francisco*.[1] By 1930, however, Montes Claros had become the unofficial regional capital of the north. It possessed a railroad terminal, a telegraph line, a normal school, banks, textile mills, and several newspapers. This progress is all the more remarkable considering that just a century earlier Montes Claros was a sleepy hamlet, a distant third in regional importance to neighboring Januária and São Romão.

Velloso's predictions contain both political and economic significance. The envisioned improvements in education, transportation, communication, and industry were typical aspirations voiced by imperial politicians. The possession of such infrastructure implied economic progress from which might also flow social order and political influence. The isolated co-marca of Rio São Francisco seemed an unlikely candidate for order and progress. It suffered from both periodic flooding and drought. Its geography, climate, and disease environment represented ecological constraints that could not be overcome, barring major technological and medical advances. Of course, geographic and ecological factors did not solely determine the political and economic development experienced by the three communities of Montes Claros, Januária, and São Romão. The region was integrated, albeit loosely, into broader patterns of settlement, trade, and influence established during the colonial period.

The São Francisco region was one of the earliest areas settled in Minas Gerais, first explored by the Spinoza expedition of 1554. Cattle ranchers from Bahia quickly followed, migrating inland along the Rio São Francisco.[2] Bandeirantes, mestiço slavers, and prospectors also traversed the sertão mineiro, opening a route from São Paulo through the Minas interior to Bahia. By 1707, twenty *sesmarias* (royal land grants) had been given in the area, many to reward bandeirantes for wiping out Indian populations.[3] Revealingly, São Romão's name commemorates a wholesale massacre of Indians that had occurred on that saint's feast day.

After the discovery of gold in central Minas Gerais in the 1690s, the São Francisco valley became an important supplier of cattle, hides, and salt to the mines and also served as a way station en route to the colonial capital, Salvador da Bahia.[4] By 1720, numerous small sugar mills marketed *cachaça* (sugarcane brandy) and *rapaduras* (brown loaf sugar) for local consumption. Traders extended roads from the mining centers to the northern sertão, one following the Rio São Francisco, passing through Januária and São Romão, the other along the Rio Verde, passing through Montes Claros. Slaves, trade goods, cattle, horses, leather, salt, and dried fish flowed southward, and contraband gold entered the interior, without the Portuguese government taking its share. The São Francisco region may have even generated more income and trade than did the gold district.[5]

The volume of this enthusiastic contraband complicates any detailed reconstruction of the political economy of northern Minas Gerais.[6] The essayist Licínio Cardoso has even characterized the sertão as the "tax-free zone" of the eighteenth century.[7] Sertanejos zealously defended their economic autonomy in 1736, when Governor Martinho de Mendonça attempted to enforce collection of the miners' head tax in the north. Prominent *fazendeiros* (estate owners) implemented a revolt and managed to set up a provisional alternative government in São Romão for a short time before the movement was contained. The sociologist Carla Anastacia has interpreted the revolt as a protest against a specific policy rather than an anticolonial movement per se. Her analysis of the sedition as a clash between private and public power, however, could be pushed even farther.[8] The north was a site of independent capital accumulation and the private rule of large landowners, beyond the mercantile pale and of nominal interest to the crown. Because it was nearly self-sufficient economically, it could afford to be autonomous politically. For example, one of the leaders, Maria da Cruz, capably managed several estates, had them policed adequately, and even promoted education and cultural entertainments in the region. The presence of public power in the sertão was neither necessary nor desired by its inhabitants.

This autonomy provides a stark contrast to the dependency that the region would face in the following century. The sedition coincided with the beginning of a temporary economic decline of the São Francisco region. As gold output peaked in the 1730s and gradually diminished thereafter, the economic focus of the frontier shifted northward to the neighboring provinces of Bahia, Pernambuco, and Goiás. Formidable mountain ranges separated the upper São Francisco from the mines to the south, presenting a daunting geographic barrier that few were willing to risk without the lure of payment in gold. The area also suffered out-migration resulting from the great floods of 1736–37 and the discovery of gold to the west in Paracatú in 1744. The São Francisco region slid into relative obscurity, becoming progressively isolated from the center of Minas Gerais over the course of the eighteenth century. At the time of Brazilian independence, it commanded little interest on either the national or the provincial level.

Development and Change during the Empire

An accurate understanding of the economic dynamics, growth, and change of the São Francisco region is crucial to the reconstruction of its political development during the nineteenth century. How could an area that seemingly had little to offer economically to the emerging state of imperial Brazil develop any degree of political influence or integration? This question applies equally well to Minas Gerais as a whole, which was long assumed to be economically depressed following the decline of the gold mines yet managed to play a robust and influential role in imperial politics.[9] Recent scholarship reevaluating the economic history of nineteenth-century Minas has revealed a pattern of economic diversification and non-export-oriented trade.[10] Far from being stagnant, the economy of Minas Gerais was able to sustain the largest slave population of any province in the empire.[11] It experienced impressive demographic growth generally, which contributed to the province's political clout on the national level.

Following the decline of gold mining, Minas Gerais experienced a fairly widespread silent "protoindustrial" revolution in the form of cottage cloth production and small-scale iron foundries. Weaving became an almost universal female occupation, and the coarse and durable "Minas cloth" was consumed in both internal and external markets.[12] Minas Gerais produced cotton for export during the first two decades of the nineteenth century and during the U.S. Civil War.[13] During the last two decades of the empire, twenty-five textile mills were established. However, in the 1870s and 1880s, railroads spread rapidly in southern Minas Gerais, lowering transport costs to the interior, thereby reducing the price of imported manufactures. Protoindustrial small forges and cottage cloth producers lost their competitive advantage in local markets and did not survive the transformation to industrialization. Some regional agricultural specialization also took place. The *zona da mata* to the south became an important coffee producer, increased in political stature, and was the major recipient of provincial modernization efforts.[14] The south, or *sul*, raised livestock for the growing market of Rio de Janeiro.[15] The *triângulo*, in the west, also became a producer of meat and dairy products.

This economic diversification, which the historian Douglas Cole Libby has characterized as a "process of accommodation to adversities," seemingly did not occur in the São Francisco–Montes Claros area, which remained the least commercialized and possessed the fewest slaves. Libby maintains that it was distinct from the other nine subregions of Minas Gerais: "The regions that constituted the immense mineiro north dedicated themselves to the same activities, but . . . commercialization was limited to a large extent to products destined for export. . . . One could say that the north was unable to achieve the transition to an economy of accommodation, as happened in the rest of the province. . . . The north continued to depend on more classically colonial economic structures. . . . In this manner, the north of Minas made great strides toward the miserable underdevelopment that characterizes it even today."[16]

In his study of the mineiro northwest, Bernardo Mata-Machado goes to the other extreme, describing the sertão as "precapitalist or archaic compared to the coast, which adopted capitalist relations of production more rapidly."[17] Further inquiry shows, however, that it was neither a self-sufficient, sealed-off, precapitalist Eden nor an inert economy narrowly based in self-subsistence, mired in colonial patterns, and divorced from regional markets.[18] The São Francisco region did expand production opportunistically to participate in minicycles of exporting such products as cotton and rubber. It also increased cultivation of basic agricultural staples during droughts in the Bahian sertão. European travelers attested to the widespread existence of regional and interprovincial trade networks emanating from the São Francisco valley and commented on the availability of imported goods. Although conditions of material existence were Spartan, they were not unlike those faced by contemporaneous planters on the expanding Paulista coffee frontier.[19]

The region also offered mineral resources of a more humble nature than gold and precious gems. The area exported tons of sodium nitrate to powder factories in Ouro Preto and Rio de Janeiro. Salt was also important to the economy of the São Francisco valley. *Barreiros*, beds of salty earth, yielded *sal de terra*, which was used to cure dried beef and fish. Historically, the cities along the Rio São Francisco had imported rock salt from Bahia and resold it locally and to mining communities farther south. This commerce was essential to the commercial well-being of the river port towns and to the health of the region's livestock.

The São Francisco area also participated, albeit on a modest scale, in the protoindustries discussed by Libby. At least one iron foundry functioned in Montes Claros for an indeterminate period of time. Cottage production of cloth was widespread in both Januária and Montes Claros, and cotton cultivation expanded after about 1850. Local capital funded the construction of a small textile factory in the 1870s.

The economic fortunes of the São Francisco region, however, should not be romanticized. The area suffered from a number of drawbacks, some natural and others man-made. Geography and climate presented formidable challenges to development. The terrain of the São Francisco region is varied, crisscrossed by multiple river systems and mountain ranges, interspersed with plateau regions known as *chapadas*. An uninterrupted navigable stretch of the mighty Rio São Francisco begins at the southern edge of the comarca at the falls of Pirapora and extends 480 kilometers to the Bahian border. In Minas, most of its major tributaries, the Carinhanha, Verde, Pardo, Urucuia, Paracatú, and Jequitaí rivers, are shallow and interrupted by rapids, suitable only for small craft. Only the tributary Rio das Velhas offers relatively unobstructed navigation.

The São Francisco river valley is separated from the Rio Doce by the Serra do Espinhaço to the east. From this range extends a vast plain of semiarid tablelands (*taboleiros* and chapadas), punctuated by wetter oases (*veredas*), that slopes downward toward the west. Its pastures are divided by minor mountain ranges.[20] The communities of São Romão and Januária are located at the edge of the São Francisco; Montes Claros lies one hundred kilometers to the east at the headwaters of the Rio Verde. The region has two seasons, hot and dry from April to October and rainy from November to March, with the heaviest rains falling in December and January. Rainfall averages about 120 centimeters annually, about twice the average of the Bahian sertão, but fluctuates markedly from year to year.

The comarca of Rio São Francisco was too arid to grow coffee or cacao. The dry and hilly landscape was best suited to livestock ranching, which required large spreads in order to be profitable. It also, however, possessed a variety of microenvironments, enabling the cultivation of varied crops, including sugar. During the nineteenth century, the Rio São Francisco's banks were still heavily wooded and fertile. In the river valleys, farmers practiced *vazante* agriculture, the planting of subsistence crops, cotton, and tobacco in the rich deposits of silt left by annual floodwaters. The drier *cerrado* supported manioc, cotton, and castor seed. Swampy *brejos* provided fertile ground for sugar, rice, tobacco, melons, and grapes. Hunting, fishing, and the extraction of natural products such as timber, medicines, dyes, herbs, honey, pelts, and fibers augmented the agricultural base.

The region also suffered from two major environmental disadvantages, flooding and droughts. Montes Claros suffered most from the direct effects of droughts, which struck at roughly ten-year intervals. Disease was another negative natural factor. Although epidemic and endemic diseases such as smallpox, measles, hepatitis, chicken pox, fevers, and tuberculosis were common throughout Brazil, some ailments such as malaria were particularly prevalent in the river valleys of the comarca and struck annually during the rainy season.[21] The remoteness of the sertão was both blessing and curse. Low population density slowed the spread of epidemic diseases—for example, although smallpox struck Minas Gerais five times between 1811 and 1874, the São Francisco region was seriously affected in only two of these outbreaks. However, geographic isolation limited the availability of medical aid to alleviate crises.

The unpredictable environment and physical isolation of the area also limited the range of profitable markets for agricultural products. The São Francisco region was located approximately one thousand kilometers from both Rio de Janeiro and Salvador da Bahia, too remote to engage in profitable export. Small-scale mills produced coarse brown sugar and cane brandy for internal trade in Minas Gerais and neighboring Bahia. Although the region produced a superior variety of long staple cotton, careless harvesting and packaging combined with adulteration damaged the reputation of the mineiro product in foreign markets. Transport costs also consumed profits except when the world market price of cotton was exceptionally high, for example, during the U.S. Civil War. The area did not generate sufficient capital to invest in technological improvements or to import large numbers of slaves.

The area also suffered from a scarcity of capital, credit, and currency. The first bank in Minas Gerais, a branch of the Banco do Brasil, was established in the provincial capital only in 1856, and it was a month's journey distant. Northern Minas acquired most of its currency from Bahia. This situation became especially troublesome in the 1820s and 1830s, when falsified copper coin from Bahia flowed into the sertão mineiro. Periodically, the imperial government recalled copper currency when it suspected counterfeiting and set up exchange houses to trade coin in circulation for new money provided by the government. The burden of currency exchange fell heaviest on the poor, who possessed only the small copper denominations. The effect could be devastating when coupled with drought and elevated food prices.[22]

Currency crises prompted a number of responses. Some merchants refused to comply with compulsory exchange, declaring the measure "anticonstitutional" and a "direct attack against property rights."[23] Others reverted to barter rather than accept copper coin or promissory notes of dubious value. Barter trade remained common, and items such as salt and cotton were used as currency. During times of monetary crisis, private individuals issued promissory notes as a substitute.[24] One influential cattle rancher issued small paper notes worth two and five hundred réis to make up for the lack of small bills in circulation.[25]

The São Francisco region attracted few domestic or foreign investors because of its economic and ecological limitations. In the nineteenth century, the bulk of investment capital went to the emerging coffee sector, which in turn provided tax revenues for the financially squeezed Brazilian state. The coffee frontiers also defined patterns of foreign investment and were the major beneficiaries of railroad construction and the development of other forms of infrastructure.[26] British mining companies also came to central Minas Gerais to exploit gold deposits that had been left untapped because of technological limitations.[27] The national and provincial governments were reluctant to invest in infrastructure in northern Minas because of its limited tax base. This created a negative spiral: isolation limited production, which discouraged the investment necessary to improve transportation networks.

Many of the problems faced by the São Francisco region were endemic to the entire province. Annual reports written by provincial presidents identified primitive agricultural methods, lack of capital, poor roads, insufficient labor, and difficulty of tax collection as the principal ills facing the mineiro economy.[28] Over the course of the century, the improvement of roads and navigation and the modernization of agricultural, industrial, and mining methods became top priorities.[29] Authorities from the São Francisco region attempted to tap into these provincial goals, but the region's perceived backwardness proved difficult to overcome.

The provincial government, in turn, was constrained by a small budget and the burden of constant debt. Public works were often started but not completed for lack of funds. In addition, municipal projects, approved by provincial assemblies, often floundered because of administrative changes between approval and execution. Lack of credit, limited internal markets, and poor communications resulted in undifferentiated regional economies based in local self-sufficiency rather than integrated markets.[30] It was these factors, rather than the supposed inherent inertia of the sertanejo, that limited the development of the region.

Land and Labor

The historical reconstruction of patterns of settlement, population growth, production, and trade is complicated by the fact that the geographic boundaries of the region were in a constant state of flux. When the comarca of São Francisco was created in 1833, it consisted of three municipalities—Januária, São Romão, and Montes Claros—and the judicial district (*julgado*) of Barra do Rio das Velhas.[31] Montes Claros was designated the administrative seat of the comarca. Each municipality headed a number of districts, an area of jurisdiction designated a *termo*. *Municípios* were also divided ecclesiastically into parishes (*paroquias* and *freguesias*). These units did not always coincide with their secular counterparts, and, over time, boundaries were altered to make them correspond more closely. No fewer than sixty-five clauses in provincial laws passed between 1834 and 1889 relate to administrative alterations and divisions within this particular region.[32]

Over time, administrative units tended to contract in size as the populations that they served grew. The comarca population grew from approximately 19,000 in 1825 to more than 70,000 by 1872, a rate consistent with that of the province as a whole, which tripled between 1835 and 1889, from 619,775 to almost 2 million.[33] However, the comarca diminished in size simultaneously, and it underwent a process of subdivision beginning in 1866.[34] Each municipality also lost districts: by the end of the empire in 1889, São Romão had been reduced from five districts to three, Januária from six to three, and Montes Claros from twelve to five. Territorial boundaries also fluctuated owing to the different rates of demographic and economic growth experienced by rival communities. Districts were created, suppressed, or incorporated by neighbors, motivated by local initiative and sanctioned by provincial representatives.

To determine growth on the municipal level would yield too imprecise a measurement to be meaningful, although the increase in size of the county seats provides some indication. Between 1832 and 1872, Montes Claros nearly doubled in size from 5,519 to 10,101. São Romão grew from 1,143 to 3,063. Pedras dos Angicos (São Francisco), which overtook São Romão to become the county seat in 1873, expanded more than sixfold from 677 to 4,310. The two principal urban centers of Januária, Porto do Salgado and Brejo do Salgado, grew from 1,570 to 3,893 and from 1,171 to 8,589, respectively. Population density remained low, less than one person per square kilometer as late as 1872.[35]

A sparse population, however, did not translate into greater availability of resources for all. Socioeconomic inequities are especially apparent in patterns of land tenure, patterns that were by no means unique to the São Francisco region. During the nineteenth century, access to land came through sale, inheritance, squatting, sharecropping, tenancy, or peonage. The historian Warren Dean estimated that, by 1845, 44 percent of the land in Minas Gerais was held by squatters.[36] In 1850, the imperial government passed a law requiring all landowners to register their holdings with the government. Affecting more than just those who held land through crown grants, this law also allowed cultivators who effectively occupied, yet did not actually own, holdings to file claims of ownership. The motives behind this legislation were to identify so-called vacant lands that the government could sell to interested Brazilians or European colonists, to force indigenous peoples to give up their extensive territories in exchange for small registered parcels, and to crack down on illegal squatters.[37]

Unfortunately, the land registers from the parishes of Montes Claros, São Romão, and Januária provide only imprecise and inconsistent information and have almost no statistical validity.[38] Ideally, the parish priest was to record the name of the owner, the location, the size and value of land, as well as the means by which the property was acquired; typically, only name and location are provided. Boundaries were defined according to natural landmarks such as streams, clumps of trees, and oddly shaped rock formations. Those holding small parcels of land or parcels with undefined dimensions or value typically stated, "I possess a piece of land on the following *fazenda*" (ranch or estate), suggesting that ownership was not absolute or involved obligations to the owner of the estate.

The majority of the population did not hold formal title to land. In the mid-1850s, the parish of Montes Claros had a free population of 12,220 but only 952 landowners possessed titles, distributed among 219 fazendas. Men, women, and children were registered as owners. Assuming an average household size of five persons, roughly two-thirds of the adult free population of Montes Claros did not hold legal title to land.[39] Population data for Januária and São Romão for the 1850s are inconsistent or incomplete.[40] The parish of N.S. do Amparo (Januária) had 619 landowners on 170 separate estates. In São Romão, only 561 persons registered parcels of land.

The land registers and other sources suggest a bifurcated pattern of a small number of immense estates and a larger number of small holdings. The estimated value of entries in the land registers varied from as little as 5$000 (£1.00, or 2.5 percent the annual wage of an artisan) to 5:000$000 (£1,000). Some properties were immense, measuring up to six hundred square kilometers. A few members of the rural elite also boasted numerous estates. For example, Lieutenant José Lopes da Rocha possessed property worth a total of 17:800$000, including an *engenho* (sugar mill), a water-powered manioc mill, a half league of lands under cultivation, and some two-story buildings in a district of Paracatú. In Januária, he owned another league of land on the fazenda of Itapirassaba on the banks of the Rio São Francisco with two hundred head of cattle and forty horses, a second league of territory called Rancharia with fifty more cattle, a town house, and thirty-six slaves. His kinsman Captain José Lopes da Rocha Castro owned property valued at 10:800$000. He possessed a fazenda in the parish of Morrinhos with two and a half leagues of land, one thousand cattle, eighty horses, a corral, and some simple houses. In Januária, he owned the plantation Bom Jardim (planted with wheat), a grain mill and a run-down sugar mill and ten slaves, two additional decrepit sugar mills, a few modest houses, and a half league of uncultivated lands worth another 900$000.[41]

Land remained cheap for lack of credit and buyers. One fazendeiro explained to the British traveler James Wells that his family owned a vast estate, including forest and pasture lands, houses, and farm buildings, but that the land market was so sluggish that he was unable to sell it for the low price of £200.[42] Conflicts over land were infrequent, except for the occasional dispute among fazendeiros. Aspiring landowners occasionally attempted to expropriate Indian lands as well.[43] Even modest land prices, however, were beyond the reach of many of the poor, especially given the fact that much land in the São Francisco region was dry and infertile, requiring extensive acreage or capital improvements to earn a profit. Many small landowners who registered their holdings indicated property values that were virtually insignificant. Registrants who did not indicate the value of their land may have owned even smaller portions. The tendency toward subdivision to less than subsistence size continued and intensified during the early decades of the twentieth century.[44]

Although formal access to land may have been limited, the frequent complaints of labor-hungry landowners suggest that the free poor did have alternatives that allowed them to meet their subsistence needs. The municipal council of Januária complained of "the existence of a considerable free and proletarian population that works as little as possible, sufficient only to sustain a miserable and disgraceful existence. . . . current laws aren't sufficient to oblige them to constant and regular work."[45] The authorities of São Romão similarly lamented, "Besides the lack of slaves, the free population don't want to subject themselves to labor because of the facility in sustaining themselves by hunting, fishing, and wild bees."[46] So acute was the need that, in 1854, the municipal council responded enthusiastically to a government circular that raised the possibility of establishing a penal colony in the region.[47]

Labor became less scarce, however, when rational economic incentives existed. Foreign travelers readily found help if they were willing to pay a decent wage.[48] Authorities who complained about idleness noted with surprise the industriousness of the local peasants during drought years, when food crops commanded higher prices enabling temporary expansion of markets beyond normal transportation barriers. Apparently, limited markets, poor communications, and lack of credit explain labor scarcity and low productivity in the sertão mineiro more accurately than complaints of sertanejo laziness.

Unfortunately, the activities of the landless rural poor remain obscure. It is likely that these individuals either squatted, lived on uninhabited land, or hired themselves out as occasional laborers.[49] Some settled in small villages and towns and worked as artisans. Female-headed households constituted

Table 1. Slave and Free Populations of São Francisco Communities, 1833–34 (unless otherwise noted)

	Free	Slave	Total
Montes Claros			
Montes Claros (1832)	5,001	518	5,519
Contendas (1838)	3,914	430	4,344
Pedras dos Angicos	556	121	677
Olhos d'Agua (1838)	719	212	931
Santo Antonio de Gorutuba	730	178	908
Tremendal	3,270	811	4,081
Coração de Jesus	2,603	650	3,253
Boa Vista	1,264	108	1,372
Bomfim de Macaubas	2,063	680	2,743
Morrinhos	825	219	1,044
Barra do Rio das Velhas	1,638	368	2,006
Extrema	736	628	1,364
TOTAL	23,319	4,923	28,242
Januária			
Porto do Salgado			1,570
Januária (Brejo)	893	278	1,171
Mucambo	578	239	817
Santo Antonio da Vereda	358	38	396
São João da Missão	481	189	670
TOTAL	2,310	744	4,624
São Romão			
São Romão (1838)	946	197	1,143
Santo Antonio da Manga	840	391	1,231
Brejo da Passagem	788	176	964
Senhor do Bomfim	392	132	524
São Sebastião das Lages	722	158	880
São Caetano do Japoré	1,566	520	2,085
TOTAL	5,254	1,574	6,828

Sources: Martins, "Revisitando a província," 27; Botelho, "Demografia"; APM, SP PP 1/33, cx. 287, 1 Aug. 1833, cx. 152, p. 41, 15 Oct. 1834.

approximately 25 percent of urban residences and in some districts could reach up to 40 percent. These urban women toiled in domestic service, worked as spinners, weavers, seamstresses, and laundresses, sold cooked foods, processed castor oil, and engaged in prostitution.

Capital and credit scarcity limited the availability of slaves to supplement labor needs. Although imperial Minas Gerais had an abundant slave population that exceeded that of all other provinces, including coastal regions producing for export, the São Francisco region possessed a disproportionately

Table 2. Slave and Free Populations of São Francisco Communities, 1872

	Free	Slave	Total	% Slave
Montes Claros				
Montes Claros	8,821	1,280	10,101	12.6
Contendas	13,403	543	13,916	3.9
Coração de Jesus	5,964	1,050	7,014	15.0
Bomfim	5,110	715	5,825	12.3
Olhos d'Agua	2,973	458	3,431	13.3
TOTAL	36,271	4,046	40,317	10.0
São Romão				
São Romão	2,829	234	3,063	7.6
Pedras dos Angicos	4,111	199	4,310	4.6
TOTAL	6,940	433	7,373	5.9
Januária				
Januária	3,761	132	3,893	3.4
Brejo do Salgado	7,914	675	8,589	7.9
Morrinhos	3,495	308	3,803	8.1
TOTAL	15,170	1,115	16,285	6.8
Barra do Rio das Velhas	6,701	484	7,185	14.8
Grão Mogol				
Grão Mogol	16,030	1,758	17,788	9.9
S. José de Gorutuba	13,132	808	13,940	5.8
Brejo das Almas	10,768	674	11,392	5.9
Itacambira	9,374	511	9,885	5.9
TOTAL	49,304	3,701	53,005	7.0

Source: Recenseamento de 1872.

low share.[50] In the 1830s, over 36 percent of the provincial population of Minas Gerais were captives, but, by 1872, that proportion fell to just 21 percent. Rates in the São Francisco–Montes Claros region, however, fell far below the provincial average, just over 17 percent in the 1830s and 7 percent by 1872.[51] It was one of the few regions where slavery definitively declined after 1830 (see tables 1 and 2).[52]

The São Francisco slave population diminished for a variety of interrelated reasons. Slave prices rose substantially in the nineteenth century, especially after the closing of the transatlantic trade in 1850. Moreover, prices commanded in the coffee regions of Minas Gerais, Rio de Janeiro, and São Paulo were sufficiently tempting to induce locals to sell their slaves elsewhere. Januária, which had the highest proportion of slaves in the 1830s, began to export its slaves after 1860. Several individuals in the comarca also participated in an illicit trade in illegally enslaved free persons between 1850 and

1870.[53] The economic effects of this labor drain are difficult to ascertain. Most owners in the region held fewer than five slaves. There were exceptions to this generalized pattern, such as José Ignacio do Couto Moreno of Januária, who possessed forty slaves. Pedro José Versiani, a fazendeiro from Montes Claros, registered 138 slaves in 1831.[54]

The rural elite could not afford to replenish its slave population, and it was not willing or able to offer wages that were sufficiently high to ensure that its demand for labor would be met. It did, however, possess noneconomic means of coercion. In a region with a large, transient, river-borne population and increasing rates of violent crime, physical protection was of paramount concern to most people. Between 1850 and 1870, free people of color risked being kidnapped and sold into slavery by passing traders. A powerful patron could protect such a victim's interests by appealing to the local courts. Landowners offered protection for their dependents in return for services and votes. Poor men could gain access to land by joining a landowner's personal security forces.

The rural elite could threaten the stability of poor families as well. Municipal officials had authority to recruit rootless "vagrants" into the military. The poor, unemployed, and homeless were especially vulnerable. To survive, it made sense to bind oneself to a powerful protector and suffer whatever social, political, or economic obligations that entailed. Over the course of the empire, rural dependents acquired some bargaining power of their own. Those who met the minimum property or income requirements necessary to vote exerted some leverage, albeit minimal, in the unequal reciprocity that existed between patron and client.

A Tale of Three Towns

Although São Romão, Januária, and Montes Claros all faced the common challenges of poor transportation and communications, inadequate capital, and labor scarcity, each would follow a different economic trajectory during the imperial period. São Romão's economy declined, and Januária remained stable, but Montes Claros grew and expanded, despite the fact that it did not enjoy direct access to a river network. Each community engaged in a regional trade in basic necessities that yielded a steady if unspectacular prosperity.

Much of the following information is derived from European travel narratives written by naturalists and engineers who faced the challenges of constant provisioning, hiring guides and porters, and arranging transportation and lodging. Such needs gave travelers a heightened awareness of regional trade networks and scarce urban amenities.[55] These travel narratives, however, are imbued with cultural superiority at best and smug racism at worst. Foreigners highlighted isolated cases of economic or cultural progress to support the view that the laziness and immorality of the Brazilian poor were matters of choice rather than the products of economic, social, or environmental circumstances. Such attitudes were not limited to Europeans, however, being also shared by the modernizing political elite of Rio de Janeiro.

Januária

Before the gaze of these "imperial eyes," Januária made the most favorable impression in the early part of the century.[56] As the principal river port between São Romão and Joazeiro, Bahia, it was active in the salt trade and the importation of European manufactures from Salvador. Traders exported sugar products, cereals, and legumes. The Bavarians Spix and Martius praised the cultural sophistication of Januária and attributed the quality and frequency of church festivals, plays, and impromptu concerts to the wealth generated by commerce.[57]

Januária was considered the most fertile of the three municipalities. It favored the production of subsistence crops and sugar over livestock raising. The São Francisco valley boasted the first sugar mill operating in Minas Gerais, constructed in 1694. Januária was one of the earliest major producers during the colonial period. Its small-scale, primitive mills produced sugar, rapaduras, and *aguardente* for local consumption and export to other provinces. Regional prominence continued into the early decades of the nineteenth century, as Januária marketed thousands of rapaduras per year and possessed the largest number of water-powered mills in the comarca. With greater access to distant markets via the Rio São Francisco, investment in more advanced technology was possible, yet a generalized lack of machinery and technicians and inadequate numbers of slaves hindered modernization. Januária boasted eighty-six *engenhocas* in 1855 and one hundred by 1870.[58] Riverine traders and peddlers marketed aguardente in local shops and taverns. Proprietors in the district of Mucambo even sent their slaves out door-to-door to market sugar products.[59]

Local producers traded basic foodstuffs widely to more arid points in the sertão. During periods of serious drought, profits could be fantastic. In 1860, for example, Januária's town council reported that local prices of basic foodstuffs rose 500–800 percent over the course of weeks as starving migrants poured into town. Opportunities for speculation in staple foods, of course, benefited those with capital and resources and weighed heavily on the poor, who could not keep up with such rapid inflation. Periodically, the municipal council intervened by enforcing prohibitive taxes and fines and careful regulation of the town market to keep speculators from exporting large quantities of food at the expense of the local population.[60]

The rural elite of Januária also sought to diversify its agricultural production. Its town council requested cuttings and seeds to propagate cloves, cinnamon, nutmeg, camphor, tea, pepper, and anise from the provincial government.[61] It identified such untapped commercial resources as the valuable woods *jatoba*, *cedro*, *aroeira*, and *pau d'arco*.[62] At midcentury, the municipal council of Januária proposed the foundation of an agricultural school in the district of Amparo do Brejo do Salgado. The council emphasized the favorable climate and soils, appropriate for the cultivation of even "delicate European vegetables," and the district's suitability for livestock breeding. Its abundant water supply would facilitate irrigation and provide energy to run modern machinery. The district of Brejo do Salgado also boasted native plants suitable for commercialization, a favorable disease environment, and access to ready transportation along the Rio São Francisco. The council glowingly described its natural advantages:

> *This municipality is, in the opinion of very competent persons, the most fertile in the province. . . . (According to St. Hilaire) . . . the lands of Salgado are inexhaustible and are the only ones in the province of Minas that enjoy this privilege. . . . sugarcane, manioc, and other subsistence crops have been planted constantly for more than 150 years in the same area, without the slightest aid of fertilizers. With plant rotation, no reduction is perceived in successive harvests. . . . A quart of rice planted commonly yields a hundred* alquieres. . . . *the sugar of Salgado is preferred in Minas and Bahia, to where it is exported. Our coffee, aside from being sparse and poorly cultivated, is nearly equal in quality to mocha. . . . the system of cultivation followed by the inhabitants is the most miserable, simple, and even negligent that could possibly be imagined.*[63]

Januária's bid to improve productivity through education and the introduction of new crops fell on deaf ears in the provincial assembly. There is also no evidence to suggest that any of the imported spice and dyestuff cultigens enjoyed any commercial success. The presence of mineral resources, however, did permit some limited diversification of the economy. Saltpeter production expanded in the 1830s, and, by the 1850s, Januária's six factories exported an average of two thousand *arrobas* per year.[64] Local officials also reported deposits of iron ore that remained unexploited owing to insufficient capital and high local interest rates. Manganese, antimony, and sulfates reputedly were abundant yet underexploited. Amethysts existed on Indian lands in the district of São João da Missão, but the inhabitants barred prospectors. Authorities periodically sent unknown specimens to the provincial government for testing, hoping to strike it rich or at least attract a little official attention.[65]

The municipality sustained an active commercial center, importing dry goods, tools, sugar, aguardente, salt, bacon, livestock, leather, cheese, marmalade, coffee, and basic staples from other regions of Minas and then reexporting these goods to neighboring comarcas and to other provinces, including Bahia, Pernambuco, Piauí, Goiás, and Rio de Janeiro. Municipal products like saltpeter, sugar, tobacco, and basic necessities were exported either overland or along the Rio São Francisco in canoes and barges.[66] At midcentury, the annual value of exports and imports came to roughly 125 contos. The municipality possessed twenty-four shops, twenty taverns, ninety-eight cattle fazendas, and eighty-six small engenhocas. It had no textile factories, but household production of cloth was widespread.

By the 1860s, Januária boasted seven hundred houses and a population of five thousand. It exported slaves to Rio de Janeiro. From Bahia, it imported dry goods, salt, pottery, armaments, and iron tools and, from Goiás, livestock, sweets, cheese, coffee, cotton, and some wheat. Locally grown cotton, sugar, rum, tobacco, rice, and manioc dominated its exports. In the final decades of the empire, it seemed that Januária was the only town along the Rio São Francisco that would retain any lasting importance. Carlos Ottoni, nominated district judge in 1877, described populous and prosperous Januária as the "princess of the São Francisco river."[67] Even James Wells, a fussy and critical British civil engineer, praised Januária, in a departure from his typically unflattering portraits of Brazilian rural poverty and inertia.[68] His colorful portrayal of Januária's bustling population of six thousand inhabitants, well-dressed and prosperous traders, bronzed cowboys, mulatta hawkers, and water bearers is worth quoting at length:

> At the landing-place there were a number of canoes, ajojos and barcas from both up and down-stream, bringing hardware, Manchester goods, crockery, salt and minor articles of various natures, brought overland to the upper and lower river from Rio de Janeiro and Bahia, and much of which will be forwarded to Goyaz from Januária. There were also dark-skinned sinewy boatmen of the river; countrymen from the Geraes; gaudily but semi-clad

washerwomen, black brown and yellow; naked moleques *(Negro lads) all chattering, smoking and expectorating. On the flat ground above are the long streets of brilliantly-painted houses and* vendas *[shops], the passing trains of mules, wandering stray goats and pigs, horsemen on gaily-caparisoned fast-pacing steeds, that stir up the hot dust of the sandy streets into thick clouds. Such signs of life, even with the many idlers lounging at door and window, or squatting on their heels on the banks of the stream, made up a scene of movement and business that I had long been unaccustomed to.*[69]

Januária began to lose ground, however, in the 1870s when its sugar industry entered into a period of crisis. Dr. Otto Wagemann, a German immigrant and sugar estate owner in Januária, blamed the decline of municipal sugar production on the sale of Januária's slaves to the coffee plantations to the south and competition with modernizing Bahian mills to the north. Backward technology combined with a slump in sugar prices reduced productivity and profits and limited mill owners' ability to pay competitive wages.

Wagemann offered a solution to Januária's economic woes. He had invested over seventeen contos to erect a modern mill and purchase property. Having exhausted his financial resources, Wagemann could not afford local interest rates of 3 percent per month. He requested assistance from the provincial assembly to purchase four abandoned mills bordering his property and to invest in centrifuges, vacuum pans, and other modern equipment. Wagemann then proposed to "offer these lands to the people" for cultivation of food crops and sugar, "thus creating an ample number of honest workers who will develop interest and love for the steady labors of sugar mill production." His bid to rehabilitate the free poor in exchange for a low-interest loan fell on deaf ears, however, and his request was denied.[70]

Wagemann beat considerable odds to modernize his sugar operations but was unable to negotiate successfully with the provincial government, despite the fact that it had subsidized the construction of modern sugar factories in other regions of Minas Gerais. The provincial government had even imported a centrifuge at its own expense, but it remained in storage for years because nobody was willing to pay the transportation costs of retrieving it.[71] It may be that the provincial assembly remained skeptical about the viability of reviving Januária's sugar sector, given continuing transportation limitations.

Sugar processing also exacted high environmental costs. The fuel needed to refine sugar contributed to deforestation in the area, which in turn could lead to erosion, worsening the effect of floods and also exacerbating the effects of drought. Sugar also exhausts the soil relatively quickly, requiring periodic replantings in virgin soil to remain productive. Multiple factors contributed to Januária's sugar crisis, a development that marked a turning point in the fortunes of the municipality, which began to decline in importance in comparison to Montes Claros in the 1870s.

São Romão

São Romão, also a port on the Rio São Francisco, never achieved the prominence of its neighbor to the north, Januária. In the early decades of the century, it was a simple settlement that housed about a thousand people in wattle and dab one-story huts and supported a small number of prosperous merchants. Its economy was based on cattle and the limited exporting of dried freshwater fish.[72] The municipality also produced a small amount of sugar but never became a major producer. In the 1830s, it possessed only four primitive mills and most likely had to import aguardente to supply its twenty-three taverns.[73] It reported a few primitive engenhocas at midcentury, precarious operations mostly operated by family or wage labor with rented cattle that barely cleared a year-end profit.[74]

São Romão also lagged in regional commerce. One report from the 1840s alleged that merchants preferred Januária over São Romão because of perceived disease risks.[75] Regardless of the reason or reasons, São Romão's commerce amounted to less than one-quarter of Januária's trade at midcentury. It exported mostly cattle, leather, hides, and diamonds but, by the 1850s, no longer produced a surplus of fish. Unlike Januária, which exported food, São Romão frequently had to import basic staples. The town possessed only seven dry goods stores, one *armazen* (warehouse), and four taverns.[76]

In the first half of the century, mineral resources remained insignificant, consisting of only a few sporadically worked saltpeter deposits.[77] Typically, mineral wealth existed only as a possibility, used as a bargaining chip by local authorities to attract provincial funding. For example, in the 1830s, authorities from São Romão communicated that untapped deposits of gold and diamonds could be exploited if the provincial government granted a subsidy to construct a canal.[78] A diamond rush did occur in 1863 when deposits were discovered on the border of São Romão and Paracatú. The fact that the value of some of the individual diamonds discovered exceeded that of the annual salary of a small farmer or artisan quickly attracted more than two thousand prospectors. The discovery contributed to the rapid depopulation of São Romão but also generated substantial commerce.[79] The profits earned through these mineral discoveries, however, were not used to develop the municipality. Migrants who were lucky enough to strike it big tended to leave with their newfound wealth. Benefits were limited to short-term profits earned by locals who charged exorbitant prices for basic staples and tools.

São Romão suffered from multiple and sequential natural disasters. Although it was able to withstand a drought in 1833 by relying on local supplies of fish, the drought was followed by a cattle plague that allegedly reduced the herds by over 90 percent. A flood followed in 1839, bringing malaria and local food shortages.[80] Three years of flooding from 1854 to 1857 provoked famine. The town was then hit by the effects of the drought of 1859–60. By midcentury, the economy of São Romão had begun to stagnate and was reverting to subsistence.[81]

Outsiders had little good to say about São Romão. In the 1860s, Richard Burton deemed the town "God-forsaken" and barely viable with three general stores, a single blacksmith, a garrison, and a greatly reduced population of 450 inhabitants.[82] Carlos Ottoni, a magistrate posted to the area in 1877, described São Romão as a "decadent ruin."[83] Owing to São Romão's decline, a neighboring district, Pedras dos Angicos, was able to convince the provincial government to transfer the municipal seat there in 1873. Although the citizens of São Romão resisted the transfer and some modest revival of trade did occur in the 1880s, it was insufficient to regain its former status. It exported a modest amount of dried fish and sugar and sugar by-products from its fifteen mills. Its manufacturing remained limited to a few craftsmen: tailors, carpenters, blacksmiths, shoemakers, goldsmiths, and masons.[84]

Montes Claros

While São Romão's fortunes declined and those of Januária remained relatively stable, Montes Claros expanded. In the 1810s, the Bavarian travelers Spix and Martius had been distinctly unimpressed with Montes Claros, describing the small settlement as "a few rows of low mud huts, ill-famed for its banditry, seeming not to possess the lovely virtue of hospitality of its neighbors."[85] By the 1820s, the town consisted of two hundred simple houses, three or four *sobrados* (two-story houses), several dry goods shops, and a population of about eight hundred people.[86] In the 1830s, the population reached one thousand, and the center boasted a square urban layout, church, jail, and roofed marketplace.[87] All visitors reported an active regional trade in livestock and leather goods and highlighted Montes Claros's favorable location on the road from Diamantina to Bahia.

The município of Montes Claros had a varied terrain of mountains, high plains, and river valleys but relatively poor soil. It relied more on horse and cattle ranching but was an agricultural producer as well. The predominant cattle variety was called *zebu*, a tough, drought-resistant strain with a humped back, apparently introduced by the Portuguese from India during the colonial period. In the 1830s, a group of self-defined progressive farmers in Montes Claros established an agricultural society that had as one of its goals the introduction of new breeds of cattle. Ranchers from the municipality demonstrated interest in agricultural diversification and experimentation. In the 1840s, the municipal council responded positively to offers made by the provincial government to provide tea, vanilla, and indigo seeds to stimulate production of new crops for export. One fazendeiro from a district of Montes Claros expressed interest in these exotic plants and in *cochinel* and the manufacture of soap from a native fruit called *tingui*.[88]

A few fazendeiros diversified and modernized their holdings, allowing them independence from foreign imports. For example, the fazenda of José Vieira de Matos, located between Montes Claros and Grão Mogol, boasted herds of cattle, sheep, and pigs, warehouses, water-operated mills to grind corn, wheat, manioc, and castor beans, a sugar mill and still, and even a small iron foundry. According to the visitor Johann Pohl, this "fazendeiro by vocation" maintained a fruit orchard that met European standards and employed up-to-date scientific methods.[89] The French naturalist Saint-Hilaire also commented on this owner's self-sufficiency, raising sheep and cotton for domestic cloth production and smelting his own iron. The Frenchman commented admiringly, "Except for salt, it was unnecessary to buy anything. Sr. Vieira was not, however, the only inhabitant who had so many things made to order in his home; many fazendeiros want their slaves to learn trades and, through this means, eliminate outside manufactures."[90] Vieira did expend some of his profits on imported creature comforts, serving wine to his guests and retaining slave musicians for entertainment.

Another model fazendeiro was Captain Pedro José Versiani, the son of a former diamond intendant. As a youth during the late colonial period, he had worked in the Diamond District as a courier.[91] He accumulated sufficient wealth to become the largest slaveholder in the region, possessing 138 captives in 1831. Versiani was one of the few proprietors to possess a steam-operated sugar mill on his diversified estate, St. Eloi. He also cultivated cereals for domestic consumption. His son-in-law reported that the property yielded fifteen thousand calves annually. Versiani also was sufficiently prosperous to buy luxury imports. He adorned his house with fine imported textiles, silk, lace, and silver utensils.[92]

Progressive members of the landed elite contributed to the wealth of the municipality. By midcentury, Montes Claros possessed a lively commercial sector with forty-six shops and taverns. Its diverse occupational base included 100 merchants (including owners of small taverns), 74 civil servants, 120 artisans, and 200 miners. Some primitive factories produced coarse cotton cloth. The largest, located on the fazenda of Canoas, turned an annual profit of 200$000 per year. Montes Claros exported thousands of arrobas of sodium nitrate to powder factories in Ouro Preto and Rio de Janeiro in the 1810s, and saltpeter continued to provide export income for decades.[93]

During the 1850s, Montes Claros imported and exported eighty to one hundred contos of goods annually from Rio de Janeiro via Diamantina. Local manufactures included saltpeter, leather, tobacco, cotton cloth, hammocks, sugar, aguardente, rapadura, cheese, cereals, and modest amounts of coffee and wheat. Although Montes Claros took second place to Januária in the value of its exports during the 1850s, it regulated its trade more effectively, collecting more taxes on the products that it sold. During the 1850s, its tax revenues on trade goods amounted to 52:815$315, compared to Januária's at 27:283$245 and São Romão's at a modest 9:453$612.[94]

By midcentury, Montes Claros had begun to surpass Januária in demographic and commercial importance. Initially a nominal producer of sugar, it had come to rival Januária, possessing one hundred mills, a few of them steam powered. By 1873, Montes Claros had become the regional leader, possessing 148 engenhos in its five districts. The municipalities of Januária and Guaicuí each reported only thirty-one and São Romão a mere three.[95]

A few other towns in the municipality of Montes Claros gained some minor commercial importance, notably its outlying districts of Guaicuí and Brejo das Almas, each with forty sugar mills. Guaicuí (formerly Barra do Rio das Velhas), located at the juncture of the Rio das Velhas and the Rio do São Francisco, began to expand its participation in the trade between Rio de Janeiro and the northern sertões in the 1850s.[96] A modest trade in diamonds contributed further to its growth.[97] However, most subsidiary towns in the municipality remained small hamlets consisting of simple mud and straw dwellings, their economic resources barely meeting the needs of local consumers.[98]

Montes Claros also became actively involved in cotton cultivation and textile manufacturing. Cotton was better suited to the semiarid environment than sugar, requiring less water, and was better adapted to marginal soils. It also did not depend on economies of scale given the simple technologies of the era. Small producers with limited capital could grow and process the crop on a modest scale. The variety of cotton grown in the area produced a high-quality, long staple fiber that held up well in mechanized textile production.

Montes Claros also managed to establish a textile factory in 1879, facilitated by a provincial subsidy. A local Liberal politician, Gregorio José Velloso, formed a society to raise the initial capital of 150:000$000, which required pledges from 145 investors (8.2 percent of them women) from Montes Claros and neighboring communities. Most subscriptions were quite modest. Sixty-three percent of the investors put up 600$000 or less, and, of these, 31 percent pledged only 200$000. The greatest and most costly challenge faced by the enterprise was not the purchase of the "most perfect and modern" machinery imported from the United States but the cost of its overland transport from Rio de Janeiro.[99] By 1883, the factory was transforming 650 kilograms of cotton into 900 meters of diverse fabrics daily. It employed seventy-two employees of both sexes, preferring homeless orphans. The factory also boasted a night school, funded by a government grant. Local demand for the cloth was brisk, and the enterprise quickly began to show a profit.[100] In 1884, the company expanded, building a warehouse in Pirapora (south of São Romão) for the sale of cloth and the purchase of raw cotton.[101]

The establishment of a textile factory in a comparatively isolated area with supposedly low levels of capital accumulation was quite a feat. Even more impressive was the reconstruction of the enterprise after a disastrous fire in 1889. Rather than take advantage of provincial laws that enabled businesses to use government capital, the Montesclarenses rebuilt on their own. In 1897, the journalist and politician Antonio Augusto Velloso proudly recounted: "The business had only its own resources, relatively scarce in an interior zone where wealth is very dispersed, consisting for the most part in land, and where credit operations are nearly unknown. In addition, it faced obstacles of every kind, such as the cost of transporting heavy machinery, the lack of technical personnel, and many others." The steam-powered mill produced twelve hundred meters of cloth per day and employed eighty workers, mostly orphans. It earned nearly 200 percent in profits annually.[102]

As the empire drew to a close, Montes Claros had acquired many of the urbane trappings of modern society—a jail and a town hall, schools, hospitals, cemeteries, and a textile factory. The local paper, the *Correio do norte*, rhapsodized about the arrival of barber shops and the first trolley car. The editor exclaimed, "Every day we progress closer to civilization, bringing to the inhabitants and the persons who arrive here the same comforts that are enjoyed in more advanced locations."[103] (Those visitors, however, still had to arrive by mule train.) At the turn of the century, the municipality generated a regional commerce worth two thousand contos annually in agricultural and extractive products. Local manufactures included cotton cloth, ceramics, leather hats, saddles, hammocks, tobacco, sugar, and cachaça. The weekly market attracted up to one thousand noisy buyers, sellers, and hangers-on, attracted by a wide array of local and imported goods.[104] Although a new capital of Northern Minas Gerais was never created, Montes Claros had become the informal capital of the north. During the First Republic, it never obtained a university, but it did have a number of secondary schools, technical courses, and an *escola normal* (teaching college). It published a number of newspapers. By 1930, it approximated Antonio Augusto Velloso's rosy vision for the future.

External factors also contributed to the ascendancy of Montes Claros and the relative demise of Januária and São Romão. The São Francisco River became a less decisive factor in the commercial landscape as the province of Bahia entered into economic decline in the mid-nineteenth century.[105] Towns located further to the east and south, such as Montes Claros, Guaicuí, and Pirapora, profited from the rise of Rio de Janeiro. Trade with Paracatú and Goiás to the west diminished as these areas made the transition from mining to ranching economies. Overall, towns located on the east side of the river grew and those on the west declined. Montes Claros replaced Januária as the regional center, São Romão gave way to São Francisco and Guaicuí, and Pirapora gained in commercial and demographic importance.[106] Pirapora replaced Januária as the most dynamic city on the Rio São Francisco. It developed an economy based on cotton cultivation, possessed baling and warehousing facilities, refined cottonseed oil, and enjoyed railway access to the new capital, Belo Horizonte.[107]

When the coffee boom came to Minas Gerais, the province began to modernize and develop its infrastructure. The construction of railroads and communication systems expanded from south to north. Telegraph and phone service reached Montes Claros by the turn of the twentieth century, but the municipality remained comparatively isolated, receiving news and trade goods by mule train into the 1930s. The extension of the railroad, first discussed in the provincial assembly in the 1880s, reached Montes Claros only in 1926, thanks to the efforts of transport minister Dr. Francisco Sá, a "son of northern Minas."[108]

The development of Montes Claros, however, took place in the context of the increasing economic marginalization of Minas Gerais. During the First Republic, coffee interests came to dominate Brazil politically and economically. São Paulo, the leader in coffee production, diversified and industrialized. In so doing, it flooded neighboring Minas Gerais with cheap manufactures, upsetting local production, which could not compete effectively. Although Minas Gerais also experienced some modest industrialization in Juiz de Fora, the state was reduced to being a supplier of primary products for the center-south. Ultimately, within Minas Gerais, the arid and isolated São Francisco region became a peripheral producer.

CHAPTER 2

The Marginalization of the Municipality, 1822-50

The comarca of Rio São Francisco faced formidable challenges to its aspirations for regional development in the postindependence era. The constitutional monarchy that ruled Brazil from 1822 to 1889 imposed a new political system from above that required substantial adaptation on the part of the rural elite. Although the constitution of 1824 expanded political representation and introduced relatively broad suffrage, subsequent legislation limited the powers of municipal corporations and authorities. How, then, were municipalities to develop the political capital necessary to secure the provincial and national resources necessary for the development of infrastructure and the expansion of local economies? How did municipal officials rework themselves to adapt to their reduced circumstances?

In order to understand change at the local level, the structures and ideology of the imperial political system require some initial analysis.[1] When Brazil declared its independence in 1822, it consisted of a group of disparate regions each with its distinct identity. Under colonial rule, the various captaincies had been discouraged from communicating with one another, and each developed stronger ties to Lisbon than to its neighbors. Out of this patchwork, the architects of independence had to construct a nation. Against formidable odds, Brazil retained its political and territorial unity. Only recently have scholars begun seriously to question Brazil's "exceptionalism" (in comparison to the fragmentation of the Spanish republics) and to take a closer look at the regional challenges that erupted throughout Brazil in the 1830s and 1840s.[2]

Brazil did have one advantage, a national elite that was unified in class and education. No universities had been established in the colony, so members of the elite had to send their sons to Portugal to Coimbra University. This system provided an opportunity for prominent members of society from different regions to meet and served as a glue to hold together the immediate postindependence state.[3] This political elite assisted the self-proclaimed Emperor Dom Pedro I to create an independent nation that retained considerable continuity with colonial society beneath the surface of new liberal institutions. Brazil was a slave society, and the new state depended on export taxes levied on tropical commodities for much of its revenues. In order to assure a smooth, unified political transition, traditional planters needed to retain their captives.

Liberalism as it developed in Brazil was an amalgam of borrowed European precedents and traditional colonial privilege. The constitution of 1824 drew on the French Rights of Man with modifications to allow for the perpetuation of slavery and monarchical rule. Free trade and property rights received considerably more support than did democratic reforms.[4] The leaders of the new nation were more concerned with the consolidation of a strong, unified state and the economic and political integration of the center-south than in promoting representative institutions.[5] Key to the developing Brazilian conception of liberalism was a modernizing ideology that emphasized order, progress, and, eventually, the adoption of European culture.[6]

Concessions to elite interests reflect the circumstances behind the constitution's creation. A constituent assembly had been convened in 1823, but, impatient with its slow pace, and apprehensive about the projected limitation of his personal powers, Dom Pedro I had it disbanded. The revised constitution drafted by the Council of State followed the original version but with some important modifications that granted the emperor more extensive prerogatives. Freedom of the press, representative government, equal rights under the law for the free population, and the guarantee of trial by jury were among the most democratic reforms.

The constitution divided government into four branches: the executive, legislative, judicial, and monarchical. The emperor was invested with the moderating power (*poder moderador*), allowing him arbitrarily to dissolve the parliament and to nominate senators, thereby limiting the autonomy of elected representatives. The executive and legislative powers consisted of an elected Chamber of Deputies, an appointed Senate and Cabinet, and the Council of State. Provinces elected representative councils (*conselhos gerais*), which were supervised by centrally appointed provincial presidents.

The electoral system operated indirectly through the establishment of electoral colleges that selected provincial and national representatives. The constitution allowed for a fairly broadly based electorate, comprising slightly over 50 percent of the adult free male population by 1872.[7] Property requirements were minimal, and suffrage was contingent on neither race nor literacy. All free adult male Brazilian citizens, by birth or naturalization, enjoyed *votante* status if they earned a minimum annual income of 100$000, a requirement that most artisans and small holders could meet. The minimum voting age was twenty-five years, except for married men, military officers, university graduates, or priests, who could vote at twenty-one.

Despite the establishment of new representative institutions, Dom Pedro I frequently acted autocratically during the 1820s, imposing his authority through an appointed Council of State.[8] His favoritism toward Portuguese-born advisers, his preoccupation with the royal succession in Portugal, and the drawn-out Cisplatine War added to his growing unpopularity. By 1828, nativist *exaltados* began to organize street protests against him. Dom Pedro I abdicated in 1831, and a three-member regency was appointed to rule until his five-year-old son, Dom Pedro II, attained his majority. During the regency (1831–40), ethnic and ideological differentiation between political factions became more pronounced. Some of the less extreme nativists and Brazilian-born Coimbra graduates formed the *moderado* party. Defenders of traditional privilege, many of them Portuguese born, formed the Restorationist party (*caramarús*), which called for the return of Dom Pedro I. Radical and stridently anti-Portuguese exaltados became increasingly marginalized.

After the death of the exiled Dom Pedro I in Portugal in 1834, the moderado marriage of convenience broke down. A series of regional revolts in the 1830s further widened the split between nativists, who favored a more decentralized form of government, and conservatives, who advocated strengthening the power of the center. By the late 1830s, more distinct political parties began to emerge.[9] Liberals favored broader voting rights, greater power of elected officers, expanded local powers, increased freedom of trade, and stronger guarantees for individual choice. Conservatives emphasized monarchical and constitutional authority, empowering jurists and magistrates, centralizing fiscal authority, and limiting suffrage. The relative degree of state centralization was the point of greatest contention between Liberals and Conservatives, especially during the formative decades of the 1830s and 1840s.[10]

Some historians maintain that the regency was a period of informal "republican" decentralization operating within an overarching monarchical framework.[11] Although a formal shift to a united federation of provinces within a republican model never occurred, regents and politicians experimented with a number of reforms that strengthened regional power at the expense of the center. One of the major triumphs of this "Liberal decade" was the Additional Act to the Constitution, passed in 1834. The act has long been interpreted as a major decentralizing victory because it conceded greater administrative and financial autonomy to the provinces with respect to Rio de Janeiro.[12] It redefined the provincial assemblies (*assembléias legislativas*), giving them control over public education, the postal service, public works, roads, navigation, prisons, hospitals, churches, and associations, the municipal police, and the National Guard. Provinces fixed municipal and provincial budgets and taxes, created and suppressed civil service posts, and set administrative salaries. They could judge, fire, or suspend magistrates for abuses of authority and had the power to demarcate civil, ecclesiastical, and judicial boundaries. The power of elected assemblies was tempered, however, by the veto power exercised by provincial presidents, who were nominated by imperial appointment.

The full significance of the Additional Act, however, requires analysis beyond the national and provincial levels of government. Incorporation of the municipality, an essential component of the Brazilian state, shifts the meaning of such reforms and the framework in which they occurred. Although provinces gained autonomy with respect to the nation in the 1830s (and lost much that they had gained through counterreforms of the Conservative Regresso in the early 1840s), municipal polities experienced a steady loss of political autonomy and self-determination with respect to both provincial and national governments.

This diminution of formal municipal autonomy may explain why historians of imperial Brazil have dismissed the municipality as a politically significant entity. Although municipal government has received ample treatment by historians of colonial and republican Brazil, the topic has inspired little interest among scholars of the imperial period.[13] This lacuna is all the more surprising in view of the fact that nineteenth-century politicians, jurists, and publicists considered municipal administration to be a matter of vital importance.

Municipalities did not benefit from the "decentralizing" reforms of the 1830s but rather lost many privileges that they had gained over the course of the colonial period. The municipal council (*câmara municipal*) had functioned as the basic administrative unit of Brazil—indeed, of the entire Portuguese empire.[14] Under the Philippine Ordinances of 1603, câmaras were empowered to implement sanitary measures and urban improvements, levy taxes and fines, inspect weights and measures, and regulate local markets. Councilmen supervised local judges and nominated officers (*capitães-mores* and *mestres do campo*) to lead rural militias (*ordenanças*). The councilman who received the most votes served as lay judge (*juiz ordinário*). The *homens bons*, white, legitimate, Catholic, property owners, free of Jewish, Muslim, or African ancestry, selected council members through indirect elections.[15] Although merchants, craftsmen, non-Catholics, foreigners, and people of color were officially denied membership, these niceties were frequently ignored in Brazil. Over time, the município of the Brazilian interior also developed political and judicial functions, attaining the height of its powers in the mid-seventeenth century.[16]

The autonomy of the councils in colonial Brazil should not be idealized. Rather than acting as an expression of the ideals of self-government, effective local power flourished because of anarchy, poor communications, and limited resources. The Portuguese crown lacked the means to control the strongmen of the vast interior, and it was often in its best interests to permit *mandonismo* (arbitrary private rule) of patriarchal rural proprietors over local populations. In 1696, the Crown began attempts to curb municipal excesses by substituting for the elected juizes ordinários royally appointed circuit judges (*juizes de fora*). This measure proved largely ineffective because Portuguese control over subordinates remained attenuated at best. Although Crown-appointed judges were prohibited by law from marrying locally, they frequently disregarded such restrictions and were incorporated into prominent clans. Formal institutions were thereby absorbed into local interest groups and customary informal networks.[17]

Not unmindful that regional interests had the potential to undermine national stability, the imperial government sought to reverse this worrisome trend toward local autonomy through the passage of the regulatory *lei dos municípios* of 1828.[18] The law stripped the councils of most of their powers and redefined them as purely administrative units. The municípios became subject to provincial tutelage, which likened the municipality in the administrative order to a minor in the civil order. The "adult powers" of the province and nation were to strictly supervise administrative measures proposed by the councils, especially in the area of fiscal legislation.[19] All municipal initiatives had to be approved by elected provincial assemblies and centrally appointed provincial presidents. The Additional Act of 1834 further diminished municipal autonomy. Town councils, reduced to subaltern status, had to submit for approval all proposed budgets, municipal ordinances, and projects for public works to the provincial legislative assemblies.[20]

Municipalities lost even more ground in the 1840s as part of a broader trend spearheaded by the Conservative party to centralize state power. The so-called Liberal decade came to an end when fifteen-year-old Dom Pedro II assumed the throne in 1840. The young monarch soon succumbed to Conservative pressure and deposed the Liberals, who had pushed successfully for his premature (and unconstitutional) coronation. He dissolved Parliament, appointed a Conservative cabinet, and called for new elections. When the Liberals again won the majority of seats in Congress, the cabinet refused to accept the results and maintained that the Liberal victory at the polls had been achieved fraudulently. This act was coupled with the reinstatement of the Council of State, an entity that symbolized the absolutism of Pedro I's reign.[21]

The Conservative party, with its emphasis on strong, centralized government, proved to be the most attractive alternative to the elite who wished to preserve the status quo. Influential Liberals such as mineiro Bernardo Pereira de Vasconcelos turned Conservative after witnessing the rapid corruption of local institutions such as elected justices of the peace and the jury system. In this regard, a Pernambucan party publicist pithily observed, "The people of Brazil are as likely candidates for democracy as the Moslems are to recognize the authority of the Pope."[22] Regional revolts that broke out during the 1830s and 1840s also provided a convenient justification for Conservatives to limit local autonomy.

The Conservatives took advantage of their brief tenure in the early 1840s to pass the Interpretative Act, the first major Conservative step to create a centralized bureaucracy. Under this constitutional reform, which "reinterpreted" the Additional Act of 1834, provincial assemblies lost many of their prerogatives. The assemblies could no longer make general pronouncements about municipal economies and policies. Everything had to be submitted piecemeal, ordinance by ordinance, budget by budget. For the provincial assemblies, it was, as historian Thomas Palmer has aptly remarked, more of a nullification than an interpretation.[23]

The reformulation of the Criminal Code passed in 1841 further strengthened the center through the creation of an ever more extensive and centralized police and judicial bureaucracy. The Conservatives implemented an administrative infrastructure based on clientelism to preserve unity and stability in a nation that was overwhelmingly rural, illiterate, and lacking in trained and educated administrators. By 1850, municipalities lost their rights either to elect or to nominate the personnel who were responsible for maintaining law and order, including magistrates, police delegates, and officers of the National Guard. The linking of municipal institutions of social control to national political interests would have far-reaching consequences. Through these reforms, the centralizing national elite gained the ability to manipulate electoral proceedings through their municipal appointees. In the words of the Brazilian jurist and scholar Victor Nunes Leal: "The law of 3 December 1841 was not merely a procedural code of judicial and police administration; it was, above all, a political instrument, a powerful apparatus of domination, capable of giving to the government overwhelming election liberties, be it the Conservatives or Liberals in power."[24]

The year 1850 marks a critical juncture within Brazilian politics. Within three decades of independence, Brazil experienced profound institutional changes that culminated in a centralized state, maintained through the manipulation of a complex political machine and the moderating power of the emperor. Although municipalities retained few independent prerogatives within this framework, they were not completely without influence because they continued to perform a number of useful functions for the state. Politically, municipal officials organized, publicized, and supervised parochial elections. Councils regulated law and order through the appointment of attorneys, accountants, bailiffs, and jailers. They swore in state-appointed policemen and judges. Municipal authorities also provided a continuous flow of information to the provincial assemblies. Periodically, justices of the peace and parish priests compiled statistical surveys about agricultural production, land distribution, and household censuses. In the economic realm, councilmen administered municipal property, regulated local markets, submitted annual accounts, imposed and collected municipal taxes, provided limited social services, and regulated public health.

Councils also defined the development priorities of their municipalities. In addition to supervising public works and authorizing contracts, they submitted proposals to the provincial assembly for more extensive funding. The councils encouraged improvements in agriculture, the introduction of new technology, imported seeds, and improved breeds of livestock. They directed urban planning, proposing the construction of churches, prisons, town halls, charity hospitals, roads, and bridges. Councils defined educational needs, including schoolhouses, the donation of materials for charity pupils, and the appointment of primary school teachers. Municipal budgets, however, barely covered operating costs. Even the most minor projects, such as repairs to the church roof, depended on provincial subsidies, always in short supply and attainable only through protracted negotiation.

Funding came predominantly from the provincial treasury, which collected local taxes levied on agricultural products and then reallocated a portion of these monies back to the municipalities. In the 1840s, the budget allocated for municipal councils in the entire province varied between 50:000$000 and 60:000$000 (approximately £25,000–£30,000). By the 1880s, this sum had risen almost ten times, averaging roughly 500:000$000 annually, although some of this increase was due to inflation, currency devaluation, and a proliferation of the number of municipalities. This increase did not benefit all municipalities equally. Communities in the zona da mata to the south received funding for railroads and other projects commensurate with the export taxes collected on coffee. Rarely did the São Francisco region capture more than 1 percent of the provincial budget allocated to meet municipal costs.[25]

Rural municipalities had neither the income nor the autonomy to initiate large projects independently. The alternative was to appeal for funds to the provincial president by using well-argued proposals, emphasizing the liberal goals of order, progress, and profit. This tactic proved largely futile owing to the lack of continuity in the provincial government. The tenure of provincial presidents in Minas Gerais was notoriously short. Only rarely did a president complete an entire year in office before being posted elsewhere. The extent to which provincial presidents could gain knowledge of and respond effectively to municipal concerns, even if they had been willing to make the effort, was extremely limited. If any continuity in provincial government existed at all, it lay in the Ouro Preto bureaucracy, a branch of government that deserves a study of its own.[26]

A survey of provincial laws in Minas Gerais reveals that petitions for municipal projects seldom yielded the desired resources, especially prior to 1850. Initiatives that exacted low or nonexistent costs, such as the shifting of municipal boundaries or the revision of town statutes, were easy to push through. More costly endeavors, such as the improvement of urban space, the expansion of transportation networks, the promotion of economic growth, and the enhancement of public education and hygiene, stagnated until the consolidation of electoral machinery based on patron-client relations.

Municipal Strategies in the São Francisco Region

In the decades following independence, the municipalities of the São Francisco region responded in very different ways to their reduced circumstances. São Romão communicated but rarely with the provincial government, and extant documentation fails to provide a clear picture of that community. In contrast, officials from Januária and Montes Claros generated abundant and detailed correspondence that reveals markedly different approaches in their interactions with the provincial government. In the decades following independence, the Montesclarenses readily adopted the language of liberalism, emphasizing civic duty, fiscal responsibility, and social order in their correspondence with provincial officials. They invoked lofty social and political imperatives to achieve mundane pragmatic objectives. For example, investment in transportation would facilitate civic duties such as voting, attending council meetings, or jury participation by easing the travel burden of citizens in outlying districts. Expanded public education would inform the young about their responsibilities in a liberal society and would result in a more modern, enlightened, and productive population. More efficient taxation would promote development.

In the words of Benedict Anderson, the municipal elite identified with a wider "imagined community," although it is doubtful that the center initially "imagined" Montes Claros as an integral part of its national project.[27] Strikingly, the Montesclarenses seem to have made this ideological shift in the absence of immediate or tangible material rewards. They incorporated new concepts of governance, citizenship, order, and progress into a dialogue with a larger political community. Notables from Januária, in contrast, seemed unwilling or unable to see beyond their parochial horizons and demonstrated a commitment to localism and petty intrigue. They proved unwilling to participate in broader provincial imperatives or fiscal initiatives from which they did not immediately benefit.

The political evolution of the two municipalities found expression in multiple contexts such as the manipulation of municipal boundaries, fiscal administration, adherence to official protocol, commitment to law and order, and cultural norms. The following detailed comparison of the political styles articulated by Januária and Montes Claros from the 1830s through the 1850s demonstrates that rural peoples of the interior did not respond to political change in a unified or homogenous fashion and were anything but politically inert. The actions of the Montesclarenses ran counter to many prevailing regional stereotypes, while Januária's residents tended to reinforce pejorative notions of the unruly sertão.

Januária's commitment to localism becomes abundantly clear in a decades-long struggle between the districts of Brejo do Salgado and Porto do Salgado for control over the municipal seat. Each district had ample opportunity: the seat alternated between them in 1833, 1836, 1845, 1850, 1853, 1871, and 1885.[28] After a transfer, be it to Brejo or to Porto, the victorious district temporarily assumed the name *vila* Januária. Interestingly, the rivals did tap into liberal rhetoric in their petitions. Both sides linked urban development and civic virtues with responsible government in their game of one-upmanship. Extensive documentation about this conflict also reveals that, to gain their objective, locals quickly resorted to petty intrigue of the lowest sort.

By definition, incorporated towns were sites of both civil and ecclesiastical power and needed to be formally invested with tangible symbols of their status. The *matriz*, the main church of the parish, not only provided spiritual services and moral guidance but also served as the site of elections. The town hall not only provided a place for councilmen to deliberate but also did double duty as a prison. Both buildings occupied prominent positions on the town square and were the symbolic embodiment of civic and ecclesiastic power. The lack of such amenities threatened community status as an acceptable site of local government.

This particular game of representation began in 1833, when Brejo do Salgado first lost its status as a vila, or incorporated town, after the provincial assembly transferred the municipal seat to Porto do Salgado. Demoted to the status of a mere hamlet, it lost the privilege of local representation, embodied in its municipal council. Brejo's inhabitants protested in a petition addressed to the young Dom Pedro II. Although the petitioners grudgingly admitted that Porto was more populated, they added that its citizens were unlettered farmers and artisans, unsuited to hold public office. Brejo, they alleged, had experienced a longer period of settlement and had a better-educated population. It possessed a great number of slaves who might rebel if the judicial center were relocated. It supported a lively market and craft manufacturing, was well watered and fertile, and possessed eight engenhos and three grain mills.

The Brejenses also highlighted Porto's environmental dangers. They complained of fevers borne by the fetid vapors of the Rio São Francisco that plagued Porto and kept travelers and merchants away. The Brejenses recalled how their rivals had to carry their possessions away by canoe every year to escape the winter floods. The banks of the river suffered serious erosion, causing buildings to slide into the river from time to time. Petitioners supported their claims with eyewitness testimony describing the floods of 1780, 1791, 1792, 1802, 1832 and 1833.[29]

The inhabitants of Brejo revealed much about their priorities and values in their petition. Criticism of Porto do Salgado's deficiencies highlighted exactly what qualities a vila should have. The municipal seat should be a hub for commerce, industry, and agricultural markets. It needed public buildings commensurate with its status as a secular and ecclesiastical center. A large settled population was not sufficient; a vila also needed educated men to fill administrative posts. Finally, it should provide a minimum level of security from ecological drawbacks such as periodic flooding and an unhealthy disease environment.

The truth behind the Brejo-Porto rivalry is difficult to ascertain. Each characterized the other as a pocket of urban poverty, neglect, and depopulation. Two household censuses dating from the 1830s offer a more objective comparison of the rival communities.[30] In 1838, the district of Porto contained 257 tightly clustered households and had a population of 1,016. About 12 percent of the population were slaves. In comparison, Brejo boasted over 400 dispersed households and a population of 1,974 inhabitants, 23 percent of them captives. In Brejo, some ranches and plantations were hamlets in their own right. For example, the engenho of Santo Antonio do Boqueirão had a chapel and 178 residents, including men, women, children, slaves, *libertos* (freed slaves), and gypsies.

European travelers' accounts generally favored Porto over Brejo, despite Brejo's greater population. It became clear that Porto's superior facilities for river-borne trade offset the risk of flooding and an unfavorable disease environment. Richard Burton aptly summed up the debate when he visited Januária in the 1860s, commenting: "The water side objects to the hill side that it is too far from the seat of trade; the hill side retorts that at least it is in no danger of seeing even its saints swept into the river."[31]

Rivals emphasized the limitations of churches in either district. In 1834, the inhabitants of Brejo had complained that Porto possessed only a small adobe chapel covered with thatch, unsuitable for the "celebration of the sacred mysteries of our religion and for the solemnities that the nation demands."[32] Brejo, in contrast, possessed the spacious church of Nossa Senhora do Amparo and two auxiliary chapels. In 1845, when the county seat reverted to Porto, the priest José Lemos da Silva resisted the transfer by refusing to hold mass in Porto. The padre later insisted that the church was little more than a bundle of sticks and mud, bound together with vines. It lacked adornment save a relic that had been stolen from the corpse of a deceased priest. He also predicted eternal damnation for one of the Porto ringleaders, whom he accused of attempted murder and the seduction and prostitution of orphan girls.[33]

When the county seat reverted to Brejo do Salgado in 1850, the vicar of

Januária, Francisco Xavier da Silva, refused to move as well. The padre justified his actions, declaring that the church in Brejo was in danger of collapse
and that only a dozen of the sixty-six houses in Brejo were in decent repair.
The remainder were "ridiculous, and some wouldn't serve even as chicken
houses." The vicar asserted that only one hundred "miserable souls" lived in
Brejo, compared to two thousand persons in Porto. Church attendance in
Porto reached two to three hundred parishioners, compared to only twelve
to sixteen in Brejo.[34] Padre Silva's perceptions were exaggerated if not erroneous. It seems unlikely that Brejo's chapels would have fallen into such disrepair over the course of only fifteen years. Moreover, as late as 1872, the population of Brejo was more than double that of Porto.

Representatives from rival districts also invoked petty legal technicalities
to resist change. In 1833, after Porto became the new site of the vila, the councilmen of Brejo do Salgado continued to hold meetings of the town council
in their own district, often in private homes. The stubborn Brejenses defended their actions by pointing out that Porto did not have a town hall.
Even the district judge of the comarca had to hold criminal trials in his own
home in the absence of an appropriate public building. Jurors from Brejo refused to travel far to observe trials held illegally in private residences. Adherence to such niceties was selective, however, as illustrated by their willingness to hold official meetings in Brejo in the home of a respected Portuguese
merchant, José Luiz da Costa Araujo e Arcos.[35]

Some individuals even resisted by destroying municipal and private property. In 1836, when Brejo do Salgado became the new municipal seat, some
townspeople threatened to tear down their houses and rebuild them in
Porto.[36] Commander Pedro Antonio Correia Bittancourt, a Porto resident,
retaliated by refusing to swear in justices of the peace unless his district regained municipal control.[37] When Porto regained authority in 1845, José Ignacio do Couto Moreno of Brejo do Salgado destroyed the *pelhourinho*
(whipping post) rather than see it relocated.[38] The Brejo-dominated municipal council responded to a subsequent transfer in 1853 by taking the remaining office supplies and archives when it left office, leaving the new council
without paper, ink, or other materials.[39]

The tempo of this drama slowed after the death of José Ignacio do Couto
Moreno in 1854. Couto Moreno had become active in politics early on and
emerged as the Conservative party leader in Januária in the 1840s. He was
one of the principal leaders of the Brejo contingent and one of the few Januarenses to have personal contacts with provincial and national politicians.
Shortly after his death, the mineiro assembly again debated the fate of Jan-

uária. Legislator Figueiredo, who had lived in the comarca and apparently allied himself with Liberal chief Manoel de Souza e Silva, pushed successfully for the retention of Porto, arguing that the seat had remained in Brejo only because of Couto Moreno, who had monopolized all public jobs for himself and his family.

The Brejo contingent lost, perhaps owing to the assembly's irritation and fatigue. The legislator responsible for preparing background reports failed to do so in this case because, after so many transfers, he believed that nobody could be unfamiliar with the claims of each side.[40] The Liberal Porto faction also enjoyed the support of the district magistrate of the comarca and the occasional provincial assemblyman from Montes Claros, Jeronimo Oliveira e Castro, interestingly despite his personal affiliation with the Conservative party. Castro died in 1866, and, after a Conservative administration assumed power at the federal level in 1868, the Brejenses subsequently wrested control of the municipal seat in 1871. In 1885, the saga of the seesawing municipality came to an end with Porto as the ultimate victor.[41]

What does this story of local intrigue and backbiting reveal about the tenor of municipal politics in Januária? Prior to 1850, local rivals couched their appeals in terms of trade, civic duty, public hygiene, and security. The dispute began to take on a more overtly partisan tone by the 1850s. After Conservative Couto Moreno's death, the Porto Liberals took advantage of the Conciliation cabinet to press their claims and held on until the Liberals were overturned on the national level in 1868. Conservative Brejo was then able to reassert its hegemony. Political connections gave the two districts bargaining leverage in their efforts to win control of the municipality.

Sustained contentiousness in Januária, however, was not limited to the Brejo-Porto rivalry. The local elite's capacity for petty bickering, infighting, and not-so-subtle accusations of corruption on the part of rivals ultimately hurt the municipality politically. Despite the ability of rival factions to tap into partisan politics by midcentury to achieve limited victories within the municipal ambit, local officials remained so hopelessly embroiled in mutual backstabbing that it is hard to believe that any provincial authority took them seriously. Unrelenting petty intrigue also called into question the elite's ability and willingness to integrate itself into a larger political whole.

Officials from Januária exhibited a notable disregard for the letter of the law, the enforcement of municipal regulations, and their fiscal responsibilities. The conduct of the municipal council could be highly irregular, as the following series of complaints lodged against councilman Francisco Paula Proença shows.[42] On one occasion, two aldermen reported that Francisco and his cronies Candido José Pimenta and Joaquim Lopes da Rocha frequently skipped meetings, "preferring to gamble and fish." Moreover, Proença, who was only an alternate, had illegally usurped the council presidency after Henrique de Sales had died in 1847. He was known to conduct meetings with fewer than the five councilmen required by law, sometimes presiding over as few as two. Legally, close kin were prohibited from serving on the council concurrently, yet Proença allowed substitute councilmen (*suplentes*) to serve alongside their relations. More than once, the council had expelled Proença from the town hall for acting out of order during meetings. Similar irregularities continued well into the 1860s.[43]

Municipal regulations defined a number of "incompatibilities" (*incompatibilidades*, or conflicts of interest) that were designed to prevent certain factions or individuals from wielding too much influence. The prohibition against kin serving simultaneously noted above was one such measure. Individuals were also forbidden to hold more than one office simultaneously. Yet the councilmen of Januária frequently bent the rules defining "incompatibilities" when it suited them. In 1839, the municipal council explained that, for lack of other suitable candidates, it allowed one individual to serve as both jailor and bailiff.[44] In 1852, José Ignacio do Couto Moreno requested that he and Felipe José de Santana be sworn in as councilmen even though they served as alternates to the municipal judge and police delegate. He also asked the following intriguing question: Could the father of the council secretary serve conjointly with his son if they belonged to two different political parties? At midcentury, Couto Moreno raised the possibility that political opposition could obviate family interest, thereby nullifying one reason behind incompatibility regulations in the first place.[45]

The council also adopted a rather lax attitude toward its employees, perhaps because of kinship or party affiliations. For example, it delayed firing municipal secretary Antonio Gomes Ortega for forgery, alteration of official documents, and selective tax collection until 1850 despite documentary evidence of incompetence dating back to 1846. For two years running, he had failed to submit municipal accounts to the provincial assembly, thereby incurring heavy fines, as well as neglecting to request provincial subsidies to sustain poor prisoners.[46]

The municipal elite of Januária also fell short in fiscal matters. It did make some attempts to augment the town treasury through expansion of its tax base, but those attempts rarely succeeded. For example, in 1839, the council began to implement plans for a weekly fair at Porto in order to tax the commercial traffic that passed through the area more efficiently, but the project ground to a halt for lack of municipal funding.[47] In 1842, the council asked for a monopoly on river passages and tolls on the São Francisco and Carinhanha rivers in exchange for establishing new ports and maintaining existing ones. If awarded the concession, the council agreed to provide free passage to government employees.[48] (The municipality finally gained this privilege under a provincial law passed in 1855.)[49] In the late 1840s, the council repeatedly proposed local taxes on cachaça, tobacco, beef, and fish to augment the depleted municipal treasury.[50]

The council blamed its poverty on careless justices of the peace who kept inadequate records and were lax in collecting taxes and fines. It maintained that municipal employees went unpaid, and the council could not repay the "favors and loans" extended by its members. As a result of the council's monetary difficulties, the number of men willing to pledge themselves to public service had declined. The provincial assembly remained unimpressed and failed to grant the council's request to raise taxes, probably owing to frustration with the ineffectual and somewhat disingenuous council. The petitions discussed above also described a constant flux of immigration and lively trade at odds with its portrait of administrative poverty.[51] The council complained that the municipality was too vast to collect taxes and fines effectively, yet it made no effort to repress corruption or demand better performance from its tax collectors.[52] During the 1850s, the volume of trade generated by Januária exceeded that generated by Montes Claros by an estimated 25 percent, yet Montes Claros collected almost twice as much tax revenue for the province.[53] Nor did Januária keep its books regularly, and it often resorted to the convenient excuse that archival materials disappeared every time the municipal seat changed or was flooded.[54]

Januária's requests could also be contradictory and self-serving. For example, in 1837, the municipal council of Januária protested the imposition of new provincial taxes on sugar mills and producers of aguardente, claiming that they weighed too heavily on the poor. The council claimed that most mills were so small that the tax would exceed their profits and that fear of taxation would prevent them from distilling liquor from the by-products.[55] Such objections, however, seemingly vanished twenty years later when it petitioned the assembly for permission to levy taxes on sugar products for the benefit of the municipal treasury.[56]

Januária's unwillingness to collect provincial taxes probably weakened its bargaining position with the assembly. The town had proved equally uncooperative when the provincial government attempted to establish a customs house in the region in the 1830s. Although sales tax was not charged on produce marketed within Minas Gerais, interprovincial trade was subject to customs fees to be paid at provincial borders. As the river port closest to the Bahian border, Januária was a logical location. Local authorities tried to avoid the responsibility of a customhouse because of the costs involved in constructing, provisioning, and manning a garrison. They also disingenuously denied the existence of trade between the region and Goiás, dismissing the need for an additional checkpoint.[57] (A few years later, the same council requested money to build a bridge to expand existing trade with Paracatú, Cuiabá, and Goiás.)[58]

The council also attempted to bargain on the strength of the hardships that maintaining a customhouse would provide. In 1837, it tried, and failed, to negotiate the elimination of provincial taxes on fresh beef, tavern owners, and aguardente producers in exchange for their cooperation.[59] Despite sustained protests, the provincial government finally decided to set up a checkpoint at Escuro, located to the north on the west bank of the Rio São Francisco at its junction with the Rio Verde. A number of logistic problems cropped up. Provincial funding for the barracks never arrived, and most councilmen did not want to donate money and materials. Nobody from the local National Guard wanted to assume leadership of the post.[60] Finally, José Antonio da Silva Couto took over the garrison, but, owing to bureaucratic delays holding up his men, several herds of livestock evaded him by passing along the western side of the river.[61]

On arriving with his squadron, Commander Domingos Fernandes de Melo had a very different story to tell. Allegedly, Silva Couto had falsified accounts, exchanged legitimate money for counterfeit, and corrupted soldiers under his command. He also threatened to kill the commander but fled after the county prosecutor charged him with embezzlement. Silva Couto's successor, Serafim Alves Neves, resigned in frustration, unable to halt the cattle trains and unwilling to neglect his own lands. Fernandes e Melo assumed temporary command of the barrier, and, during the next forty years, it continued to function precariously with reluctant and short-term personnel, yielding only marginal revenues.[62]

Corruption also siphoned away provincial funds that were deposited in municipal treasuries. In the 1840s, Januária received minor provincial subsidies to construct a town jail. The treasurer embezzled the monies by producing falsified and inflated receipts for donated materials.[63] Other funds allocated to feed and clothe poor prisoners were also stolen by one of the councilmen.[64] To compensate for inadequate security, the desperate council requested permission to follow the unconstitutional example of a Bahian district magistrate and lock more dangerous prisoners in stocks and chains.[65]

If such departures from the rule of law were not sufficient, authorities from Januária, in their efforts to discredit one another, also provided evidence to the provincial government of elite participation in Afro-Brazilian culture. In particular, the Portuguese military officer and planter José Ignacio do Couto Moreno frequently criticized his neighbors who failed to meet his enlightened expectations. For example, during a nativist conspiracy that took place in Januária in 1831, he reported that some slave owners allowed their captives to participate in political meetings. When some Brazilian fazendeiros set out to harass a Portuguese merchant, José Joaquim Loredo, they invaded his home and demanded that he dance the *batuque*, a sensual and energetic Afro-Brazilian dance. The poor man had no knowledge of the steps, but some of the more inebriated intruders paired off and insisted that he dance with them. A prominent planter mocked him, saying, "Joaquim, you devil! You dance the batuque better than I do," as Loredo dodged gunshots aimed near his feet.

Couto Moreno's critiques of his neighbors revealed that Brazilian-born elite whites and low-status blacks often shared the same social space. Allegedly, Couto Moreno's brother-in-law Francisco Proença liked to gamble not only with freed blacks but also with his own slaves. On the Silva Gomes family's estate, both *senhores* (slave owners) and slaves indulged in the *jogo de búzios*, a Yoruba-based form of divination using cowrie shells. Slaves and freed blacks attended political meetings, socialized, danced, drank, gambled, and fought with members of elite families. Although slaves, the free poor, and planters certainly enjoyed differential access to political power and economic resources, affective distance seems to have been minimal.

Such references to Afro-Brazilian practices in the São Francisco region appeared only sporadically, usually in the context of attempts to discredit political rivals.[66] Documentation from Januária is unusual in the level of detail that it provides about alternatives to European culture that members of the elite tolerated and even embraced. Januária's indifference to emerging cultural and political norms may have been an active choice, an example of what the historian E. Bradford Burns has called the "patriarchal preference." Burns has suggested that Europeanized notions of order and progress met with stiff resistance from the rural sector in nineteenth-century Latin America. This opposition, he posits, came not only from the "folk," who resisted such misguided priorities through violence and support for traditional rural strongmen, but also from the rural elite leaders' "patriarchal preference" to retain a self-contained rural microcosm based on a precapitalist ethos.[67]

Documentary evidence from Januária suggests that at least some "traditional rural patriarchs" chose not to Europeanize their lives. Whatever the precise motives behind Januária's commitment to localism and tolerance of non-European cultural expression, the elite's obsession with petty intrigue suggests an inability consistently to surpass local concerns and to serve as useful links to a larger political system. Its failure to adapt to new political circumstances contrasts sharply with the modernizing zeal of neighboring Montes Claros.

The Evolution of Political Identity in Montes Claros

Compared to the lively chaos displayed by Januária's unruly elite, the citizens of neighboring Montes Claros seem maddeningly dull. Municipal authorities represented themselves as tireless defenders of law, order, and enlightened institutions, ever-vigilant combatants against ignorance and petty intrigue. Montes Claros rapidly adopted at least the rhetoric of detached objectivity, loyalty to the public good, and constitutionalism. For example, when lobbying for public schools in the 1830s, its council emphasized the positive role that primary education would have in political socialization. It linked good citizenship to knowledge of the law, which defined what being a citizen meant.[68] When the council of Montes Claros protested the recall of copper currency after a severe drought, instead of whining like some of its neighbors, it invoked liberal terminology: "The council understands that the laws should be regulated by customs, times, epochs, and countries and using the right to petition enabled by our Social Pact."[69] At the very inception of the municipality's creation, local officials promised to defend the rights of Brazilian citizens with their lives and concluded official correspondence with expressions of loyalty to the constitutional monarchy, declaring *vivas* to "sacred religion, Dom Pedro II, the legislative assembly, and the Brazilian nation."[70]

Local officials, such as the vicar and Liberal chief Antonio Gonçalves Chaves, even sought to recast evidence of local intrigue grounded in petty personalism into an ignoble struggle against new government institutions. For example, in a response to a complaint in which the *juiz de direito* was accused of manipulating local jurors, Chaves maintained: "This discontent, this nefarious clamor against the local authorities, is really directed against our present-day state of enlightenment and the laws that fortunately govern us. The malcontents do not dare to attack publically these sacred objects of veneration and respect because this would be the most criminal and revolting audacity. Men embedded in total ignorance and immersed in the slime of perversity and backwardness wail against the new institutions, which they hate and secretly curse because they have cut short their lives of crime."[71]

This high-minded rhetoric should be taken not as an accurate reflection of reality but rather as aspirations that select members of the municipal elite wished to attain. Cracks occasionally did appear in Montes Claros's civic veneer. Its elite, like that of Januária, generated masses of official correspondence replete with elaborate details of local intrigue, but the former were less likely to divulge embarrassing incidents that conflicted with European-inspired models of civilization, order, and progress. Montes Claros occasionally transgressed legal boundaries, but less frequently. For example, in 1843, the council of Montes Claros reported that substitute councilmen refused to attend meetings on "frivolous pretexts." Substitute councilmen and municipal judges sometimes neglected their duties as well.[72] Montes Claros also produced slates for municipal councilmen who could not legally serve together, but only rarely.

The municipal elite kept discussions of intraclass conflict to a minimum, with the exception of certain individuals who flagrantly transgressed the boundaries of the law or represented a danger to the state. Corruption was a factor, but, with the exception of election disputes (to be discussed in chapter 4), accounts were more discreet and less personalized. Montes Claros also proved willing to disassociate itself from retrograde districts like Morrinhos that did not conform to the European ideals. In 1834, the council condemned Luiz José de Azevedo, the newly appointed vicar of Morrinhos, for political subversion, disorderly conduct, and indulging in unseemly Afro-Brazilian customs.[73]

Montes Claros also initiated its fair share of attempts to manipulate territorial boundaries. Secure in its position as head of the entire comarca, it did not have to contend with serious challenges for control over the municipal seat, as had occurred in Januária. Rather, it sought to expand its territorial base by competing with the neighboring municipalities of Grão Mogol, São José do Gorutuba, and São Romão to incorporate various border districts. In one instance in 1833, the council tried to justify an exchange of territory with São Romão on the grounds of relative proximity to the respective municipal seats. The wily Montesclarenses neglected to mention that the districts that it was willing to cede suffered from poverty and endemic malaria.[74]

The community also demonstrated greater fiscal responsibility and initiatives to expand its markets and tax base. It was the only municipality in the comarca that turned in detailed accounts to the provincial government with any regularity.[75] Most municipal income derived from licenses, fees, taxes on agricultural production, fines, rental of municipal property, and voluntary contributions. Over the years, taxes levied on coffee, tobacco, sugar mills, carts, slaves, and real estate were added. Expenses included salaries for municipal employees, lighting and maintenance of the town jail, public works, the delivery of official correspondence to outlying districts, election and voter registration expenses, newspaper subscriptions, and subsidies for the care of abandoned children. By the 1870s, expenses had become more diverse, including research costs for a piped water project, the purchase of metric weights and measures, fodder for stray livestock appropriated by the municipality, and repairs to and supplies for the town jail.

In the early years following municipal incorporation in 1830, the council leaned heavily on its representatives for monetary assistance. For example, in 1834, Council President José Pinheiro Neves loaned the council money to buy a town house to serve as a county jail. During the 1830s, the council frequently complained that official salaries were too low to attract competent employees, and it had to pay additional wages out of the councilmen's pockets.[76] The council of Montes Claros frequently could not collect monies due. In 1837, it took in less than half the anticipated revenues, in 1838 only one-fifth, and in 1842 just one-third. The council held pledge drives in the 1840s to construct a secure jail and town hall but managed to collect only a fraction of the subscriptions promised.[77]

In printed government reports, municipal accounts from Montes Claros appeared balanced. For example, in 1838–39, municipal income came to 408$000 and showed a modest balance of 12$136 over expenses of 396$467. Yet unpublished manuscript sources reveal an interesting underside to this picture of fiscal health. That same year, the council was owed 5:858$960 in unpaid fines and pledged donations. It also incurred debts of 5:180$772 to nine individuals, including former councilmen and employees, merchants, and ranchers. The council did manage to free itself of economic dependence on its aldermen in the early 1840s, after ten years functioning as an autonomous municipality.[78]

Montes Claros adopted a proactive approach by petitioning the provincial assembly for permission to levy new taxes to benefit the municipal treasury. In 1848, it received authority to tax barrels of cachaça sold in the municipality.[79] In 1864, the town added taxes on hides, bacon, slaughtered beef and pork, livestock for export, and commercial establishments. The town secured the right to charge additional taxes in 1866, 1877, and 1884.[80] Montes Claros also received permission to hold an annual livestock fair at Easter from which it earned revenues by charging participants for space and pasturage and a 2 percent sales tax.

Some taxes also incorporated broader social agendas. In 1872, the Conservative assemblyman Justino de Andrade Camara proposed an increase on a graduated tax on small merchants, tavern owners, and aguardente producers.[81] It was designed to tax out of business petty merchants who, Andrade argued, encouraged vice by selling liquor to slaves. It favored mid-level traders, as would a subsequent tax imposed on traveling merchants in 1886.[82] This tax imposed on itinerant peddlers (*mascates*) charged from 10 to 30 percent of the value of inventory, with small-scale merchants paying the heftiest tax proportionately. The law encouraged the wealthiest traders to settle in town, thereby freeing themselves of the tax after two years and expanding the commercial network of Montes Claros in the process.

Montes Claros took active steps to ensure responsible administration and economic progress. It demonstrated a willingness to work with the provincial government and to follow a new political model being disseminated at the national level. In comparison, Januária remained more parochial in its thinking and less willing to participate in a broader political project. What consequences, if any, resulted from these two disparate choices?

Definitive conclusions remain elusive. Although obvious correlations exist between the political adaptions made by the elite of Montes Claros, its ability to place local sons in provincial and national government, and its ascendancy as a regional center, the causal mechanisms between these three elements remain unclear. The fact remains that the sober aldermen and officials of Montes Claros were able to build a political base that transcended local interests. It is reasonable to hypothesize that self-representation as a law-abiding, responsible, and enlightened community, and as an ally who could be counted on to deliver, inspired trust at higher levels of government. A reputation for predictability and stability may have been a crucial component of Montes Claros's credibility.

The fact that the Montesclarenses consistently invoked modern political rhetoric and principles despite that fact that this strategy did not immediately provide material rewards suggests that ideological change was at

Table 3. National and Provincial Representatives from Northern Minas Gerais by Municipal Origin and Party Membership

Year	Representative	Origin	Party
Provincial Assembly			
1835	José Antonio Marinho	Januária	Lib.
1838	José Antonio Marinho	Januária	Lib.
1840	J. M. de Oliveira e Castro	Montes Claros	Cons.
1842	Antonio Gonçalves Chaves Sr.	Montes Claros	Lib.
	José Antonio Marinho	Januária	Lib.
1844	J. M. de Oliveira e Castro	Montes Claros	Cons.
	José Ignacio do Couto Moreno	Januária	Cons.
1846	Antonio Gonçalves Chaves Sr.	Montes Claros	Lib.
1848	Carlos José Versiani	Montes Claros	Cons.
1850	Carlos José Versiani	Montes Claros	Cons.
1852	Carlos José Versiani	Montes Claros	Cons.
1854	Carlos José Versiani	Montes Claros	Cons.
1862	Justino de Andrade Camara	Montes Claros	Cons.
1866	Antonio Gonçalves Chaves Jr.	Montes Claros	Lib.
1868	Antonio Gonçalves Chaves Jr.	Montes Claros	Lib.
1870	J. M. Versiani e Castro	Montes Claros	Cons.
	Justino de Andrade Camara	Montes Claros	Cons.
1872	Justino de Andrade Camara	Montes Claros	Cons.
1874	Justino de Andrade Camara	Montes Claros	Cons.
1876	Justino de Andrade Camara	Montes Claros	Cons.
1878	Justino de Andrade Camara	Montes Claros	Cons.
1880	João Vieira Azeredo Coutinho	Montes Claros	Cons.
1882	Camilo Filinto Prates	Montes Claros	Lib.
	Francisco de Sales Peixoto	São Romão	Lib.
1884	Camilo Filinto Prates	Montes Claros	Lib.
	Francisco de Sales Peixoto	São Romão	Lib.
	Antonio J. Nunes Brasileiro	São Romão	Cons.
1886	Antonio Augusto Veloso	Montes Claros	Cons.
	Camilo Filinto Prates	Montes Claros	Lib.
	L. C. de Souza e Silva	Januária	Lib.
1888	Antonio Augusto Veloso	Montes Claros	Cons.
	Camilo Filinto Prates	Montes Claros	Lib.
	L. C. de Souza e Silva	Januária	Lib.
Provincial Presidents			
1883	Antonio Gonçalves Chaves Jr.	Montes Claros	Lib.
1884	Antonio Gonçalves Chaves Jr.	Montes Claros	Lib.
Chamber of Deputies			
1842	José Antonio Marinho	Januária	Lib.
1845	José Antonio Marinho	Januária	Lib.
1848	José Antonio Marinho	Januária	Lib.
	Antonio Gonçalves Chaves Sr.	Montes Claros	Lib.
1853	Carlos José Versiani	Montes Claros	Cons.
1857	Carlos José Versiani (sub.)	Montes Claros	Cons.
1877	Carlos José Versiani	Montes Claros	Cons.

Source: "Governo de Minas Gerais," 3–9.

least not initially tied directly to self-interest. This contradicts some of the long-held scholarly assumptions about the sertão discussed previously. Some members of the municipal elite chose to embrace new concepts and realities and provided the necessary leadership to affect the formation of the municipality's political identity. In the long term, the ability of Montes Claros to adapt ideologically did eventually pay off after midcentury, although such an outcome could not be foreseen in the decades following independence.

Montes Claros underwent vital political adaptations that Januária made tardily, if at all. Willingness to adopt new political norms also found expression in the formation of well-organized Liberal and Conservative party directorates, which emerged by the 1840s. As the next chapter will show, party differentiation and active electoral participation in the São Francisco region took decades to catch on. By midcentury, however, partisan lines had become sufficiently well drawn in Montes Claros that the provincial government stationed troops in the town to quell potential unrest during the elections of 1849. Montes Claros also managed to elect at least one representative to almost every provincial assembly from 1846 on, while Januária and São Romão secured their first legislative seats the 1880s. Getting locals elected became essential after the site of decision making shifted from the municipality to the province following the administrative reforms of the 1820s, 1830s, and 1840s. Municipalities either had to develop connections with assemblymen or get local notables elected to bargain for their hometowns. Only by gaining control of provincial assemblies were rural proprietors once again able to govern themselves (see table 3).[83]

CHAPTER 3

From Kinship to Party Politics

By midcentury, municipalities retained a single effective bargaining chip to use in their negotiations with the state. Self-representation as an upstanding civic community was not enough. Politicians at the national and provincial levels required municipal backing to stay in power. The surest road to success for a municipality was to tap into partisan networks created by the two national parties by exchanging votes for government subsidies. In the São Francisco municipalities, partisan affiliation followed closely on the heels of the centralizing measures promulgated by the national government. This pragmatism on the part of local elites has been well documented by scholars of imperial and republican regional politics. It has long been assumed that party identity was just a superficial veneer overlaid on preexisting local networks of interrelated kin. As this and subsequent chapters will demonstrate, such analyses are not incorrect but incomplete.

Social class, kinship, and party identity defined political relationships and possibilities in the São Francisco region and throughout imperial Brazil. The basis of the emerging electoral system became political patronage channeled through family networks. Hierarchical social relations mediated by patriarchal authority and family dating from the colonial era expanded to incorporate partisan affiliation and provincial and federal factions. Moreover, imperial law embedded kinship in its definition of *citizenry* as reflected in the minimum voting age, which was twenty-five if single and twenty-one if married. Marriage typically signified the creation of an independent household and the extension of family ties to another lineage.

As the Brazilian state progressed in its program of nation building and state centralization, municipal notables realized that forces beyond the region had the power adversely to affect their lives. Once the state began to intrude increasingly on local affairs and relationships through centralized appointment of county officials, further adaptation to new political norms occurred. The political party, as a nexus of patronage that was not formally defined by kinship, emerged as a new organizing principle. It did not supplant the family, but, rather, the two categories underwent a process of accommodation to one another. Parties that initially were adopted by groups of interrelated families eventually began to take on lives of their own.

At independence, the political horizon for most people was limited to the district, the parish, the municipality, or, at most, the comarca. The localized vision of the municipal authorities of the 1830s was reflected in their use of the term *country* (*país*) to refer to the São Francisco region.[1] The provincial capital, Ouro Preto, and the national center, Rio de Janeiro, remained remote, shadowy, and imagined spaces. Early postindependence responses in the São Francisco region to participation in national politics were lukewarm at best. Extant documentation suggests that voter turnout remained small in the 1820s and 1830s because the rigors involved in traveling to an election site outweighed any possible benefits. As municipal government became increasingly dependent on the goodwill of provincial assemblies, the local elite came to participate in elections with greater enthusiasm and self-interest.

The municipal elite of Montes Claros adapted to expanded political opportunities more readily than did their counterparts in Januária. In both communities, however, eligible voters put other priorities before civic duty in the 1820s. In 1824, twenty-seven Montesclarenses provided justifications for not voting. Eleven cited old age or physical ailments, including stomach troubles, skin infections, ulcerous sores, blood blisters, and swollen limbs. José Pinheiro Neves, who would be elected president of the first municipal council in Montes Claros in 1832, stayed home to nurse a loyal mestiço dependent. Several persons were conducting business beyond the municipality. Four individuals argued that it was too far to travel to the election site, and three more claimed that they had not been informed about the elections at all. Some voters had official duties to fulfill that they could not abandon in order to journey to the polls. One police delegate refused to leave his post, and a priest had been called away to administer last rites.[2]

Eligible Januarense voters also remained relatively disinterested politically until the 1830s. As late as 1828, only ten *eleitores* from Januária participated in regional elections held in São Romão. The election had been scheduled during both the branding season and the rainy season, when traveling conditions were at their worst.[3] In this case, economic self-interest clearly outweighed civic duty. José Ignacio do Couto Moreno, an autocratic rancher of Portuguese birth who had settled in Januária, implied that voters did not take the election ritual seriously by raising a series of ironic and presumably rhetorical questions about protocol. Could voters who lived a mere seven leagues distant (forty-five kilometers) be excused from voting? Were the religious solemnities that accompanied elections optional? (Many priests dispensed with this formality.) Who should pay for the music? Finally, during the session, "was it appropriate that eleitores get up, sit down, walk around, leave the room, come in, or gossip as the mood struck them? If not, what penalty should be imposed?"[4]

Couto Moreno later revealed that fourteen prominent notables, including friends and kin, had not participated in the last elections. Many of them justified their absence because of illness and were in fact ill, but not so ill as to preclude a journey to São Romão. Francisco de Paula Pereira's indigestion had not prevented him from journeying over sixty kilometers to his cattle ranch to care for his new calves, nor had elderly Francisco Pereira do Amorim's chiggers and hemorrhoids prevented him from traveling between the county seat and his home district over 150 kilometers distant. He criticized voters for their unwillingness to undertake long, arduous journeys to cast their ballots. His views mirrored those of the national elite, as he concluded that "two-thirds of the people for whom the constitution was prepared need to be prepared for it."[5]

Accounts from the 1820s point to a generalized lack of ideological commitment to the electoral process. Eligible voters became more involved as party differentiation developed in the 1830s. Again, this process began sooner and emerged along more distinct lines in Montes Claros.[6] Partisan factions became clearly defined in the 1830s following a minor judicial corruption scandal. Colonel José Pinheiro Neves became the local Conservative chief, supported by the influential Versiani family. On the Liberal side, Francisco Vaz Mourão, commander of the National Guard, won the support of Antonio Xavier de Mendonça, José Fernandes Pereira Correia, and Lourenço Vieira de Azevedo Coutinho. Montes Claros divided politically after Commander Mourão had been removed from the list of jurors for having manipulated his fellow jurors to acquit Joaquim José de Azevedo for the crime of reducing a free woman to slavery. Azevedo was the brother-in-law of the justice of the peace, João José Fernandes, who was Mourão's cousin. Azevedo's acquittal was later overruled, but it had earned Mourão the enmity of Colonel Neves, the president of the municipal council. Allegedly, Mourão and Fernandes also arbitrarily imprisoned a prominent landowner, Januário Durães Coutinho, and had the guards shoot at him "as one would shoot at a pig."

When Mourão lost his credibility in the community, so did his party. He refused to run for office again. In the following elections for municipal council, the Conservatives emerged victorious, with the Reverend Felipe Pereira de Carvalho as president and Colonel Neves as vice president. Neves took command of the National Guard as well. The Liberal priest Antonio Gonçalves Chaves Sr. also won a seat on the town council, marking the beginning of his long political career. The Liberals of Montes Claros first won a majority in the municipal council in 1840 and retained their local hegemony until 1852. After the dissolution of the Chamber of Deputies and the provincial assemblies by Dom Pedro II in 1849, the Conservatives, led by the Versianis, won the municipal elections in 1853 and controlled local government until 1880.

In Januária, political factions coalesced into formal parties slowly and remained more loosely organized. In the early 1830s, ethnic divisions erupted when Brazilian landowners led a nativist conspiracy against local Portuguese-born merchants and military officers stationed in a nearby garrison.[7] The planned uprising was not an isolated incident but part of a broader nativist backlash that took place after Pedro I abdicated the throne in 1831. Coronel Couto Moreno, a victim of Lusophobic sentiment, eventually became an ardent advocate of the Conservative party.

Factions developed, grounded largely in personal interests, although hints of ideological conflict appeared as well. In 1833, Father Custodio Vieira Leite, "in the purity of spirit of a true Christian," self-righteously asserted that an emissary of the radical *exaltado* priest José Antonio Marinho had arrived in town and was encouraging the people to form a republic. Allegedly, Francisco de Paula Pereira Proença and Joaquim da Silva Gomes had answered the call and organized an election against the precepts of the constitution, filling the electoral college with relatives and unqualified adolescents.[8]

Padre José Antonio Marinho, best known as an eyewitness chronicler of the Liberal Revolution of 1842, was a native son of Januária. He was the son of poor mulatto peasants but rose to local prominence after his godfather, a wealthy landowner, noticed his intelligence and dramatic talents at an appearance in the local theater. His patron felt that his energies would be best channeled into the priesthood, and he sponsored the youth to study at the Olinda seminary. In 1824, Marinho joined the ranks of the revolutionaries and fought in the Confederation of the Equator. As a radical Liberal, he participated in the Barbacena Revolt of 1833 and the Liberal Revolution of 1842. In the 1830s and 1840s, Marinho was elected to both the provincial and the national assemblies. He was a strong advocate of public education and was active in the Liberal press. Marinho died in 1853, at age forty-nine, during a yellow fever epidemic in Rio de Janeiro.[9]

Marinho's rise to prominence coincided with the emergence of formal political associations and parties in Januária in the 1830s. In 1832, some prominent citizens founded the Society to Promote Unity and Defense of the Center (Sociedade Promotora da União e Defensora do Centro). Its principles were similar to those of socially conservative societies founded in Rio de Janeiro in the 1820s and 1830s. The society emerged in response to the social disruption and increased incidence of crime associated with increasing migration to the region. It hoped to restore law and order and to limit corruption among municipal officials. The society subscribed to newspapers from neighboring provinces to supplement those already being provided by José Antonio Marinho, giving them access to information about a larger national community.[10]

The Liberal party quickly gained support in Januária, probably owing to the influence of the radical Padre Marinho, who was instrumental in establishing lines of patronage between Rio and the Januarense elite. In 1838, a justice of the peace alleged that a group of Liberal notables had collected over 500$000 as a "gift" with which to "purchase" the transfer of the county seat from the Conservative district of Brejo do Salgado to the Liberal-dominated Porto do Salgado. Two free men of color had been sent to Rio to deliver the money to three prominent Liberal deputies from Minas, José Antonio Marinho, Teófilo Benedito Otoni, and Joaquim Antão Fernandes Leão.[11]

The prolonged rivalry between the districts of Porto do Salgado and Brejo do Salgado contributed to patterns of partisan differentiation. Initially, family factions coalesced along spatial lines, forming parties loyal to the rival clans of each district. The Conservative party under the leadership of José Ignacio do Couto Moreno, a Portuguese military officer turned planter, dominated Brejo do Salgado. The Liberal chief and regionally well-connected merchant Manoel Souza e Silva led the Liberals from his base in Porto do Salgado. Control over the municipal council seems to have been organized more along kinship lines than partisan preferences. Correlations between family and party were not absolute, and, by the 1850s, political parties began to take on a life of their own beyond kinship or district affiliation. By the 1860s, violent confrontations between the two parties became commonplace.

The historical record yields few clues about the political evolution of São Romão. The community did not produce the same number of garrulous commentators as did Montes Claros or Januária, or, at any rate, detailed documentation has not been preserved. Like the elite of Januária, the Romanenses formed a society to uphold the tenets of government in 1833, the Society of the Friends of Beneficence and Opposition against Illegality (Sociedade dos Amigos da Beneficencia e Opositora da Ilegalidade). Its statutes emphasized defense of the constitution.[12] The evolution of formal political parties remains unclear, but distinct Liberal and Conservative parties had formed by the 1860s. Like the case of Januária, Liberals and Conservatives divided themselves between two districts, São Romão and Pedras dos Angicos, respectively.

At midcentury, partisan identity in the three communities of the comarca remained ideologically vague. Montes Claros, Januária, and São Romão voiced support for liberal institutions and the constitutional monarchy, presenting themselves as uniformly socially and politically conservative. Local representatives and officials stressed their support to the system of constitutional monarchy. They showed their loyalty by informing higher authorities about elite transgressions and subversive behavior. Every time a new provincial president was sworn in, the councils dutifully sent their congratulations. Party preference seemed of secondary importance.

The three communities also demonstrated their conservatism in festivals organized to commemorate significant political events, publicly expressing their loyalty to the state in rituals of affirmation. For example, in 1834, São Romão responded to news of the Additional Act to the constitution with festivities including fireworks, a religious ceremony, and lighting the town at night with lanterns and torches. Bands took to the streets playing "consti-

tutional hymns." Each municipality also underwrote festivals to commemorate the coronation of Dom Pedro II. Montes Claros sponsored religious
ceremonies, parties, dances, "sumptuous" illumination, equestrian parades,
vivas, musical bands, and recitations of political essays in honor of the
young monarch.[13] The municipality of Januária funded four days of festivities, including an equestrian show (*cavalhada*), an opera, town illumination,
the singing of hymns, and shouting vivas in the streets. The whole town
turned out in its Sunday best, adorned with a Brazilian touch—sprigs of
coffee in lieu of flowers—to hear the vicar celebrate mass. Women and children joined in the festivities. One official produced an organ-grinder to ac-
company the merrymaking of the people.[14]

Januária, São Romão, and Montes Claros also avoided involvement in the
"subversive" regional revolts of the 1830s and 1840s. In 1833, the National
Guard of Montes Claros proposed that anyone who spread the doctrines of
the Restorationist party should be arrested and subject to a fine of twenty
milréis. Montes Claros and Januária remained aloof from the popular
Sabinada Revolt as it spread outward from Salvador da Bahia into the sertão
and celebrated when it was suppressed. Januária commemorated the "triumph of legality" over the Sabinada with fireworks, illumination of the
church, and a special mass, while the municipal council of Montes Claros
congratulated itself for governing "sensible inhabitants."[15] None of the
three communities participated in the Liberal Revolution of 1842. Local historians have maintained that Chaves was an intimate of the Liberal priest
and one-time regent Diogo Antonio Feijó and that Chaves had been given a
role to play, but no concrete evidence has been uncovered to support this
claim. In any event, as president of the council, Chaves publicly supported
the government.[16]

The unified social conservatism of the municipal elite of the São Francisco
region began to break down at midcentury. Prominent individuals began to
make partisan distinctions, especially targeting individuals believed to be
antimonarchical. For example, a letter from the Conservative commander of
the National Guard of Januária dating from the 1850s denounced his fellow
officers who were Liberals, emphasizing their predilection for red hats, ties,
and other garments. Reputedly, Manoel Caetano Souza e Silva, the *chimango* (Liberal) leader, had imported these offensive scarlet trappings from
the Liberal reduct of Diamantina and had also spread republican propaganda.[17] Yet, at midcentury, such ideological observations were still rare,

and kinship remained the primary criteria for the formation of political alliances.

Kinship, Landownership, and Political Factions

Politically ambitious members of the local elite mobilized partisan support through two interlocking mechanisms: kinship and landownership. Extended kin networks cannot be reconstructed from household censuses alone because small nuclear households were the norm in eighteenth-and nineteenth-century Minas Gerais.[18] Land registers dating from the 1850s, however, enable the reconstruction of extensive kinship ties and also provide information about how many potential voters each estate owner might have commanded. The registers reveal a spatial pattern of interrelated families, each residing on separate plots of land but located on the same large estate or neighboring estates.[19]

As noted in chapter 1 above, small landholders did not seem to have absolute title to their land, be it inherited or purchased. The typical formula was "I possess [*sou possuidor*] a piece of land on the estate owned by *senhor de tal* [so-and-so]." The meaning of such a statement in terms of ownership rights is unclear. It may reflect the fact that such owners were tenants, registering usufruct rights to land and ultimately recognizing the authority of the head fazendeiro. It may reflect the subdivision of estates through partible inheritance and the subsequent sale of some of those holdings. Or it may represent a combination of the two patterns. The registers do not provide enough information to tell for certain. What owners invariably did mention were the name of the estate on which they were located and the name of the patriarch with whom they were associated. From there, we can reconstruct the number of registrants on a given estate and, in most cases, the predominant proprietor. These data, then, suggest the extent to which principal landowners may have exerted influence on poorer relatives and dependents at election time. For the small landholder, the protection offered by an estate owner was a reasonable trade-off for the deferential behavior, occasional labor, and potential votes demanded in return.

A comparison of land registers of São Romão, Januária, and Montes Claros dating from the mid-1850s shows significant differences in the spatial distribution of landholdings.[20] Montes Claros recorded 1,323 parcels of land on 203 estates. In São Romão, 554 owners registered parcels on 159 estates. Januária revealed a similar distribution of 610 owners divided among 170 properties. In all three samples, estates divided among one to five owners predominated: 69.5 percent in Montes Claros, 80.6 percent in Januária, and 81.1 percent in São Romão. The number of middling estates (shared among six to ten owners) among the three communities also was comparable, ranging from 11.9 percent in Montes Claros to 13.5 percent in Januária. Montes Claros, however, far outstripped its neighbors (by a factor of three in percentile terms) in its number of large subdivided estates (eleven to forty owners). The largest fazenda in São Romão, Gameleira, was divided among thirty-four proprietors. In Januária, the most populous spread was Itapirassaba, divided among thirty-five owners. In Montes Claros, however, seventy-eight landowners and their families resided on the fazenda Canabrava, mostly descendants of the patriarch Januário Durães Coutinho.

The contrast between the three municipalities is even more striking when we compare the distribution of people on these estates. In Montes Claros, only 20.8 percent of the landholding population resided on estates divided among one to five people, compared to 46.2 percent in São Romão and 46.7 percent in Januária. In Montes Claros, 65.4 percent of all landholders lived on estates divided among more than eleven owners. The eight largest estates held 448 individual subproprietors, 33.9 percent of the total. In comparison, only 26.2 percent of landholders in São Romão lived on fazendas shared by more than ten owners. Januária had a similar ratio; 25.4 percent of its landowners resided on its ten most populous estates.

Differences in the distribution of people may represent a crucial element to Montes Claros's relative political dynamism. In Montes Claros, owners of vast subdivided estates controlled a large number of dependents and consequently wielded a great deal of personal and political power.[21] Dependent retainers were more likely to cast their votes reliably for their patrons but also ran the risk of running afoul of rival families and factions. One example of such a potentially powerful network was the Durães Coutinho clan, which, in addition to controlling the populous and extensive estate of Canabrava, was spread out over seventeen different properties. Joaquina Ferreira de Barros, the widow of João Durães Coutinho, registered four pieces of property on three estates. Januário Durães Coutinho's wife, Maria Leite Pereira, inherited land on five separate estates. Seven other heirs held multiple claims to these properties.

The Velloso and Versiani clans, the leaders of the Conservative party in Montes Claros, had married into the influential Durães Coutinho network, becoming even more numerous and far-flung. The Vellosos controlled the extensive estate of Canoas, divided among thirty separate owners, some of them Versianis. The descendants of the patriarch Pedro José Versiani spread out from the family seat, the fazenda of St. Eloi in the district of Bomfim. Francisco José, Antonio Augusto, and José Maria stayed in Bomfim. Their brothers, Carlos José and João Antonio Maria, moved to Montes Claros, where they acquired portions of four separate estates. Finally, João Antonio settled in the district of Contendas. The Vellosos divided themselves between Bomfim and Montes Claros, Jeronimo Francisco residing in the former district and Gregorio José, Antonio Augusto, Aleixo José, Custodio José, Bento José, Francisco José, and João Francisco occupying a total of eight different fazendas in Montes Claros. A numerous clan called the Velloso Falcãos, perhaps unrelated, also spread throughout the districts of São Romão.[22]

The Versiani, Velloso, Durães Coutinho, and Azeredo Coutinho families were intricately bound through marriage.[23] Bento José Velloso, a Portuguese, migrated to Montes Claros in the mid-eighteenth century. He married Vitoria Azeredo Coutinho, and they had eleven children. The next generation married with the Cardoso de Souzas and Durães Coutinhos. One politically notable grandson, Gregorio Velloso, had two sons, Antonio Augusto and Felipe Agostinho, who married into the Versiani and Caldeira Brant clans, respectively. Conservative patriarch Pedro José Versiani had numerous sons who married Vellosos and Durães Coutinhos. His grandson Antonio Durães Coutinho married Maria Velloso, and their grandsons also married Versianis and Vellosos. The Versianis were also linked through marriage to the descendants of Patrício Rodrigues Frois, one of ten brothers who had settled in the sertões of Bahia and Minas Gerais in the early nineteenth century. Patrício's descendants also made kin alliances with the Pereira dos Anjos and the Azevedos.

Outsiders were incorporated into these extensive networks as well. The district magistrate, Jeronimo Maximo de Oliveira e Castro, married one of the daughters of Pedro José Versiani. On being widowed, he remarried into the prominent Orsini family of the district of Contendas. Rita Camara, the daughter of Justino de Andrade Camara, a Conservative lawyer who served multiple terms in the provincial assembly, wed Torquato, Oliveira e Castro's son from his second marriage. The merchant João Alves Maurício also hailed from outside the comarca. He migrated from Paracatú in 1860 with the impressive sum of sixty-seven contos of investment capital. Not surprisingly, he was able to attract a bride from among the most notable families of Montes Claros. He married twice into Conservative families, first to Carlota Cardoso de Souza and, once widowed, to Firmina Versiani.[24]

On the Liberal side, the two most dominant families were the Chaves and the Prates clans.[25] Hermelegildo Rodrigues Prates, a Dutchman, had migrated to Brazil around 1800 and had married Maria, Reverend Antonio Gonçalves Chaves Sr.'s sister. They had nine children, some of whom married into the Goulart and Sá families. One of Hermenegildo's sons, José Rodrigues Prates, eventually became the Liberal chief of Montes Claros. He married the daughter of a wealthy fazendeiro from São Paulo, José Joaquim Marques. The prolific Reverend Antonio Gonçalves Chaves Sr. had ten children with Maria Florença de Assunção. Three children married their Prates kin. The son Antonio Gonçalves Chaves Jr. and the daughter Maria Chaves de Queiroga married into influential Diamantina families. Antonio Gonçalves Chaves Jr. and Camilo Filinto Prates, two of the most prominent second-generation politicians from northern Minas, were brothers-in-law. First-generation Liberals Antonio Xavier de Mendonça and José Fernandes Pereira Correia were also brothers-in-law.

In Januária, a select group of interrelated families that controlled heavily populated estates also dominated local politics.[26] The Bittancourt, Couto Moreno, Pereira Proença, Silva Gomes, Pimenta, and Lopes da Rocha families, bound through marriage and godparentage, contentiously dominated Conservative politics for decades. Together, they held portions of the Morro sugar estate and engenho, divided among nineteen owners; the fazenda Santo Antonio, divided among eleven titleholders; and Itapirassaba, owned by José Lopes da Rocha but divided among thirty separate individuals, including his kin José da Silva Gomes Bittancourt, Sebastião, Sebastiana, and Pedro Antonio Silva Gomes, and Pedro José Pimenta. Descendants Felipe José de Santa Anna, Ignacio José do Couto Moreno, José da Silva Gomes Bittancourt, Pedro Antonio Silva Gomes, Pedro José Pimenta, and Sebastião da Silva Gomes all inherited portions of the Pandeiros estate from the patriarch Colonel Pedro Antonio Correia Bittancourt. Ignacio José do Couto Moreno and Joaquim Lopes da Rocha also inherited portions of a large estate in São

Romão. Liberal kinship networks in Januária are more difficult to construct owing to sparse evidence. Manoel Souza e Silva and his son Manoel Caetano, both regionally well-connected merchants, dominated Liberal politics for decades. The grandson Lindolfo Caetano contended for a seat in the provincial assembly in the 1880s.

Kinship networks shaped local politics in Januária in a highly exaggerated form if the constant complaints of local officials are any indicator. A formal accusation submitted to the provincial governor in 1833 provides an illustrative example. The council treasurer maintained that the election for members of the electoral college had been fixed by the justice of the peace, Francisco Paula Pereira Proença, his brother-in-law Captain Joaquim Gomes, and an alternate justice, João Felis Setubal. Those elected included Captain Joaquim's two brothers, Lieutenant José da Silva Gomes, Padre Sebastião do Carmo, and two brothers-in-law, Bernardo José Pimenta and Antonio José Correia. Correia was also Proença's son-in-law and nephew by marriage to the family of Manoel Gomes. Coronel Pedro Antonio Correia Bittancourt, the father-in-law of Captain Joaquim Gomes, had also been elected, as had José Ignacio, the grandson of Manoel Gomes. A complex web of brothers, in-laws, grandparents, and grandsons woven by the Gomes clan managed to secure eight seats as eleitores. Two cousins through marriage, Captain Manoel Carneiro and Luiz Garcia de Matos, were also elected. Among the runners-up were five more relatives, including Felipe Antonio Correia, who was simultaneously brother-in-law to the Gomeses, son of Coronel Bittancourt, and uncle of José Ignacio.[27]

In São Romão, the connection between domination of large estates by kin groups and participation in municipal politics is less clear.[28] The Silva Caxito, Silva Brandão, Silva Lemos, Costa Alkmim, and Souza Landim families dominated successive electoral colleges and town councils, yet none was listed as a prominent landowner. Their wealth may have come from river-borne trade. Conversely, the Pereira da Cunha and Velloso Falcão families registered numerous lands yet do not appear on the political scene, although the Velloso Falcão interests may have been represented by their kin through marriage—the Fonseca e Melo, Pereira Salgado, Pereira da Silva, and Pereira da Souza clans. Given that the land registers do not provide consistent information about land values, it is impossible to determine whether these families held so many titles because their lands had undergone subdivision or because they were truly wealthy. Still, the data raise the possibility that some prominent landowners may have chosen to remove themselves from local politics, perhaps owing to the potential trouble involved and the correspondingly minimal returns.

Other landowners in São Romão embraced political life more enthusi-astically. Pedro Gonçalves de Abreu owned the fazenda Agua Branca and partial title to nine other estates. José Pereira da Silva Lameirão owned three properties independently and was the main owner of a fourth. Both the Abreu and the Silva Lameirão families were among the most active munici-pal officeholders. Manoel Alves Pamplona, an influential local politician, was one of four heirs to the Gameleira and Barra estates. Teofilo de Sales Peixoto, another prominent notable, owned two fazendas outright and pos-sessed a sizable chunk of a third, and these holdings were not divided among numerous owners.

Some family webs extended throughout and beyond the comarca, such as those dominated by the Bittancourts, Caldeira-Brants, Alkmins, and Mourãos. The Azeredo Coutinhos hailed initially from Ouro Preto. The Caldeira Brants and Mata Machados migrated north from Diamantina and the Queiroga clan from Serro.[29] In Montes Claros, the Chaves-Prates clan intermarried with the Sás from Grão Mogol and the Machados and Felício dos Santos families from Diamantina. The Sá-Prates branch also had con-nections in the municipality of Teófilo Otoni to the east.[30]

The role of kinship is evident in the voting patterns for elected municipal office in the São Francisco region. Extant election returns available in the Arquivo Público Mineiro include the majority of elections from the 1840s through the 1870s, providing a sample of 2,419 officials.[31] Rates of turnover in elected municipal office were surprisingly high, qualifying the assump-tion that power was confined to the hands of the few. A total of 1,096 indi-viduals filled 2,419 elected municipal offices over a period of forty years, an average of little more than two terms per candidate. Fifty-four percent of of-ficeholders participated in municipal government only once. The number of persons who served either one or two terms reaches the rather high figure of 75.7 percent. Individuals who occupied municipal office more than five times constituted only 7.3 percent of the sample. The top 7.3 percent, how-ever, occupied a total of 648 positions, 26.8 percent of all locally elected posts. Of the seventy-eight top officeholders, thirty-five came from Montes Claros (fifteen of these hailing from the district of Bomfim), twenty-two from São Romão, and twenty-one from Januária.

Although individuals may have held office only once or twice, certain families monopolized a disproportionately large number of official posts. Five members of the Versiani clan of Bomfim occupied a total of forty-eight positions. Their in-laws, the Vellosos, filled an additional twenty-four spots.

In Januária, the Souza e Silvas—the grandfather Manoel, his son Manoel Caetano, and grandson Lindofo Caetano—occupied twenty municipal offices spanning four decades. The three Pimenta brothers of Januária, Bertoldo, Firmiano, and Josino, also held twenty more positions between them.

The Brazilian state attempted to exploit these preexisting family and social networks in the interests of national politics. Yet it took decades to harness successfully such a dense matrix of interrelated kin to serve the needs of national parties. Even after midcentury, institutional mechanisms remained imperfect, and state control over local electoral outcomes was never absolute. Finally, some kinship groups never transcended family interest to serve the interests of national parties.

Profile of the Municipal Electorate

Reconstruction of the municipal electorate, its motives, and its behavior remains extremely complex and fragmentary. In addition to source limitations, imperial electoral policy manipulated the size and composition of the electorate and constantly redrew the boundaries of electoral colleges and districts. Scholars had long assumed that the voting population in imperial Brazil was exceedingly low, as little as 2–4 percent of adult males.[32] Recent research by Richard Graham, however, reveals surprisingly high national voter registration figures dating from 1872 that corresponded to more than 50 percent of the adult male population.[33] The size of the voting population, based on a modest minimum income requirement, tended to grow over time as the Brazilian currency suffered devaluation. Not until the Saraiva reform of 1881, which introduced a literacy requirement, were voting rights restricted dramatically.

The appearance of broad suffrage, however, was deceptive. Elections were based on a two-tier system, direct at the municipal level and indirect at higher levels. *Votantes* had the right to vote in primary elections that selected justices of the peace and municipal councilmen. They also elected the members of the electoral colleges from the eligible pool of eleitores, a second category of voter. Eleitores needed a minimum annual income of 200$000 to qualify, double that of the votante. Libertos and men with criminal records were not eligible for eleitor status. Eleitores could run for town councilman or justice of the peace and, of course, could participate in electoral colleges, which voted for national and provincial congressmen and senators.[34] Under these guidelines, artisans, cowboys, farmers, and even ex-slaves could vote on the municipal level but not hold office. The number of voters who also qualified as eleitores was approximately one-fourth of the total.

Voter registration lists document changes in the size and composition of the voting population in the São Francisco region.[35] In 1842 and 1844, voter registration lists enumerated household heads, votantes, and eleitores. The 1842 list, the more complete and reliable of the two, demonstrates that, on average, 25 percent of all male heads of household were eligible to vote.[36] The aggregation of data, however, obscures wide variations across parishes and districts, variations that seem to be linked to population density. In the municipality of Montes Claros, for example, voter registration varied from 12.2 percent in the sparsely populated district of Coração de Jesus to 52 percent in the more commercially oriented ranching district of Brejo das Almas. The two most urbanized parishes, Januária and Montes Claros, led the region in registration, tallying 31 and 37.1 percent, respectively. In the entire comarca, nearly 24 percent of votantes were also eligible to serve as eleitores, totaling 6 percent of all male heads of household.

After a major electoral reform passed in 1846, voter registration forms and requirements changed. Lists of heads of household were dropped, and more information about voters was added, including age, civil status, occupation, and, in a very few lists, income and race. Lists from 1847 show a fall in the number of registered voters that may have resulted from the new requirement that minimum annual income of 100$000 be calculated in silver, not copper or paper. From 1842 to 1853, voter registration in Montes Claros rose only slightly over time. The number of votantes in São Romão peaked in 1850 and then began to decline. Only in Januária was there a substantial increase over an eleven-year period, from 314 to 904 voters.

Because consistent and reliable population data for the 1840s through the 1860s is lacking, it is difficult to gauge accurately what percentage of the male population qualified as "active" citizens after 1844. Data from the 1870s suggest that the electorate remained relatively constant in the county seats, despite currency devaluation and inflation, which supposedly had resulted in the expansion of suffrage.[37] In 1876, Montes Claros registered 1,333 voters, or 38 percent of the 3,500 free adult males enumerated in the 1872 census. In Januária, 1,020 voters registered in 1870, 33.3 percent of its total male adult free population of 3,063. In São Romão, only 219 voters registered in 1865, 28 percent of its 763 free adult men.[38] Finally, broadly based participation was also curtailed by the electoral reform of 1881, which reduced the number of voters by over two-thirds to 467 in Montes Claros and 234 in Januária. Comparative data for São Romão are unavailable as the town lost its position as county seat. The new municipal center, São Francisco, registered 206 voters in 1881.[39]

Information about the occupational breakdown of the electorate is scarce, but some tentative conclusions can be drawn. A series of registration forms from 1847 from seven São Francisco parishes reveals that nearly 80 percent of votantes pursued agriculture, 7.6 percent were engaged in commerce, 10.9 percent worked in crafts and services, and fewer than 2 percent were bureaucrats or worked in the liberal professions.[40] São Romão stands out for its unusually high number of wage workers and artisans: over 22 percent fell into the vaguely defined category *indústria* (although diamond prospectors and day laborers were probably lumped into this category).[41] Data from the 1850s, 1860s, and 1870s demonstrate little change in this general profile.[42] Roughly 80 percent continued to be employed in the agrarian sector as farmers, ranchers, or cowboys. Artisans and day laborers constituted 10–20 percent, depending on the community, merchants between 5 and 10 percent, and liberal professionals and bureaucrats no more than 2–3 percent. These 2 percent, however, enjoyed power disproportionate to their numbers. The general profile that emerges from this partial data set demonstrates that a broad segment of the free male adult population was able to vote and that most voters were humble sorts: small farmers, artisans, prospectors, and peddlers. Until the 1881 reform, the voting population remained relatively constant in percentile terms, although it increased in absolute numbers as a reflection of general population growth.

Although votante status seems to have been easy to obtain, it bears repeating that real political power beyond the municipality lay with the eleitores. In addition, many more men met the basic requirements as potential eleitores than actually served in the electoral colleges. The 1846 electoral reform established the national quota of 1 eleitor for every 40 votantes, with a minimum of 20 eleitores per electoral college. Local statistics conformed to these criteria. For example, in the mid-1850s, the electoral district of Montes Claros consisted of six parishes with a free population estimated at 46,210. It boasted 2,635 votantes, or 17.5 percent of the total. Only 57 eleitores were permitted to serve on the college, or 1 eleitor for every 46 votantes, or every 811 inhabitants of the municipality. In this instance, less than 0.12 percent of the municipal population participated in choosing provincial and national representatives.[43]

On the provincial level, the number of eleitores per inhabitant diminished as the population grew. In 1871, there was 1 eleitor for every 401 people in Minas Gerais and, by 1874, 1 eleitor for every 551 mineiros.[44] In 1875, the number of eleitores per electoral college was standardized to 1 eleitor for every 400 residents, regardless of sex, age, or condition, or 0.25 percent of the mineiro population. The government was able to make this more precise calculation by using data from the first national census, compiled in 1872. The appearance of broad suffrage, even prior to restrictive reforms passed in 1875 and 1881, was deceptive. Even if over 50 percent of the adult free male population enjoyed either votante or eleitor status nationwide, the number that could participate in provincial or national elections was minute.

Voting Patterns

Voting patterns varied according to the type of election (municipal, provincial, or national) and the category of voter (votante or eleitor). Richard Graham has persuasively interpreted elections as public displays of power and influence. Voters acted as players in an elaborate social drama, which confirmed status and reinforced social hierarchy within the framework of liberal institutions. During most of the empire, elections took place in church, opening and closing with the celebration of mass and other religious solemnities, thereby linking the social hierarchy to spiritual authority. This measure not only served to highlight the relation between church and state but may have been adopted for practical reasons as well. Public buildings in interior towns were often too small or decrepit to hold such weighty ceremonies. Only in 1881 did the Saraiva reform banish elections to secular space, perhaps anticipating the separation of church and state that would take place under the republican constitution of 1891.

Voting was very much a public process, taking place in full view of observers with the church doors wide open. Voters approached the supervisory board (*mesa*) one by one and identified themselves. On confirmation of eligibility, the voter wrote the names of his candidate(s) on a ballot, which was then examined by the board before it was deposited into an urn on the top of the table. If the voter was illiterate, he made his choice out loud, and the board wrote down his selection for him. After voting was completed, the number of ballots was compared to the number of voters. An auditor drew votes one by one, passing them to the president to read aloud, who then handed them to the other auditor.[45] All registered voters were required to participate or formally justify their absence to avoid being fined by the municipality.

Obviously, the meaning of casting a vote varied according to social status. The humble yet respectable votante was placed in an especially vulnerable position because he voted openly. Failure to comply with the wishes of a *patrão* (patron) would quickly become common knowledge, making it highly unlikely that the typical votante exercised any true freedom of opinion in casting his vote. The participation of votantes was also limited to elections for municipal councilmen, justices of the peace, and members of the electoral colleges. From the point of view of the national parties, the most crucial municipal elections were those that selected members of the electoral colleges. Rates of voter turnout, however, were much higher for elections of municipal councils than for those elections in which eleitores were chosen who would vote for provincial and national representatives. The average votante seemed much more likely to cast a vote for an influential relative or his patrão than for an eleitor who would select distant candidates to fill remote posts.

The extent to which party motivated municipal eleitores in selecting provincial candidates is difficult to ascertain because no comprehensive political history of imperial Minas Gerais exists. Reconstruction of the party affiliation of provincial politicians would require painstaking research beyond the scope of this book. It is possible, however, to track the level of support that candidates from the comarca of São Francisco received from the three municipalities in provincial elections. The number of votes that such prominent Liberals as Antonio Gonçalves Chaves and Camilo Filinto Prates garnered, compared to the ballots cast for such well-known Conservatives as Jeronimo Maximo de Oliveira e Castro, Carlos José Versiani, and Justino de Andrade Camara, may serve as a barometer to gauge the effect that party affiliation exerted on eleitores.

During the 1830s and 1840s, representatives from the three communities seem to have been motivated more by regional loyalty than by political party. Election returns reveal that eleitores voted for prominent locals irrespective of partisan affiliation in provincial races. Yet electoral colleges did not necessarily support every local aspirant, and many notables ended up at the bottom of the list for provincial assemblymen. They might also support candidates from opposing parties simultaneously. For example, in the election for provincial assemblymen for the term 1834–36, the electoral college of Montes Claros cast votes for a Liberal priest originally from Januária, José Antonio Marinho, and their own juiz de direito, the Conservative Jeronimo Maximo de Oliveira e Castro. Such prominent local landowners as the Conservatives Pedro José Versiani and José Pinheiro Neves and three members of the Liberal Vaz Mourão family received only a few votes apiece.[46] The electoral college of São Romão also supported Padre Marinho and the magistrate Oliviera e Castro but cast a high number of votes for José Pinheiro Neves and a local fazendeiro, Tomas da Conceição Araujo, as well.[47] Similarly, in 1838, the electoral college of Januária voted for two candidates from Montes Claros, the Liberal priest Antonio Gonçalves Chaves and the Conservative magistrate Oliveira e Castro. Eleitores also supported their own José Ignacio do Couto Moreno, a Conservative fazendeiro, but did not enthusiastically endorse Couto Moreno's influential father-in-law, Pedro Antonio Correia Bittancourt, or a landed priest from the district of Morrinhos, Ciriaco Antonio de Araujo.[48]

The influence of party affiliation in candidate selection seems to have affected voting patterns earlier in Montes Claros than in other municipalities. In the 1840s, personalism and regional affiliation still reigned as the principal behind local electoral support. For example, in the 1840s, the Liberal Antonio Gonçalves Chaves Sr. received widespread support as candidate for the provincial assembly, but so too did prominent Conservatives from Montes Claros and Januária.[49] In 1849, after Dom Pedro II deposed the Liberals and nominated a Conservative cabinet, voters in Januária, guided more by personalism than by party, still supported Chaves, although the Montes Claros electorate did not.[50] In 1851, electoral colleges of São Romão and Januária continued to cast votes for Chaves but supported three Conservative candidates as well.[51] Chaves retained his popularity among the Januarenses in 1855, despite the fact that its electoral college was at that time dominated by Conservatives, demonstrating that regional loyalty still outweighed party loyalty for many.[52] In contrast, Montes Claros, also Conservative dominated at the time, did not put aside partisan loyalties to support a local son.[53]

Not only were eleitores swayed by party affiliation, but they also consid-

Table 4. Voting patterns for Provincial Assemblymen in Northern Minas Gerais by Profession of Candidate

	1830s		1840s		1850s		1860s		Total	
	N	%	N	%	N	%	N	%	N	%
No information	25	16.0	26	5.6	15	4.5	1	1.1	67	6.3
Landowner	23	15.0	53	11.0	36	11.0	0	0.0	112	10.7
Merchant	16	10.0	50	11.0	31	9.2	11	12.0	108	10.3
Civil servant	6	3.8	12	2.6	20	5.9	6	6.7	44	4.1
Law/magistrate	41	26.0	134	29.0	76	23.0	42	47.0	293	28.2
Professor	7	4.4	7	1.5	0	0.0	1	1.1	15	1.3
Clergy	36	23.0	130	28.0	71	21.0	3	3.3	240	23.1
Politician	2	1.3	12	2.6	3	0.9	0	0.0	17	1.5
Military	0	0.0	0	0.0	0	0.0	1	1.1	1	0.0
Medical doctor	2	1.3	40	8.6	85	25.0	25	28.0	152	14.6
Engineer	0	0.0	1	0.2	0	0.0	0	0.0	1	0.0
	158		465		337		90		1,050	

Sources: APM, SP PP 11, cxs. 77, 79–87, 89, 93, 98, 100–101, 103–11, 156, SP AL 1/4, cx. 10, and SP 664–65, 765–66, 835, 891, 1001, 1003, 1058.

ered the profession of potential officeholders. An analysis of a sample of 1,050 provincial and national candidates elected by colleges of the São Francisco region from the 1830s to the 1860s reveals trends that are very similar to those discovered by José Murilo de Carvalho in his study of the national political elite.[54]

Lawyers and magistrates constituted roughly one-quarter of all elected candidates from the 1830s to the 1850s. The percentage of lawyers rose dramatically in the 1860s, although these figures may be misleading given the small size of the sample for that decade. Political participation of medical doctors also increased from 1.3 percent in the 1830s, to 8.6 percent in the 1840s, to 25.3 percent in the 1850s, to 27.8 percent in the 1860s. Priests, in contrast, composed about 25 percent of elected candidates for the first three decades, but their numbers then dropped sharply to 3.3 percent in the 1860s. The presence of landowners also declined gradually, from 14.6 percent in the 1830s to 10.7 percent in the 1850s, dropping to zero in the 1860s. The proportion of merchants remained relatively constant over the four decades, at around 10 percent. The tendency to declare a profession also increased over time. In the 1830s, 15.8 percent of the candidates did not list occupation, compared to 1.1 percent in the 1860s.[55] Changes in voter preference indicate a growing trend toward professionalization and secularization, suggesting the internalization of ideals of order, progress, and modernization (see table 4).

From Fraud to Violence

In 1849, a dramatic shift in municipal electoral dynamics became evident. The year before, Dom Pedro II had exercised the moderating power, dissolving the Liberal-dominated Chamber of Deputies and appointing a Conservative cabinet. The following election represented the first contest in the São Francisco region where public authority was overtly misused to manipulate electoral outcomes. Up to that point, elections had proceeded in a relatively orderly fashion, and only occasionally were results contested, usually on the grounds of fraud or some minute technicality.[56] For example, in 1833, a former justice of the peace of São Romão was accused of tampering with the ballots of the electoral college. The ex-justice, in collusion with the town vicar, allegedly had opened the sealed envelope, removed the twenty-one ballots, and substituted others.[57] In 1844, the municipal council of Montes Claros questioned the legality of voter registration in the district of Bomfim on the grounds that the presiding justice of the peace was a substitute.[58]

Given the potential for abuse inherent in the electoral procedure, it is surprising that such irregularities did not occur more often. Despite the public nature of the voting process, supervisory electoral boards had ample opportunity to manipulate the procedures if they wished. *Mesários* (board members) could deny voters by claiming that they had not registered. Illiterates had no way of knowing whether their choices had been accurately transcribed. Elections could drag on for three or four days as distant voters straggled in, allowing for ballot tampering at night.

The appearance of electoral honesty had to be maintained, however, in order for elections to function successfully as public displays of power. The use of excessive or arbitrary force would erode the legitimacy of the election ritual and undermine the authority of its principal actors. On the other hand, some members of the municipal elite argued that excessively orderly elections were unfair because voters had been intimidated. A minimum level of disorder suggested that some autonomous expression against vested interests was permitted. Fraud was more common than violence, and methods included discrediting members of voter registration boards, refusing to recognize voters from the opposing party, falsifying election minutes, neglecting to inform voters about upcoming elections, substituting alternative voter registration lists, ballot stuffing, and bribery.

Prior to 1849, election-related violence occurred occasionally but was not yet endemic. In Januária in 1838, Councilman João Henriques de Sales appeared at the church with a group of armed dependents, vowing to make widows out of the wives of any who opposed him.[59] In Montes Claros, on 14 April 1839, an appropriately melodramatic dark and stormy night, a shadowy figure fired bullets and lead shot at the Conservative chief José Pinheiro Neves. The culprit escaped on horseback under the cover of darkness, the sound of hoofbeats gradually receding into the gloom. The Conservative district judge surmised that the attempt was grounded in political motives, but nobody was ever arrested. Neves recovered and, shortly thereafter, proposed a municipal law that would prohibit the carrying of arms, including guns, knives, daggers, and other stabbing instruments. On completion of his term, he moved to Diamantina, where he subsequently served on its municipal council.[60]

After 1850, politically motivated violence became endemic in the São Francisco region. Municipal authorities routinely began to violate legal restrictions designed to limit the physical coercion of voters. Laws were passed prohibiting the bearing of arms, stationing nearby military troops, or staging punitive army recruitment drives prior to or following elections. Authorities applied such protective legislation selectively according to their own partisan identity and that of the voters involved. Elite members of the opposition party responded in kind, employing personal security forces to ensure their own safety and that of their clients at election time. They also began to use private mercenaries to coerce and threaten common voters from the other side.

Significantly, elections in the comarca of Rio São Francisco were the most tranquil and the least corrupt during a period that traditional historiography characterized as formative and unstable. Regional revolts threatened Brazilian unity beginning with the Pernambucan revolution of 1817 and concluding with the Praieira Revolt of 1848. By midcentury, the Brazilian state had been consolidated through the formation of a centralized administrative and electoral system. Only when this machinery was in place did elections in the region become violent.

The next few chapters will demonstrate that the presence of the state became more intrusive at the local level by providing municipal officials with the coercive power to manipulate electoral outcomes. Excesses and abuses perpetuated during elections came to be seen as increasingly illegitimate and engendered both elite and popular resistance. Accordingly, the pageantry of electoral ritual, as documented by Richard Graham, began to break down. Responsibility lay, however, not solely with rustic sertanejos operating beyond the reach of law and order, but with a state system that institutionalized electoral violence and corruption.

CHAPTER 4

Centralized Bureaucracies and Electoral Corruption

As the empire became consolidated, municipalities became integrated into broader political networks. Just as municipal councils were reduced to dependency on provincial assemblies, public employees became absorbed into a political system that required them to participate in electoral politics in order to retain their appointments. The price of political patronage was an increase in election-related corruption, violence, and partisan impunity. An electoral dispute that took place in 1849 suggests some of the potential social costs involved in patronage politics and foreshadows a pattern of corruption and violence that intensified in following decades.

In 1848, Dom Pedro II both dissolved the Chamber of Deputies and appointed a Conservative cabinet. This act ended a four-year period of Liberal dominance at the national level and foreshadowed political turnover at the local level as well. In Montes Claros, Liberals dominated the town council and all branches of administration. Consequently, the newly appointed provincial president ordered that the community be placed under military occupation to ensure a Conservative victory in the upcoming elections of 1849. The commander of the provincial special forces, Lieutenant Manoel Joaquim Pinto Pacca, rode into town with his contingent of armed cavalry shouting vivas to the caramarús (Conservatives) and death to the chimangos (Liberals). Conservative municipal authorities, such as District Magistrate Jeronimo Maximo de Oliveira e Castro, collaborated with the occupying force.

Antonio Gonçalves Chaves Sr., the vicar and Liberal chief of Montes Claros, fled to neighboring Diamantina and, while in exile, detailed his woes in a ten-page missive to the provincial president of Minas Gerais.[1] Reverend Chaves was a person of stature in his community. Born in Minas Novas in 1803, he had migrated to Montes Claros as a young man and was appointed vicar to the community in 1834. He fathered ten children, many of whom married into prominent Liberal families throughout the region. Locally, he had attained some fame as a satirical poet and self-educated lawyer. He served as president of the municipal council from 1840 to 1852 and was elected provincial assemblyman in 1842 and 1846. Chaves had assumed leadership of the regional Liberal party by 1842, serving until his death in 1877, when the mantle was passed to his brother-in-law Colonel José Rodrigues Prates. Antonio Gonçalves Chaves Jr. followed in his father's footsteps, becoming a radical Liberal and achieving provincial and national political status.

The vicar's account anticipated an emerging genre of electoral narratives that would evolve in the mineiro political press in the 1860s. Such accounts highlighted the connections between kinship- and party-based patronage, the corruption of the judicial system by centrally appointed officials, and the forms of coercion used by the elite to intimidate voters. Although the details are no doubt exaggerated, beneath his literary license lay a bedrock of politically motivated violence. In keeping with his clerical status, Chaves's denunciation took the form of a morality play. He portrayed his adversaries as victimizers of women, children, slaves, and the elderly, disrespectful of church, state, and monarch. The vicar claimed that Pacca arbitrarily harassed Liberal families, including their women, children, and slaves, and attempted to ransack the homes of prominent Liberals under the pretense of searching for illegal arms. Chaves was placed under house arrest but managed to flee in the wee hours of the morning.

The vicar asserted that Pacca also victimized more humble citizens. In league with the Conservative police delegate, he roamed the streets at night, roughing up poor folk. The locals, however, did not passively accept Pacca's insults. After one soldier twice assaulted a local resident, the victim retaliated and stabbed the soldier to death. Lieutenant Pacca tracked down the culprit and turned him over to his troops, who proceeded to hack the man to death; the pieces were later reassembled for burial. Pacca blamed his soldier's murder on the Liberal camp. Had the assassin not been found, his troops threatened to take ten Liberal lives to compensate for the loss of their comrade. Many Liberal families subsequently fled on foot to Diamantina, a Liberal-dominated community to the south.

Pacca also tried to implicate one of the principal Liberal families in an attempted jailbreak by forcing one of the culprits to "confess" Liberal involvement. When the man refused, he was tortured and crucified, "akin to the supplication of the Redeemer, if not for the nails and cross." Four stakes embedded in the ground in rectangular form substituted for the cross. In place of nails, strong cords bound the victim's hands and feet to each of the stakes. In Chaves's description of the "crucifixion," the elderly victim becomes Christ-like and Pacca and his horde godless. Pacca's men even disrespected the sanctuary of the church, insulting Chaves in prayer, in the confessional, and during celebration of the mass.

Aided and abetted by the Conservative lieutenant colonel of the National Guard, the juiz de direito, and the municipal judge, Pacca's henchmen threatened the people with violent reprisal if they did not vote progovernment. On election day, Pacca subjected the inhabitants of Brejo das Almas and Montes Claros to forced searches. In contrast, Conservatives from Bomfim, the seat of the powerful Versiani clan, were greeted with music, fireworks, and celebration. Pacca also invaded the ranch of a respected octogenarian, the Reverend Joaquim Correia Burgos, where his soldiers attacked unarmed tenant farmers with "incomprehensible fury." Chaves concluded by reporting an act of treason, claiming that the Conservatives had taken the "sacred name" of the monarch in vain, saying that "whoever did not vote for the *governistas* (the party in power at the national level) would be considered enemies of HIS MAJESTY!!!"

Pacca's efforts bore fruit. Only 200 of 949 registered voters cast ballots. The Conservatives won control of the electoral college, and Chaves later lost his seat in the provincial assembly to the Conservative Carlos José Versiani, brother-in-law to the juiz de direito of the comarca. Although Chaves had three years remaining as president of the town council in 1849, a political turnover at the national level eroded his local authority. Centrally appointed magistrates, police officers, and troops brought in from the outside broke him and his allies, thereby securing electoral victory for the Conservative party. In 1851, Chaves resigned his position as council president, probably because his situation had become untenable.[2]

This election marked the first full-blown episode of blatant electoral corruption and violence in the region since independence. A close analysis of the event provides the opportunity to explore a number of interrelated changes in electoral and administrative procedures that evolved during the early decades of the imperial period. The central government imposed two interlocking policies to control elections. The first was to control appointments of municipal authorities, and the second was to limit suffrage. The justification behind these separate initiatives was the same: isolated rural peoples were incapable of intelligent self-government and electoral responsibility.

The reality was the evolution of a political system that became more violent and corrupt as mechanisms of accountability broke down. Independent locals had, since colonial times, always managed to work the system to serve their own interests. However, once municipal official appointments became linked to partisan affiliation and electoral outcomes, regional tendencies toward violence and corruption became institutionalized. After midcentury, the region reported increasing levels of social strain and disorder as it coped with a judicial and policing system that was ineffective and untouchable, barring a national political turnover.

Dynamics of Local Administration

The Conservative victory of 1849 as described by Antonio Gonçalves Chaves would have been much more difficult to achieve without the collusion of the local authorities. By the time that election occurred, the imperial government had gained control of most official municipal appointments and could place political allies strategically in positions of social control. This process took place during the 1830s and 1840s, reversing an earlier trend that permitted municipal populations to participate in the selection of many of their officials. By the 1840s, few locally elected officials remained; moreover, they had lost many of their privileges. This process is perhaps most obvious in the case of the justice of the peace (*juiz de paz*).

The office of justice of the peace had been created in 1827 as the first and only experiment that left the selection of judges to the people and not to central appointment. Every four years, each district elected four justices of the peace, each serving a one-year term. Although the justices of the peace occupied the bottom rung of the judicial hierarchy, they were endowed with fairly broad policing powers. In 1832, the moderado code of criminal procedure further expanded their jurisdiction. They could arrest people if caught in the act of committing a crime, set bail, hold summary judicial hearings, pass judgment, and impose sentence for violations of municipal codes and petty misdemeanors. Justices of the peace could call up the National Guard to assist them in their duties. They also performed the more mundane tasks of obliging vagrants to work, drying out drunks, upholding moral standards, and gathering local statistics. Justices of the peace also supervised municipal electoral boards and elections for officers of the National Guard.

The position of justice of the peace, modeled on borrowed European precedents, decentralized judicial power and placed it in the hands of locally elected citizens. The state anticipated that, as representatives of the people, justices of the peace and jurors would act in a fair and impartial way. Unfortunately, the system did not function as the imperial statesmen had so optimistically envisioned. Reports quickly filtered back to the central government that justices and jurors were easily co-opted and intimidated by powerful rural landowners. Local bosses overruled judges or co-opted them by offering the possibility of marriage into an elite family. Influential landholders compromised jury verdicts through threats and the use of hired thugs (*capangas* and *jagunços*).[3]

Within a decade of the institution of the office of justice of the peace, the Brazilian parliament declared the experiment to be an administrative disaster. What was at issue, however, was not so much the fact that locals manipulated the system, which had therefore become corrupted, but that the office functioned beyond the control of the central government. The statesman Joaquim Nabuco's criticism is revealing: "Justices of the peace are judges who, according to the constitution, should be purely conciliatory and men of peace and harmony [but who] have been converted into law enforcement officers . . . *without any ties to a unified center, obedient only to local interests and passions*, in open conflict with district magistrates in the comarcas, and disobeying the orders of even the provincial governors."[4]

Recognizing its limited ability to control the actions of elected justices, the state responded by limiting the powers of the justices of the peace through the establishment of a multilayered judicial system that placed the juizes de paz at the bottom of the hierarchy.[5] The Criminal Code of 1832 created centrally appointed district judges (*juizes de direito*) with jurisdiction over entire comarcas. The position required a law degree. For most juizes de direito, the post represented the first step in a long political career that, with luck and connections, would eventually culminate in a parliamentary or ministerial position in Rio de Janeiro.

Below the district magistrate existed a host of lesser judges. Each municipality had a *juiz municipal* (municipal judge) responsible for both criminal and civil cases. The *juiz de orfãos* (probate judge) handled civil cases, specifically wills, probate inventories, and the administration of property inherited by minors until they reached their majority. These two offices were eventually combined into a single position, the *juiz municipal e orfãos*. The comarca also had a *promotor público* (county prosecutor), who determined which cases should be brought to trial. Ideally, both municipal judges and county prosecutors possessed university degrees, although in the early decades in the sertão mineiro they rarely did.

Any tendency toward local autonomy within the justice system was reversed under the centralizing Regresso in the early 1840s.[6] Prior to 1840, town councils had some say in the selection of magistrates, submitting three nominees for each position to the provincial president, who made the final selection. The Interpretive Act to the constitution transferred power of appointment outright to the provincial presidents, who in turn were selected by the emperor in consultation with his cabinet. Not only were appointed judges now to be selected by outsiders, but the locally elected justices of the peace also lost many of their prerogatives under the reformulation of the Criminal Code in 1841, which created police delegates (*delegados*) and subdelegates (*subdelegados*). They assumed many of the duties formerly performed by the juizes de paz.[7] Each town had an appointed delegate and each district a subdelegate. These officials did not serve fixed terms but were appointed and dismissed according to the interests of the central government.

Unless they witnessed a crime in process, the police delegates and subdelegates did not have independent powers to arrest but served as intermediaries who carried out the orders of judges and country prosecutors, who were responsible for drawing up warrants. In such a capacity, they could assist a politically allied magistrate in carrying out punitive arrests or could impede the judicial process to thwart an adversary. Thomas Holloway aptly sums up the broad powers enjoyed by the civilian police from 1841 to 1871, stating, "For petty crime and the sorts of behavioral restrictions embodied in city ordinances, then, the Police Chief or his delegate was accuser, investigator, arresting officer, prosecutor, as well as judge, jury, and jailer."[8]

In the small communities of the interior, owing to budgetary constraints, the delegados did not have the luxury of a permanent police force under their command. They received assistance from block inspectors, one appointed for every twenty-five households, who reported suspicious happenings. Should a delegado require backup, he could request a temporary force of National Guardsmen or auxiliaries from the provincial military police.

The military police was created in 1834 after the provinces gained control over their own defenses under the Additional Act to the constitution. Institutionally, the provincial police were distinct from the appointed police delegates, who were considered civil authorities. The military police acted as a standing army that provincial authorities could send to trouble spots when needed. Small infantry contingents (*pedestres*) were also permanently stationed in sparsely populated and isolated frontier regions. The military police suffered chronic underfunding and manpower shortages and almost never attained the quotas designated by provincial law. Even under the best of circumstances, the number of military police for the entire province of Minas Gerais was vastly inferior to that of National Guardsmen enlisted in the São Francisco region.[9]

The National Guard, an unpaid citizen militia, was created in 1831 by the regent Padre Feijó as a substitute for the colonial militias (ordenanças). Based on the French model of a reserve force of citizen-soldiers, it was designed to compensate for the weakness of the imperial army.[10] Dom Pedro I's arbitrary use of Portuguese troops to further his absolutist policies in the 1820s left reformist Brazilian politicians reluctant to create a powerful military. The relative poverty of the central government and the fear that Brazil could go the way of the Spanish-American republics served as additional deterrents. In comparison with neighboring republican armies, Brazilian imperial forces were absurdly undermanned and underfunded.

By law, the National Guard was to "defend the constitution, liberty, independence and integrity of the empire; to ensure obedience to the law, to preserve or reestablish order and tranquility, and to assist the army in the defense of frontiers and coastlines."[11] It proved to be only minimally effective in fulfilling its stated purpose and in certain locales even participated in some regional revolts against the central government. The National Guard had almost no formal autonomy. It was prohibited from arming itself or mobilizing without orders from a superior officer, who, in turn, required authorization from a civil authority. Police delegates and justices of the peace were permitted to call up the guard to combat municipal unrest or to escort criminal suspects, prisoners, or military recruits. Provincial presidents and the Ministry of Justice had authorization to muster the guard during periods of internal upheaval or external war, for example, during the War of the Triple Alliance (1865–70).

Municipal civil authorities, including the justice of the peace, the parish priest, and members of the local electoral colleges, also supervised guard enlistment. All free men aged twenty-one to sixty who earned a minimum annual income of 100$000 were required to serve unless they occupied administrative or judicial offices that had the authority to mobilize the guard. Clergy, jailers, magistrates, and police delegates were thereby exempt but qualified for the reserves, as did civil servants, lawyers, physicians, university students, provincial and national officials, persons over age fifty, and the infirm. The guard depended largely on local and voluntary funding for arms, munitions, uniforms, and training, although by law the provincial government was supposed to fund them. The result was an ill-trained mass of humble citizens, armed by local poderosos, thereby available for both public and private shows of force.

The minimal local autonomy of the National Guard dwindled further over time. The regulatory law of 1831 had given ordinary members the right to vote for noncommissioned officers below the rank of lieutenant. Junior officers elected senior officers for four-year terms, except for commanders and legion majors, whom provincial presidents selected on the basis of local recommendations. Under a reform passed in 1850, however, the rank and file of the National Guard lost the right to elect its own officers.[12] Instead, company *comandantes* submitted nominations for provincial approval. Oddly enough, senior officers were granted life tenure, a reform that had important consequences because officers could no longer be deposed following political turnovers. Perhaps, the makers of this law were more interested in controlling the leadership of the National Guard following the participation of some units in the regional revolts of the 1830s and 1840s than they were concerned with future electoral outcomes.

The National Guard also became more elitist in its membership. In 1850, the minimum annual income necessary to enlist increased to 200$000.[13] Reserve status was also extended to include large landowners, ranchers, and managers of large factories. Enlistment in the guard brought immunity from infantry recruitment, making membership very desirable. Service also became less onerous following a subsequent reform passed in 1873. Recognizing the guard's prominent role in voter intimidation and coercive military recruitment, the government prohibited its intervention in local affairs, limiting its participation to foreign wars or to quelling rebellions, sedition, or insurrections. Police delegates could still request its services, but only in case of emergency. The span for active service was reduced to ages eighteen to forty. Finally, the guard was to mobilize for training only once a year, never during the two months preceding or following an election.[14] Many rural municipalities, however, ignored the new directive and continued to function according to the regulations of 1850.

By 1850, control over the National Guard, civilian municipal police, and judiciary had become highly centralized. The municipality had lost the power to elect or nominate officers of the National Guard, county prosecutors, police officers, and judges. Only the justices of the peace were still elected, and their formal powers had been greatly reduced. These changes in the administrative structures of the state made possible the establishment of a political machine at the national level that produced significant levels of violence in the municipal ambit but that posed almost no threat at all to the stability of the state. By 1850, once a party assumed power at the national level, it was in position to control almost all municipal appointments. Local appointees controlled the judiciary, police, and National Guard only as long as the party that appointed them remained in power. It was, therefore, in their best interests to deliver election results favorable to the dominant party, thereby ensuring their continuing tenure. As the account by Antonio Gonçalves Chaves demonstrates, such control allowed municipal officeholders and their family and friends virtual impunity and permitted them to castigate their enemies with ease.

The key figure in this electoral machinery was the provincial president, whose primary function was not to administer but to secure votes. Presidents were directly appointed by the monarch and, as representatives of the emperor, had the authority to promote or dismiss police officers, judges, and National Guard officers. They also had the power to annul election results if they were achieved fraudulently. Provincial presidents, however, came and went with astonishing rapidity. In Minas Gerais, during the period from 1834 to 1889, 59 presidents and 63 acting vice presidents served, a total of 122 administrations, each lasting on average about six months.[15] Given such limited tenure, it is difficult to imagine that they were very effective as politicians and election riggers, much less administrators. Even if a provincial governor did succeed in installing politically compliant individuals, control was not absolute because a mixture of elected and appointed officials presided over local electoral boards.

The only viable mechanism to assure a political turnover rested in the moderating power of the emperor, which allowed him to appoint and dismiss cabinets at will, to dissolve the Chamber of Deputies, and to call for new elections. Dom Pedro II first used this power in 1841, when he dismissed the Liberal-dominated cabinet and congress. This act became one of the causes behind the Liberal Revolution of 1842, in which Liberals from Rio de Janeiro, Minas Gerais, and São Paulo cried fraud and refused to recognize election returns that gave the Conservatives the victory. The rebels set up provisional governments in their own provinces, deposing appointed provincial presidents and mobilizing the National Guard in their defense. The revolt was poorly coordinated and quickly fell apart. Pedro II pardoned most of the participants, who came overwhelmingly from the rural elite.

Table 5. National Trends in Party Control of the Cabinet, 1840–89

Year	Cabinet	Party
1840–41	Maioridade	Liberal
1841–43	Araujo Lima	Conservative
1843–44	Carneiro Leão	Conservative
1844–45	Almeida Torres	Liberal
1845–46	Holanda Cavalcante	Liberal
1846–47	Fernandes Torres	Liberal
1847–48	Alves Branco	Liberal
March 1848	Almeida Torres	Liberal
May 1848	Paula Souza	Liberal
1848–52	Olinda/Carvalho	Conservative
May 1852	Rodrigues Torres	Conservative
1853–57	Paraná/Caxias	Conciliation
1857–58	Olinda	Cons./Conciliation
1858–59	Abaete	Liberal
1859–61	Uruguaiana	Liberal
1861–62	Caxias	Conservative
May 1862	Olinda	Conservative
1862–64	Olinda	Conservative
1864	Zacarias	Liberal
1864–65	Furtado	Liberal
1865–66	Olinda	Conservative
1866–68	Zacarias	Liberal
1868–70	Itaborahy	Conservative
1870–71	São Vicente	Conservative
1871–75	Rio Branco	Conservative
1875–78	Caxias	Conservative
1878–80	Sinumbu	Liberal
1880–82	Saraiva	Liberal
January 1882	Silva Campos	Liberal
1882–83	Paranagua	Liberal
1883–84	Rodrigues Pereira	Liberal
1884–85	Souza Dantas	Liberal
May 1885	Saraiva	Liberal
1885–88	Cotegipe	Conservative
1888–89	J. Alfredo	Conservative
1889	Ouro Preto	Liberal

Sources: Fleuiss, *História administrativa do Brasil*, 241–383; and Galvão, *Relação dos cidadãos*, 22–56.

The Liberal Revolution of 1842 and the counterreforms of the Regresso intensified growing antagonisms between Liberals and Conservatives. Subsequent elections were hotly disputed, especially in situations in which either the Conservative or the Liberal party came into power at the national level through monarchical decree and then local and provincial elections subsequently followed. Following Pedro II's appointment in 1848 of a Conservative cabinet after six Liberal ones, the elections of 1849 were especially tumultuous. Although Liberals and Conservatives continued to compete at the national level, the ideological gap between them began to narrow as both parties came to recognize a need for greater national stability. A bipartisan Conciliation cabinet followed from 1853 to 1857, but this truce proved short-lived. In the 1860s, ideological differences began to resurface, and subsequent national political turnovers, especially those in 1868 and 1878, produced even more electoral violence at the local level. (National political trends from 1840 to 1889 appear in table 5.)

The state did not, however, attribute electoral violence to the centralized political machine that it had created. Politicians did not attempt to reform that system, nor did they acknowledge that it allowed for the institutionalization of fraud and abuse. Rather, it blamed escalating disorder and corruption on the least powerful element, the common voter. The solution that developed involved the restriction of suffrage over time to exclude all but the elite.

Electoral Policy

In 1874, the senator and imperial minister Paulino José Soares de Souza wrote, "The vote should be given, not to the masses incapable of comprehending the meaning of the act they practice, but to those who enjoy financial independence and guarantee not to let themselves be corrupted or intimidated, above all, by government agents, who are everything in Brazil."[16] His recommendation for electoral reform departed radically from the precedents established a half century earlier.

The political legitimacy of the newly independent state of Brazil had required the adoption of liberal institutions based on European models. Consequently, the 1824 constitution allowed for a fairly broadly based electorate, even by continental standards. Property requirements were minimal, and suffrage was contingent neither on race nor on literacy. All free adult male Brazilian citizens, by birth or naturalization, enjoyed votante status if they earned a minimum annual income of one hundred milréis, a requirement that most artisans and small landholders could meet. The minimum voting age was twenty-five years, except for married men, military officers, university graduates, and priests, who could vote at twenty-one. Men subject to patriarchal control, such as cloistered monks, estate administrators, and sons living with their fathers, could not vote.

The size and composition of the electorate fluctuated according to transformations in imperial electoral policy. Over the course of the nineteenth century, devaluation of Brazilian currency allowed the size of the voting population to increase. The government responded by increasing the minimum qualifications for suffrage. As regional challenges to the state diminished, statesmen worried less about the substance of liberal institutions as long as appearances remained intact. Once national politicians realized that the electoral process was subject to corruption, they quickly developed centralized procedures to deal with electoral violence and fraud that targeted voters of low social status.

The executive, legislative, and judicial powers shared responsibility for electoral reform. The Ministry of the Empire and its advisory branch, the Section of Empire of the Council of State, supervised the process until it was subsumed under the Ministry of Justice in 1875.[17] The legislature then approved or rejected reforms proposed by the executive. Appointed district magistrates reported municipal problems to the provincial president, who then referred such matters to the Council of State. In this manner, the central government acquired information about electoral violence and fraud from the most remote villages of the empire. National politicians responded by attempting to alter components of the electoral process, ostensibly to curtail abuses. Ultimately, they blamed, not the patronage system they had set in place, but rather the excesses of specific municipal officials and the inability of the votantes to resist coercion. Electoral reforms failed, by and large, because they strengthened centralized patronage instead of dismantling institutionalized structures that bred corruption.

Electoral guidelines underwent frequent modifications, with the most significant changes occurring in 1846, 1855, 1860, 1875, and 1881.[18] Early reform attempts focused on minute alterations in voter registration guidelines and the composition of the electoral boards. Changes typically involved reshuffling the responsibilities of the justice of the peace, the parish priest, and members of the municipal council who served on the electoral juntas. National politicians even went so far as to preoccupy themselves with the number of keys used to lock the ballot box and which authorities would hold those keys.[19] During the 1830s, numerous trivial changes were debated but failed to become law, and they need not be cataloged here.[20] The recurrence of national debate concerning such minutiae suggests that, even when adopted, such measures were ineffective or not enforced.

The electoral reform of 1846 introduced measures to minimize corruption that served as the foundation for additional reforms over the next half century. It was intended to eliminate "the anarchic confusion" associated with electoral boards that were "run by personal interests and granted the right to vote by whim."[21] The composition of the voter registration board and the board of appeals was again reorganized, but with a crucial difference, the addition of a centrally appointed official, the municipal judge, to watch over the locally elected authorities.

The 1846 reform also introduced the idea of "incompatibilities." *Incompatibilidade* translates as conflict of interest, in this case forbidding eleitores to vote for kin as senators, congressmen, or provincial legislators or face temporary suspension of voting rights.[22] In 1855, the definition of *incompatibilidade* expanded beyond kinship to include the accumulation of more than one elected or appointed office. This measure also prevented civil servants or politicians from drawing more than one government salary.

Incompatibilities ideally served to minimize corruption in the municipal ambit as well. A legal reform of 1855 prohibited provincial presidents, their secretaries, army commanders, treasury inspectors, police officers, and judges from claiming votes from their areas of jurisdiction, although they could still run for office. Candidates either had to achieve even stronger support from outside to make up the loss of their electoral home base or would have to resign their appointed administrative posts. In 1875, more restrictions were imposed on potential officeholders. None of the officials listed above could run for Congress or Senate in their jurisdiction unless they resigned from their positions six months prior to the election. Contractors assigned to public works and public school inspectors also became ineligible to run for public office.[23]

The expansion of the definition of *incompatibilidades* did not, however, resolve the problem of election fraud. In 1855, the government introduced a new strategy designed to minimize corruption, the *lei dos círculos* (law of election circles). Provinces were divided into electoral districts, each to vote for one provincial representative rather than for an entire slate. Adherents maintained that the law would diminish abuses on the local level because fraud would be limited to a single candidate. The Brazilian parliament had discussed and dismissed prototypes of electoral circles in the late 1840s and early 1850s.[24] In 1848, a Senate commission appointed to determine the constitutionality of the círculos showed great candor in acknowledging the true bases of electoral corruption. It blamed electoral fraud not on faulty legislation but on authorities who failed to enforce the law, observing that corruption was inevitable in a centralized state that controlled municipal appointments. The commission even denounced the ministers and provincial governors for perpetuating electoral fraud in order to stay in power.[25]

This assessment apparently fell on deaf ears because the possibility of implementing the círculos was still being debated in 1855. A second senatorial commission proved less candid and more elitist in assessing why the new system would be open to more local abuses: "The greatest inconvenience of the elections lies in the vestiges of intrigue, enmity, and rancor that they leave behind them. Without a doubt these inconveniences will increase with the círculos. . . . Even with free elections, as are expected, the deputies and senators may no longer come from the most notable and well-known candidates of an entire province. The subaltern employees, village notables, and protégés of local influence will be selected."[26]

The opponents of the law of the círculos were vindicated when the 1855 reform did little to reduce election unrest. Policymakers then sought a compromise by expanding the círculos in 1860. Each new district incorporated three former ones and elected three representatives instead of one.[27] This adaptation proved equally ineffective, as shown by a rise in election-related violence over the following decade. The system of patronage installed by the central government functioned all too well. Political turnovers at the national level resulted in disruption at the municipal level as locally appointed officials struggled to maintain power while aspirants from the opposing party, with provincial and national-level partisan help, sought to take over.

Opportunities for electoral disputes abounded. Parochial elections for town councilmen, justices of the peace, and members of the electoral college took place every four years. Ideally, elections for provincial and national deputies occurred every two years. Special individual elections were also held when a member of the Senate or the Congress died in office. The moderating power of the emperor, however, allowed the dissolution of Congress and the reformulation of cabinets at will. Between 1840 and 1889, Dom Pedro II convened thirty-six separate cabinets, lasting from only nine hours to up to four years. In contrast, Congress was dissolved only four times, with new elections called in 1842, 1848, 1868, and 1878. From 1848 to 1862, the center enjoyed relative stability. A coalition between moderate Conservatives and Liberals had been followed by a long period of Conservative domination. Subsequently, the two parties alternated back and forth, increasing upheaval at all levels.

Both parties partially blamed a lack of balance between Liberals and Conservatives for raising the stakes of electoral outcomes, thereby promoting disorder and violence. Parochial primary elections selected members of the electoral colleges for four-year terms. Hypothetically, the two parties might be fairly evenly matched, but, because of a small majority in a college in a given year, one party might be entirely excluded during an entire legislature. Previous reforms had not facilitated minority party representation but encouraged partisan monopolization of power. Consequently, some national politicians then called for a more radical change, a shift from indirect to direct elections. Votantes, the largest group of active citizens, would be eliminated, and the number of eleitores would be expanded. Rather than electing the colleges from a pool of potential eleitores, all eleitores would have the right to vote directly for candidates. This system, it was argued, would more accurately represent popular political opinion.

The senator, minister of the empire, and long-term Conservative leader Paulino José Soares de Souza was the most vocal proponent of direct elections. In an attempt to justify a reform that would favor only the elite, he argued that the poorer and dependent votantes would actually benefit from loss of suffrage through relief from unending repression and violence at the hands of rural landowners, who squabbled over their votes.[28] Under Souza's plan, only eleitores who met previous qualifications, payment of a graduated residential tax, and literacy would vote. University graduates, public school teachers, councilmen, justices of the peace, military officers, and clerics would be excused from the tax qualifications.

A special commission rejected the plan after prolonged discussion because it was too "aristocratic" in scope. Souza disagreed, insisting that this scheme would guarantee more *liberdade de voto* (freedom to vote). Fewer voters would qualify, but those eligible would be less swayed by local tyrants. He did not elaborate on the more relevant qualification of literacy, which would reduce the electorate far more than a modest increase in income qualifications. Proponents of direct elections, such as Souza, maintained that they would increase real political participation, despite the fact that such a measure would eliminate most of the politically active population. They dismissed the notion that the votantes cast their ballots according to personal preference, assuming that they were puppets of the wealthier eleitores. This belief served as a convenient excuse to eliminate them from the electoral process. Direct elections were not adopted, but a reform passed in 1875 virtually eliminated the majority of voters from political participation while effecting little reduction of electoral violence.

The new law doubled minimum income requirements and, what is more important, complicated the process of proving one's income beyond the ability of most votantes. Registration became a one-time event, on which one received a permanent voter registration card (*título de eleitor*). The reform, however, freed much of the elite from the burden of proving their income before the municipal judge. Government employees, military officers, liberal professionals, the clergy, schoolteachers, and established planters and merchants could vote regardless of income. Nor were officeholders, university graduates, estate owners and leaseholders, and recipients of government pensions required to prove their wealth. In contrast, the uneducated and illiterate were required to assemble legal documentation of their eligibility, which was expensive, time consuming, and complicated. As a result, men who earned the minimum 200$000 but could not surmount the necessary bureaucratic hurdles were excluded.

Politicians still continued to debate the possibility of direct elections for the wealthy and literate sectors of the population. The minister of the empire argued in 1877 that the shift to direct elections "is a guarantee of the rights of party representation. . . . The reform should confer the vote to all those who can read and write and have the necessary conditions of independence for the exercise of such an important right." To compensate for diminished suffrage, the minister promised to expand public education.[29]

Some statesmen also feared the incorporation of mass numbers of European immigrants, rural dependents (*agregados*), and the soon-to-be-freed slaves into the political process. Therefore, under the moderate Liberal cabinet of José Antonio Saraiva, direct elections became law in 1881. The income requirement was set at a flat 200$000, but required supporting documentation was extremely specific and complex. Like the reform of 1875, many civil servants and university graduates did not have to prove their income. The reform also stipulated that, after the initial registration was completed, only literates would qualify thereafter. Under the new law, only 150,000 voters registered nationwide, compared to over one million in 1870. The literacy requirement became universal under the Republican government in 1892.[30]

Causes and Outcomes

Decades of electoral reform had little real effect on electoral corruption and violence. Although the 1881 reform was hailed as a significant breakthrough by the minister of the empire, Manoel Pinto de Souza Dantas, abuses, violence, and fraud generally did not disappear. Dantas's optimistic assessment that "the country witnessed the magnificent spectacle of elections realized

with the greatest order and tranquility, profound respect for the legal prescriptions, and entire freedom to vote,"[31] was due partially to federal under-
reporting of localized electoral violence. Ministerial reports for the remainder of the decade were similarly optimistic, in part because they failed to
mention what the center deemed minor incidents.

The national political elite limited suffrage to curtail electoral corruption
despite a few dissenting voices who targeted the system rather than the
humble votante. Statesmen argued that municipal notables exercised sufficient power over the lives of most votantes to manipulate voting preferences
and even persuade them to engage in violence. In the interior, large fazendeiros enjoyed both formal and informal control over the free poor. Under
ideal conditions, this relationship was reciprocal, albeit unequal. In exchange for access to land, protection, and other benefits, local potentates
commanded votes and personal allegiance.

The accuracy of this elite reading of popular electoral participation is
questionable. Although nonelite voices appear infrequently in the documentation, some limited speculation is possible. The right to vote must have
brought status to the votantes who qualified. It implied the ability to earn a
steady living and served as a bargaining chip in dealing with one's patrão.
Politicians in Rio de Janeiro assumed that votantes engaged in election-related violence to benefit their patrons and that male willingness to engage in
violent behavior was inherent to sertanejo society. These simplistic explana-
tions failed to address popular incentives that might have motivated violence or resistance in some contexts but not others. The next two chapters
provide suggestive evidence that votantes were not acting solely as malle-
able or co-opted dupes of powerful patrons. Rather, they might have resorted to a culturally acceptable response to destabilize electoral rituals that
they saw as hollow representations of liberalism by a corrupt, hypocritical,
and intrusive government.

Elite interpretations of votante electoral motives and behavior provided
self-serving justifications to limit voting to powerful, educated members of
society. Formerly wealthy families who had fallen on hard times were not excluded from the voting process. They could bypass income requirements if
they had professional training or had been appointed to the civil service.
Traditional elites were thereby shielded from political exile regardless of
their financial status. In contrast, the barriers faced by more humble individuals increased over time. An aspiring voter needed both wealth and knowledge of the legal system in order to acquire a voter registration card. When
literacy was added, the right to vote became even more difficult to achieve.

By the end of the empire, the majority of the adult free population had been excluded from the electoral process.

Corruption of the electoral process resulted, however, not merely from the participation of an unruly and uninformed electorate, but also from a centralized administrative system that encouraged abuse. As the Brazilian state became more effectively consolidated, electoral politics became increasingly violent, chaotic, and fraudulent. The national solution that emerged was to punish the least powerful participants involved in the electoral process rather than reformulate the system of machine politics, which rewarded loyal members of the municipal elite with police and judiciary posts. As state centralization became thoroughly institutionalized, Brazilian statesmen came to blame voters for corruption, not the system. They insisted that the geographic isolation of the untamed periphery was to blame when in fact responsibility lay with the institutional connections binding dependent municipal authorities to the will of the political party in power at the national level.

The Brazilian state institutionalized an electoral system that formally adhered to the principles of liberalism yet encouraged the violation of liberal principles, such as the introduction of broadly based suffrage and elected legislative bodies. Legal codes and institutions were redefined according to European models designed to protect the basic rights of the individual. The establishment of machine politics in Brazil, however, distorted the electoral process. The state appointed judicial and police officials, not to enforce justice for all people, but to meet the imperatives demanded by political patronage, that is, to use the means of public power to deliver votes at any cost.

Centralization contributed to the development of machine politics and to the growth of politically motivated crime and election-related violence. In compensation, municipal authorities potentially gained access to provincial resources, providing that they could effectively tap into broader patronage networks. The price of such participation, as the next chapter demonstrates, was escalating levels of politically motivated violence and a higher level of impunity for municipal officials embedded in the patronage system.

CHAPTER 5

Criminality and Impunity in the Sertão Mineiro, 1822-50

In 1839, the juiz de direito Jeronimo Maximo de Oliveira e Castro threatened to resign if the provincial government did not provide him with an adequate police force. After describing various bandit gangs and murder attempts, he vowed, "Your excellency, I will not shirk from sacrificing my life in the service of my adored country, and I will do so willingly, but it must be on the field of honor. To die in a desolate place at the hands of treacherous assassins is to perish at the height of affront and dishonor. No prudent person would impose this kind of death on himself. In this comarca one sees only weak little huts that serve as jails. The National Guard is defenseless and for the most part undisciplined, composed of small farmers overburdened with poverty and family demands."[1]

Oliveira e Castro's complaints about the dangers of his position earned him a transfer in 1840. His defection inspired numerous protests from the magistrates, justices of the peace, councilmen, and National Guard officers in his jurisdiction. A judge from São Romão described him as "a magistrate with integrity who has captured the hearts of the people by administering justice with rectitude and impartiality."[2] Petitioners from the parish of Contendas also praised the magistrate "for his prudence, objectivity, impartiality, and rectitude. Without hyperbole, he may be considered a model among our esteemed judges."[3]

Jeronimo Maximo de Oliveira e Castro was the first juiz de direito to be assigned to the new comarca of São Francisco, created in 1831. He was born in Ouro Preto in 1806, graduated with a degree in law from the university of São Paulo in 1832, and received his first post in the comarca of Paracatú in

1833. In 1834, he was transferred to the comarca of Rio São Francisco. He served until 1840, with several interruptions for sick leave and to sit in the provincial assembly. During the 1840s, he served as juiz de direito in Mato Grosso and in the neighboring comarcas of Paracatú and Jequitinhonha. From 1842 to 1848, he held concurrently the appointment of municipal judge of Montes Claros, but his duties were performed by nominated substitutes. Oliveira e Castro was ordered back to São Francisco in 1850 and resumed his old post in 1852. He continued as juiz de direito, with frequent sick leaves to treat syphilis and other ailments, until his death in 1866.[4]

Oliveira e Castro's sterling reputation began to tarnish in the 1840s. In 1846, the county prosecutor accused him of disregarding the law in his zealotry to the Conservative cause.[5] In 1849, when government troops occupied Montes Claros to ensure Conservative victory at the polls, the juiz de direito condoned police brutality, stating that, if the government felt that murder and violent assault were necessary, he, as a loyal servant of the nation, would not curtail the soldiers' excesses.[6] Apparently, naked violence committed by the state was honorable, while the actions of independent, sneaky assailants, alluded to above, were not.

By midcentury, public opinion no longer unanimously supported Oliveira e Castro and his actions. A prominent citizen of Barra do Rio das Velhas sardonically described the juiz de direito as a "perfect gentleman" but an ineffectual judge.[7] How had such a personal transformation occurred? Oliveira e Castro had become integrated into the local community and had allowed private interest to supersede public duty. He had married Mariana Versiani, the daughter of the wealthiest rancher in the comarca, Pedro José Versiani, who was related by marriage to the powerful Conservative Caldeira-Brant family of Bahia.[8] After Oliveira e Castro was widowed, he remarried, taking Joana Orsini as his bride. They had a son, Torquato, who married Rita Camara, daughter of the Conservative Montesclarense deputy Justino de Andrade Camara.

After marrying into two of the most influential Conservative families of the comarca, the magistrate had to balance family loyalty and party politics with the administration of justice. His trajectory was hardly unique. During the colonial period, the Portuguese government had forbidden crown judges to marry or engage in trade, lest they become too involved with their subjects. These prohibitions were honored more in the breach than in practice.[9] After independence, the imperial government continued this futile policy by deliberately transferring district magistrates every few years. Oliveira e Castro managed to circumvent this pattern, serving intermittently in

Montes Claros over a thirty-year period. He was unusual in his regional loyalty. Rarely were district magistrates willing to forgo career advancement and certainly not in hardship posts like the comarca of São Francisco. In Oliveira e Castro's case, family ties and financial investment in Montes Claros tempered more lofty political ambitions.

Oliveira e Castro's personal trajectory provides a suggestive glimpse into the lived realities behind ideal institutions of social control established under the Brazilian empire. His career pattern was typical of many magistrates and other local authorities entrusted with the maintenance of law and order. Over his lifetime, he successfully navigated between two interlocking systems of patronage: the localized and personal and that defined by partisan networks.

Regional opinion about Oliveira e Castro's professional reputation also provides some indication of the expectations that rural peoples developed about the legitimate exercise of state power. In the 1830s and 1840s, local officials and semiliterate petitioners alike indicated their support for a judge who upheld the principle of equality before the law regardless of socioeconomic class, family, or political connections.[10] These particular representatives signaled their support for liberal legal institutions and the personnel with the will to enforce them. Oliveira e Castro's failure to uphold these principles as he descended into the sordid world of partisan politics subsequently invited censure by disappointed local citizens.

The next two chapters operate in tandem to demonstrate how electoral imperatives tainted liberal institutions ostensibly designed to uphold law and order and distribute justice equitably irrespective of income or social status. This chapter demonstrates how local officials worked the system to advance family interests during the pre-1850 period much as rural communities had done since the colonial era. Some officials continued to exploit their relative isolation, allowing nepotism and corruption to flourish. Yet the failure to distribute justice with an even hand in the mineiro interior cannot be attributed solely to the actions of a few corrupt individuals. It also derived from institutional and structural shortcomings. Local officials were generally unpaid or underpaid, poorly trained, and in many cases unwilling to serve. They lacked the most basic resources and infrastructure, including arms and ammunition, secure prisons, and funds to feed indigent prisoners. Different branches squabbled over jurisdiction and frequently worked at cross-purposes. Elite officers and officials could not always control their subordinates, who may have felt more sympathy toward criminals of their class than they did toward their superiors.

As the Brazilian state became increasingly centralized, expectations rose, accountability diminished, and the abuse of power expanded beyond intra-elite struggles to incorporate the popular classes. Chapter 6 explores these processes at the municipal level after 1850 as national parties made the system of centralized control over municipal appointments work in their behalf. Once municipal officials were required to deliver votes to retain their positions, their effectiveness in upholding the law, curbing criminality, and administering justice diminished. Incidence of recorded violent crimes rose after midcentury, especially those associated with electoral politics. Official impunity became a function, not of isolation, but of integration into partisan networks.

Moreover, these changes increasingly affected the popular classes as they too became subject to official manipulation during elections. The "respectable poor" who enjoyed voting privileges found themselves arrested, imprisoned, or forcibly recruited into the military if they resisted elite demands. Often caught in the middle between a personal patron belonging to one party and a police delegate or National Guard officer belonging to another, a poor *votante* could not count on protection from either quarter. The inability to secure reliable protection from either the state or traditional patrons may have been crucial factors contributing to increased reports of banditry and popular unrest after midcentury. Yet, despite considerable evidence of social stress, the national government showed little interest in reforming the system as long as the state's needs were met. National political parties were more interested in staffing municipal administrations with compliant partisan allies than in whether those officials did their jobs or served the interests of the citizenry.

Institutional Limitations

The criminal justice system of imperial Brazil had been crafted with some care and ideally should have inhibited some of the abuses outlined above. It consisted of a number of carefully demarcated spheres of jurisdiction that, if respected, prevented any one authority from unilaterally usurping power. For example, the National Guard could not act independently but had to be summoned by a justice of the peace, police delegate, or magistrate. Checks and balances existed to minimize the possibility of accumulation of offices. In theory, these precautions looked good on paper but did not function well in practice. A decentralized justice system required money, adequate communications, and professional training to function, resources that the new Brazilian state lacked. Educated judges were in short supply, the majority of municipal authorities unsalaried, the National Guard recalcitrant, and provincial troops were perceived as insubordinate or abusive. Town jails were flimsy, prison guards welcomed bribes, and the vast sertão seemed to have an infinite capacity to absorb fugitives of all sorts.

The imperial government's first challenge was to find adequate numbers of competent personnel to fill administrative posts. As late as 1844, temporary local substitutes filled 1,392 vacancies of a total of 4,001 centrally appointed police and judicial jobs in Minas Gerais.[11] Even the most prestigious position, that of juiz de direito, was hard to fill. Between 1843 and 1850, the Ministry of Justice nominated six candidates to the comarca of São Francisco. Three never even made it there before being transferred to other locations. One nominee spent twelve of the sixteen months of his tenure on leave. His successor received his nomination in June 1844, assumed his post in October, and spent the year of 1845 serving as provincial police chief and attending sessions of the provincial assembly. He received eleven months of sick leave in 1846 and another nine months in 1847 before he was transferred to Alagoas.[12]

When the district magistracy fell vacant, it was filled by a municipal judge, who ideally held a degree in law. First preference went to the judge from the comarca seat, Montes Claros, then the judges from Januária and São Romão. However, no university-trained lawyers resided in the comarca before 1863. Self-trained laymen (*leigos*) provided most legal services in the early decades of the empire. Their qualifications varied according to community of origin, with tiny São Romão possessing the least proficient candidates. Its municipal council recommended nominees on the basis of such vague qualities such as "alert," "able," or "upright citizen with a good reputation." Some candidates were schoolteachers, had experience as interim substitutes, or had tried cases on an amateur basis. Most were wealthy fazendeiros or merchants who held eleitor status. On rare occasions, more humble sorts received nominations: for example, a goldsmith was recommended for, but not appointed as, municipal judge of São Romão in 1841.[13]

The nominees for municipal judge and county prosecutor from Januária had better and more specific qualifications than did those from São Romão. Among the candidates were former militia lieutenants, amateur lawyers, ecclesiastical and civil notaries, officers of the National Guard, justices of the peace, and men who had already had some experience as magistrates. Some had served in other municipalities or provinces, mainly Bahia. Dry goods merchants, cattle ranchers, and sugar mill owners predominated, but men of "mediocre fortune" were also considered if they possessed qualities such as "good family man," "solid and firm with good character and morals," or "adept in the fine arts and letters." Although the law required that even lowly justices of the peace be literate, one candidate was recommended despite the fact that he "writes with difficulty" because he "had aptitude."[14]

The largest pool of educated candidates resided in Montes Claros. Nominees for magisterial positions in Montes Claros were typically fazendeiros or merchants, with an occasional *boticário* (apothecary) or goldsmith. Most had prior administrative experience.[15] Montes Claros boasted a number of competent laymen, including Padre Felipe Pereira de Carvalho, José Rodrigues Prates, Antonio Gonçalves Chaves Sr., José da Silva Souto, João dos Santos Pereira, Justino de Andrade Camara, and Francisco Vaz Mourão. Antonio Gonçalves Chaves Jr. and Pedro Fernandes Pereira Correia took formal law degrees in the 1860s.[16]

Given the lack of trained, professional lawyers in the comarca, the provincial government began to appoint qualified municipal judges from outside the region, especially after the 1841 reform of the police and judicial system. However, the position of juiz municipal remained empty more often than it was filled. For example, between 1841 and 1889 in São Romão, it was unoccupied for forty of forty-eight years. In Montes Claros, eight judges served a total of only thirteen years from 1842 to 1884. The men who assumed these posts frequently requested leave for health, business, or political reasons, and, while a judge was on leave, one of six local, formally untrained substitutes filled the office. These alternates moved up in the hierarchy as they gained seniority.

Willingness to serve as a substitute also varied among the three communities. The citizens of Montes Claros and Januária demonstrated a greater desire to serve as magistrates than did their counterparts in São Romão, perhaps because they realized the potential political advantages involved. Between 1842 and 1869, thirty-four of forty substitutes nominated to serve as municipal judge in Montes Claros accepted. Only six turned down the position, three on the grounds that they preferred to serve as officers of the National Guard. In Januária, only five of forty-eight substitutes turned down the post. In contrast, in São Romão, of forty-three substitutes nominated, eighteen were never sworn in or refused the position. Of these eighteen, only one cited conflict of interest, and one was ineligible because he was the subject of a criminal investigation. Another was relieved from his duties after he was judged to be insane.[17]

Few candidates eagerly assumed the office of elected justice of the peace. Juizes de paz occupied the bottom of the judicial hierarchy. They received no salary and enjoyed limited status after 1841, when their powers were reduced to censuring bums and prostitutes, punishing minor infractions, and compiling municipal statistics.[18] The law prohibited justices of the peace from occupying other official posts concurrently, and many candidates were reluctant to give up more prestigious and less onerous positions such as officer in the National Guard.[19] A shortage of willing and able prospects did not translate into acceptance of all takers, however. For example, in 1839, the justice of the peace of the district of Olhos d'Agua, a peddler, was dismissed because he was illiterate. Admitting that he wrote only with great difficulty, it took him five frustrating minutes with pen and paper to scrawl something resembling his name before the juiz de direito.[20]

A common strategy used by reluctant candidates to extricate themselves from serving in judicial posts was to invoke the legal prohibition against filling two positions concurrently. For example, in 1833, a captain of the National Guard refused the position of municipal judge of São Romão because, "although learned, he understood nothing about the law" and was concurrently serving as councilman and commander of the National Guard. Another nominee also declined the position of county prosecutor because he was already serving as the justice of the peace of a rural district, which was more suited to his modest abilities.[21]

Locals demonstrated considerably less reluctance to accept appointments as police delegates or subdelegates. Such positions rarely fell vacant. Typically, police delegates held office for a period of two to four years, although a few served for only a few months before being replaced. Subdelegates posted to rural districts tended to enjoy longer tenure probably because there were fewer individuals qualified to hold office. The district of Olhos d'Agua in Montes Claros had only five subdelegates over a thirty-two-year period. José Dias de Sá and his son José Jr. served ten and eight years, respectively. Five- and six-year terms were typical, and those lasting ten to twelve years were not uncommon.[22]

The position of choice among most prominent citizens was to be elected an officer in the National Guard. As the institutional successor to the prestigious militias (ordenanças) of the colonial period, the guard signified personal honor but exacted few responsibilities. The guard's minimum income requirements were equivalent to those demanded for suffrage. Guard membership also brought immunity from recruitment into the military, which was considered a most dishonorable institution. In practice, the duties required of the guard were minimal, and officers could blame its ineffectiveness on the lack of resources provided by the state.

Mundane logistic problems impeded the organization of the guard. Although the law required the state to pay for arms, munitions, uniforms, and other supplies, it rarely did. The financial burden of training and provisioning guardsmen frequently fell on the municipal elite. Consequently, organization of the guard proceeded slowly. In São Romão, the National Guard numbered 208 in active service by 1833, but, according to the municipal council, it rarely stirred itself to assist other authorities with local problems such as endemic banditry. Moreover, bad weather, poor roads, and lack of munitions impeded training. Only misplaced optimism led the council to recommend, in 1840, that a cavalry division be set up to take advantage of the superior equestrian skills of the sertanejos, who allegedly rode before they could walk.[23]

By the mid-1830s, Januária's guard consisted of only one unarmed company, which trained with fire-hardened sticks of wood in place of guns. Municipal authorities managed to register four hundred guardsmen by 1840, but factional infighting between two rival districts hindered the election of officers. By the mid-1840s, the guard still remained virtually unarmed, boasting a single army pistol belonging to the company commander of Januária.[24] Montes Claros possessed the largest National Guard, numbering by 1837 almost seventeen hundred men, divided into two battalions of six companies, headquartered throughout the municipality's ten districts. The National Guard of the districts of Montes Claros, São Romão, and Barra do Rio das Velhas was sufficiently well organized to volunteer forces to help defeat the rebel forces gathered in Santa Luzia during the short-lived Liberal Revolution of 1842.[25]

As a fighting force, the guard faced numerous limitations above and beyond the lack of basic resources. It had no autonomy and could mobilize only on receiving orders from specific civilian authorities. In addition, most members of the mineiro National Guard came from relatively modest financial circumstances and were not offered adequate financial incentives to perform their duties. Of twenty thousand members of the provincial National Guard surveyed between 1851 and 1870, 69 percent earned an annual income between 200$000 and 299$000. Seventy-one percent of the National Guard of Minas Gerais pursued agriculture and ranching.[26] Members recruited in the sparsely populated north had even lower average incomes than did those recruited in the more affluent central and southern regions.[27] Guardsmen ordinarily did not receive pay, with the exception of senior officers, instructors, and musicians. They received no compensation for mundane services such as escorting prisoners, transporting government funds, and assisting municipal police delegates. For service beyond the municipality, they earned the same meager pay as the regular infantry after three days in the field and could be required to serve for up to one year. They therefore had little motivation to offer services above and beyond the bare minimum.

The modest financial profile of most guardsmen did not, as one scholar has claimed, translate into a democratic institution.[28] Officers and enlistment authorities enjoyed considerable leverage over the rank and file. Guardsmen could not be completely uncooperative or risked being eliminated from the rolls, thereby becoming eligible for military recruitment. Members of the National Guard did, however, respond selectively to the demands of their company commanders, depending on whether they allied themselves with the authorities or with their intended targets. The rank and file were sometimes sympathetic to the plight of the vagrants, recruits, and petty criminals who found themselves in the county jail. Sometimes officers were reluctant to carry out recruitment, perhaps to protect poor clients or to retain a pool of cheap, occasional labor.

National Guard officers enjoyed multiple advantages, especially after the 1850 reform, which granted them life tenure. Thereafter, they could not be demoted for partisan reasons and enjoyed the freedom to resist civil authorities appointed by the political opposition. Only by formally resigning, leaving the district for more than six months without dispensation, moving away permanently, or committing certain crimes against the government, such as murder, fraud, counterfeiting, aiding jailbreaks, accepting bribes, or embezzling, could they be deposed. Even so, members of the National Guard routinely broke these laws, but few were punished. In fact, officer rank offered a certain degree of judicial immunity. Excessive power gained through life tenure may have been one reason for the diminution of the guard's formal powers in the reform of 1873.

Scholars have debated the purposes that the guard served, arguing either that it upheld government interests or that it became a tool coopted by the municipal elite.[29] In fact, the National Guard served both national and local interests simultaneously. Although members of the municipal elite may have used their control over the guard to settle personal scores, they used it most frequently in electoral contests in which the outcomes benefited both the entrenched local elite and provincial and national political needs. Had the center not created a political system based on patronage, the municipal

Table 6. Military Police Force of Minas Gerais, 1835–77

Year	Regular Troops (on paper)	Cavalry	Actual Number of Troops
1835	300	30	—
1840	480	40	—
1845	440	—	277
1848	500	100	—
1857	575	—	522
1860	595	—	429
1864	728	—	478
1871	1,000	—	550
1874	1,200	—	—
1877	1,200	—	750

Sources: Torres, História de Minas Gerais, 5:1017–26; LM 8, 28 Mar. 1835; LM 173, 31 Mar. 1840; LM 230, 19 Nov. 1842; LM 361, 30 Sept. 1848; Rel. PPMG, 1837, 1841, 1844–45, 1855–58, 1860–61, 1864, 1871–72, 1875, 1877.

elite would not have had reason to manipulate the guard in the first place. The nineteenth-century jurist and political commentator Tavares Bastos acknowledged this dynamic in his accurate assessment of the guard as a key repressive element in state formation and the development of machine politics that benefited the center.[30]

National Guard officers frequently disobeyed the police delegates who had the power to mobilize them.[31] Typical was a complaint voiced in 1864 by the delegate of São Romão: "The guard is ineffective. It doesn't serve, doesn't instill respect, and lacks provisions, uniforms, arms, ammunition, and discipline."[32] Police delegates blamed escalating levels of crime on the National Guard's lack of arms and munitions, negligence, and protection of friends and kin.[33] Even more relevant, some delegates plausibly argued that influential members of the National Guard were actually behind the banditry and brawling that they ostensibly combated.[34]

Civil municipal authorities constantly asked for military police troops to supplement a National Guard that was poorly trained and unwilling to serve for little or no compensation.[35] The provincial military police, however, was grossly undermanned. For example, in 1836, when the National Guard was barely five years old, it numbered 15,117 province-wide, compared to only 330 provincial military police.[36] In fact, National Guard membership in the sparsely populated comarca of São Francisco alone typically exceeded the entire provincial military police force. Troop strength never reached the quotas defined by provincial law (see tables 6–8).

Table 7. Number of Minas Gerais National Guard Members in Service, 1836–58

Year	Active Service	Reserves
1836	15,117	—
1838	32,225	—
1839	40,000	—
1840	47,000	—
1844	51,412	—
1845	58,079	—
1852	31,770	7,527
1853	46,611	10,711
1854	56,119	12,409
1855	59,099	12,664
1857	59,534	12,729
1858	63,340	13,405

Sources: Torres, História de Minas Gerais, 5:1017–26; LM 8, 28 Mar. 1835; LM 173, 31 Mar. 1840; LM 230, 19 Nov. 1842; LM 361, 30 Sept. 1848; Rel. PPMG, 1837, 1841, 1844–45, 1855–58, 1860–61, 1864, 1871–72, 1875, 1877.

In addition to inadequate resources and manpower, local authorities also had to address the reality of substandard jails that offered only minimal security.[37] Imprisoned suspects and criminals escaped all too frequently. In Januária, the murderess Maria Francisca easily escaped one rainy night by digging through the mud and straw walls, already softened by the weather. One murderer made good his escape dressed as a woman. Prisoners could leave jail if accompanied by justice officials to tend to urgent personal matters, a concession that was tantamount to an open invitation to escape. In Montes Claros, prisoners fled while being led to the river to collect water to clean their cells. Convicted criminals and suspects from "better families" not eligible for bail served sentences under very loose conditions of house arrest. Prisoners escaped when the jailor came in with food and water and when poor captives were let out to beg for their sustenance. When the town jailor went home at night, prisoners slept outside or in the council meeting room, under loose surveillance by National Guardsmen. Excessive familiarity and kinship ties between prisoners and prison guards contributed to frequent escapes. One guard in Januária aided a group of fugitives and then took the opportunity to desert himself. Jailers illegally shackled prisoners when chains were available because of the minimal security the jails afforded. Some resourceful prisoners managed to escape with their chains. Others prisoners were less fortunate; for example, one chained inmate was murdered by a gunshot aimed through the bars of his cell window.[38]

Table 8. Breakdown of the National Guard by Municipality, 1833–57

Year	São Romão	Januária	Montes Claros
1833	208	—	—
1837	N.A.	248*	1,682
1843	448	403	1,464
1846	493	406	1,463
1848	490	466	1,085
1852	417	572	—
1857	—	907	—

Sources: APM, SP PP 1/16, cx. 43, p. 47, *matrícula* of the national guard of Januária, 1850, cx. 150, p. 52, *matrícula* of the national guard of São Romão, 22 Mar. 1852, cx. 167, p. 3, 30 Apr. 1843, p. 5, 10 Jan. 1846, p. 11, 22 Nov. 1848, p. 19, 25 Apr. 1857, and SP PP 3/1, cx. 01, 17 Feb. 1836.
Note: Montes Claros's numbers declined as it lost districts to the municipalities of São Romão, Januária, and Grão Mogol.
*Districts of S. João das Missões and Japoré only.

Given the multiple factors impeding social control, municipal officials were only minimally effective in combating social unrest and violent crime. What purpose or purposes, then, did they serve? The answer varies according to the social class involved. Elite officials took advantage of their access to public mechanisms of power to resolve private squabbles. Some used their position to act with impunity, literally getting away with murder. From the perspective of the popular classes, officials coerced and intimidated more than they protected and served.

Elite Impunity

The municipal elite played out their private conflicts on the public field of the local courts. The dynamics of elite competition, corruption, and manipulation of the justice system to serve private interests can best be illustrated by examining a specific case, that of Joaquim José de Azevedo and his clan. Joaquim José was born in Goiás in the mid-1770s. He began his public career in the Goiano military but deserted when his commanding officer entrusted him with the delivery of a pay packet. Joaquim José pocketed the money and proceeded to wander up and down both sides of the Rio São Francisco. He served as a notary in Xique Xique, Bahia, but was dismissed for venality and other crimes. By 1800, he had migrated to the São Francisco region, was captured for desertion, obtained falsified release papers, and returned to settle in Januária. He married, had several children, and then abandoned his wife for a lover. Two of his sons, Luiz José and Francisco José, entered public administration, the former as a petty bureaucrat and the latter as a parish priest.

In the comarca of São Francisco, Joaquim José Azevedo occupied numerous positions, including probate judge, justice of the peace, and provincial tax collector. He served as administrator of the chapel of N.S. da Conceição until he was accused of stealing gold altar pieces and having them melted down into jewelry for his wife and daughters. Azevedo moved back and forth between Januária, São Romão, and Montes Claros during the 1820s and 1830s. He traveled under assumed names, practiced law without credentials, swindled widows and orphans, and allegedly even deflowered and prostituted an orphan girl under his care.[39]

The municipal council of Montes Claros described Joaquim José de Azevedo as "the quintessence of evil, persecutor of virtue, defender of crime, murderer of reputations." It decried "the audacity of his vituperative tongue" and branded him a "complete imposter, recognized troublemaker, incorrigible criminal, avaricious monster, and prototype of evil."[40] Padre Felipe Pereira de Carvalho, justice of the peace of Montes Claros, maintained that Azevedo "had become a monster, riding roughshod over the most sacred rights of the people of Montes Claros through the multiple positions that he exercised simultaneously in the judicial system, at the same time acting as informer and defendant, plaintiff and lawyer, adviser, judge, and jury."[41] Another priest argued that Joaquim José "seems to have been born only to flagellate humanity. . . . His birth in Brazil was either an error of nature or a punishment sent by the omnipotent hand of God to punish the dignified Brazilian nation."[42]

Joaquim José Azevedo's crimes and schemes were legion. In 1830, he arrived in São Romão with a group of armed slaves, demanding that the jurisdiction of the town be turned over to him.[43] In 1834, he was tried for the crime of reducing a free girl to slavery. His friend Francisco Vaz Mourão, who was also president of the jury, contracted a lawyer for his defense and manipulated the jurors to secure a narrow acquittal for his client. After one juror admitted that he had been "obligated" to sign in Joaquim José's favor, a second trial was set. Under the stern eye of the juiz de direito, justice was done, and Azevedo was sentenced to nine years in prison.[44] Joaquim José fled the Montes Claros jail in 1837 and hid in Januária, where he had many friends in the judiciary, who frequently were seen playing cards at his home.[45] He enjoyed enough local prestige to be nominated municipal judge of Januária in 1841.[46] Despite his unsavory, criminal past, he continued to try cases and foment intrigue, especially against parish priests who were rivals of his son, Padre Francisco José de Azevedo Lima.

Parish priests, like Joaquim José Azevedo's son, played an important role in municipal administration. They occupied both secular and spiritual roles and therefore potentially wielded a great deal of local authority. Although the church hierarchy appointed vicars, parish priests were selected by the provincial government. Their civil duties included participating in voter registration and supervisory election boards, collecting statistical information, and mentoring inexperienced or inept justices of the peace. Parish priests were supposed to perform weekly mass and the sacraments, celebrate the holy days of the liturgical calendar, provide spiritual guidance, and demand high moral standards of their parishioners. Like their purely civil counterparts, they were underpaid public servants. Priests in the comarca of São Francisco were also located at the very fringe of effective ecclesiastical authority. The comarca was divided between the distant archdioceses of Pernambuco and Bahia until the creation of the bishopric of Diamantina in 1862, located only two hundred kilometers from Montes Claros.

Parish priests were expected to uphold social order, but their moral authority often proved ambiguous at best. Priests ran the gamut from beloved, morally upright figures to knaves, thieves, and libertines. The Liberal politician and vicar Antonio Gonçalves Chaves received mixed reviews. Municipal allies characterized him as follows: "Always strong in upholding the public cause with his insights and patriotism, he never neglects the obligations of his ministry."[47] The same officials neglected to mention any political excesses, unlike a Conservative newspaper that lambasted him for coordinating a "theocracy-oligarchy" in the mineiro north.[48] Nor did they mention the existence of his ten living illegitimate children. In contrast, a priest with a lower political profile, Antonio Teixeira de Carvalho, was criticized "for appearing in public as the perfect pater familias, arriving at the church to celebrate mass dressed in clerical vestments, at the head of his numerous family of sons, daughters, and their mothers."[49]

When local notable José Ignacio do Couto Moreno declared that "only the Christian religion is capable of making men decent, obedient, and loyal to the government and their superiors," he was indulging in misplaced optimism. European-born Couto Moreno put his faith, not in the negligent parish priests, whom he blamed for the rise of moral degradation, thievery, vagrancy, and prostitution, but in visiting Azorean and Italian Capuchin missionaries.[50] Local authorities frequently chastised parish priests for not fulfilling their ecclesiastical duties. One parishioner from Januária criticized a negligent cleric for letting slaves die without receiving last rites.[51] Priests even indulged in self-aggrandizing blasphemy. In 1835, the vicar of Barra do Rio das Velhas was accused of trying to convince his more naive parishioners that he was a saint. As such, he rebaptized children, for which he charged a handsome fee, and made his way through town accompanied by a threatening armed band. The vicar might have had millenarian intentions far different than the venality ascribed to him by the local authorities. He was censured and demoted, nonetheless, for leading his flock astray.[52]

Priests also competed for jurisdiction by using connections in the municipal administration. An example comes again from the contentious Azevedo clan. The patriarch Joaquim José initiated an acrimonious dispute on behalf of his son, Padre Francisco José, to wrest control of the parish of Contendas from an elderly priest, Antonio Nogueira Duarte. Duarte had served as parish priest of Contendas since 1782, and his promotion to vicar in 1806 marked the beginning of a decades-long conflict with the Azevedos. Joaquim José even managed to bring an official ecclesiastical inquiry against Duarte but failed to dislodge the priest. Joaquim José moved to São Romão in 1812, ending for a time animosities between the two.

Troubles reemerged in the late 1820s when Padre Francisco José de Azevedo became Duarte's assistant. After Duarte tried to arrange for Azevedo's transfer elsewhere, Francisco José and his father successfully lobbied for the parish seat of Contendas to be moved to Morrinhos, requiring Duarte to abandon his properties and relocate. Duarte protested, arguing that the trip was too arduous for an elderly man in his seventies. Francisco José then informed his superiors of Duarte's disobedience and enlisted the aid of his brother, Luiz José, then treasurer of Montes Claros, the libidinous Padre Antonio Teixeira de Carvalho, and a group of parishioners to defame Padre Duarte's good name. Azevedo claimed that Duarte had not performed the sacraments for eight years and ranted against "the vicar's evil spirit and lack of moderation and his prideful, egoistic, vicious, and clutching despotism."[53] This portrayal was a far cry from the descriptions of Duarte's genteel erudition penned by European naturalists who had traveled through the sertão mineiro in the 1820s.[54]

The young Azevedo eventually triumphed over the venerable Vicar Duarte by exploiting local patron-client ties and larger political fears, claiming that Duarte preached antiliberal doctrines in the pulpit and supported the restoration of exiled Dom Pedro I. The provincial government denied Duarte's appeal to restore Contendas as the parish seat, and Azevedo ultimately did usurp Duarte's position.[55] Francisco José celebrated by assembling a group of elite allies and their more humble retinues. The group celebrated his triumph by shouting "Death to all who do not belong to our party," firing gunshots, and holding "immodest" batuques at the vicar's home for three successive nights. The gathering assumed a political flavor when the padre and schoolteacher Antonio Teixeira de Carvalho recruited his own pupils to join the revelries, threatening that resisters would be branded as Restorationist caramarús (supporters of the exiled Dom Pedro I). The gang also tried to break into Duarte's house but desisted when the justice of the peace arrived.[56]

Padre Francisco José de Azevedo ultimately was arrested and convicted in 1834 for the assault on Reverend Duarte's house.[57] While serving time in the Montes Claros jail, he nonetheless managed to keep himself entertained. In 1835, the jailor found Anna Marcelina, the vicar's mistress and an alleged prostitute, under Azevedo's bed after hours. Anna's disingenuous defense that she had been visiting the vicar as an act of mercy was dismissed when the prisoners sharing the cell with the padre corroborated the jailor's testimony.[58] Francisco José de Azevedo did not change his ways when he was released from prison. In 1837, he and his uncle, the justice of the peace, gave sanctuary to a friend who had attempted to murder a slave.[59]

Francisco José's excesses finally did catch up with him. He was murdered in 1843 at the age of thirty-six, a result of bad blood between the interrelated Azevedo and Alves Moraes families. Again, the conflict involved another priest. In the 1820s, Father Manoel Caetano de Moraes of São Romão allegedly had paid a regiment commander 200$000 to attack and kill Joaquim José de Azevedo. When the attempt went awry, Moraes went after Azevedo himself, accompanied by his mistress, a number of armed slaves, and a black accomplice of the "cabra nation." Bringing him to trial for attempted murder took time because all forty-six qualified jurors of São Romão were either accusers, witnesses, friends, enemies, or relatives of the defendant, Moraes. He was acquitted of those charges but was subsequently convicted for election fraud and defrocked as vicar.[60] Moraes apparently was none too savory an individual himself. Among other sins, he had been accused of failing to administer the sacraments, "public incontinence," swindling widows and orphans, reducing free people to slavery, embezzling church funds, and falsifying ballots. He did little to combat open adultery in his community, according to one commentator, because he had illegitimate sons of his own.[61]

Further conflict between the two families arose in the late 1830s when Joaquim José de Azevedo tried to steal the inheritance of his own nephews, Justino and Joaquim Alves. Azevedo had forged the signature of the justice of the peace in order to call up the National Guard to harass the heirs. In the confusion, Justino took a bullet to the kidneys and died.[62] Family friction ignited further when the cousins Captain Eduardo Alves Moraes and Francisco José fell out over a real estate deal. Eduardo subsequently ordered his slave, Lino, and a young male in-law to assassinate the priest. The two men beat Azevedo severely about the head and shoulders, causing his throat and tongue to swell up so badly that he could neither eat nor talk. He lingered for a few days and then died. The murderers fled across the Bahian border with the help of members of the local Liberal faction: Francisco Pereira Proença, the Pimenta brothers, the Silva Gomeses, and the interim district magistrate, João Henriques Sales. Witnesses unwise enough to testify against the culprits were ambushed and presumably silenced.[63]

The tangled saga of the Azevedo clan demonstrates how one family could monopolize civil and ecclesiastical avenues to power and therefore break the law with impunity. The Azevedos brought in priests, police delegates, magistrates, town councilmen, and National Guard officers to further their own ends. Quite literally, they got away with murder. Repeated attempts to bring the Azevedos to justice or to exclude them from positions of authority failed. Joaquim José and his two sons made plenty of enemies, but they also enjoyed the support of numerous friends. They had money and a comparatively high level of education and enjoyed local prestige. Short of killing them, there was no effective way to stop them. These disputes for position, however, were played out largely at the elite level. With the exception of some slave retainers and free rural dependents who appear largely as hangers-on and revelers, elite family conflicts apparently had little effect on the general population. Although partisan strategies, such as attempting to discredit Restorationists for treason and Liberals for aiding and abetting murderers, were voiced, the resolution of these disputes still depended more on family connections than on party affiliation.

National Guard officers also exploited personal connections to manipulate the local justice system, as the case of Lieutenant Francisco de Paula Pinheiro illustrates. Francisco had been accused of killing Antonio Fernandes in order to marry the deceased's wife. Both the juiz de direito and the local vicar upheld the innocence of the accused and recommended against prosecution. An investigation revealed that, during a family squabble, Antonio Fernandes had killed his father-in-law and then fled to Bahia to escape murder charges. When Antonio learned that Francisco had subsequently moved in with his wife, he returned, intending to kill his unfaithful spouse and her lover. The plot was uncovered by a slave, who informed Francisco's brother Lino, the justice of the peace. In the shootout that occurred between Lino and his agregados and Antonio Fernandes and his jagunços, the second group was killed. Shortly thereafter, Francisco married the widow, who incidentally was also his stepsister. The justice of the peace recommended that the case be closed because "powerful justificatory circumstances would render any criminal investigation useless." The vicar maintained that Francisco's only crime was to make an honest woman of his lover.[64]

Like the National Guard, the provincial military police proved susceptible to corruption and venality. Inadequate salaries and provisions made corruption an attractive option. The government was slow to pay military salaries and to reimburse recruitment costs. Horses died and were not replaced. Police delegates and National Guard commanders had to pay provincial troops out of their own pockets to keep them from deserting.[65] On several occasions, Commander José Ignacio do Couto Moreno provided firewood, kettles, and flour to feed and provision troops but could not afford to borrow money to pay them because local interest rates were so high.[66] Theft of military stores exacerbated the army's chronic underfunding. At one point, municipal authorities requested that the province send reimbursements to a destination other than the municipal treasury for fear that they would be stolen.[67]

The provincial police, typically sent to the São Francisco region after repeated requests for impartial external authorities, often were coopted by local authorities and engaged in corruption and brutality. For example, in the early 1830s, the provincial government sent Lieutenant Colonel Parada e Souza and a cavalry contingent to Januária to restore law and order. A local official complained that Parada e Souza quickly allied himself with some of the authorities, including officers of the National Guard. Some Januarenses accused him of torturing Indians, making arbitrary arrests, and illegally using stocks, chains, and instruments of torture. While on campaign in São Romão, Parada e Souza and his troops requisitioned livestock and demanded river-borne transport for their horses. Allegedly, they tried to rape virtuous women when their husbands were away. One woman locked herself inside to protect herself from drunken soldiers, who then set her house on fire, forcing her to leave. Other women fled into the bush.[68] Oppressed locals could and did fight back. When Parada e Souza's troops tried to break up a late evening party, a soldier was shot to death in the melee that ensued.[69]

Unruly soldiers resisted attempts by the civil authorities to curtail their excesses. In 1854, when the juiz de direito censured an infantry sergeant stationed in Januária for concubinage and beating his woman in public, the soldier retaliated by smearing manure and refuse on the judge's home. Allegedly, the sergeant's commander, Antonio Pedro César, not only arrested people arbitrarily but also embezzled public funds. He used the money allocated for soldiers' pay to purchase domestic slaves for his wife, including a cook, two laundresses, and a maid.[70] Brawls broke out periodically between his soldiers and local peasants.[71] When troops intervened to stop a poor man from beating his wife, a free-for-all ensued that left several people wounded and two jagunços dead, including Clemente "Tres Bundas" and Manoel Bravo.[72] Local complaints temporarily forced César's removal, which was later reversed following repeated proclamations of his innocence in the political press.[73]

Clearly, some officials contributed more to social unrest than to its prevention. Individuals such as one police delegate from São Romão who "meted out justice to both the strong and the weak, with much energy and independence, without the least sense of hatred, passion, or personal interest, limiting himself only to the faithful adherence to the law," were the exception rather than the rule.[74] Indifferent municipal police delegates and sluggish National Guardsmen stirred themselves to action only when the interests of the landed class were seriously threatened, for example, during a land dispute among the elite in 1862. This conflict originated when a large clan of interrelated families, the Souza Meiras, had migrated from drought-stricken Bahia to take up residence on the fazenda Gameleira, located in the district of Urucuia. Bordering the municipalities of São Romão, Paracatú, and Januária, Gameleira had been abandoned by its original owners and had reverted to the state. The Souza Meiras purchased the estate but were slow to take possession. In their absence, an extended group of interrelated agregados occupied the fazenda and founded a small hamlet, complete with chapel. The group was dubbed the Serranos because they originally hailed from the nearby Serra das Araras.

In 1863, the Souza Meira family patriarch Captain Ignacio José presented legitimate titles to the land to the municipal judge, and the Serranos retreated to a nearby fazenda. Shortly thereafter, while Ignacio José journeyed to another of his properties, the Serranos attacked Gameleira. Women, children, and slaves fled to the main house, dodging bullets as they ran for cover. For several hours, the attackers looted the remaining houses and outbuildings and then cut off water supplies to the big house and tried to set it on fire. Allegedly, the three hundred besieged women, children, agregados, and slaves resorted to drinking vinegar and even urine. Eleven were wounded and three killed. Hot, hungry, and thirsty, the Souza Meiras surrendered their property to the aggressors. The Serranos made heavy demands in exchange for peace. In addition to the slaves and property that they had stolen (valued at thirty contos), they demanded half of all the Souza Meira properties, most of their livestock, and four additional contos. Fazendeiros in the vicinity fled in fear and requested twenty National Guardsmen from Januária. Rumors quickly escalated about the intentions and strength of the Serranos, who had subsequently attacked the police subdelegate's ranch, stealing some livestock and slaughtering the rest.

The communities of Januária, São Romão, and Paracatú combined their forces to respond to this threat. Fifty members of the National Guard of Paracatú headed for the Serra das Araras, recruiting peasant volunteers on the way. Torrential winter rains and an unwilling force of impressed vagrants delayed help from São Romão for nearly two months. Although the Serranos had managed to mount a force of more than two hundred, the National Guard of Paracatú eventually captured the ringleader and sent him to the provincial jail in Ouro Preto. The remainder of the band fled into the bush along the Bahian border and continued to attack sporadically as a band of mercenaries for hire well into the 1880s.[75]

It took more than five months to neutralize the Serrano threat, allegedly because they enjoyed the protection of some members of the political elites of Januária and São Romão. The armed conflict fought over the possession of the fazenda of Gameleira was not just a simple matter of newly arrived squatters challenging landowners holding legal title to the land. A land register from São Romão dating from 1854 reveals that Gameleira was one of the largest municipal properties, divided among thirty separate owners who registered a total fifty-two parcels of land. The land law of 1850 recognized the rights of persons who had effectively occupied land, even if they had not held formal title to it. The act of registering land and paying a small fee legalized customary rights. Seven of the thirty individuals who registered parcels of land on the fazenda of Gameleira came from the Pereira da Cunha family. Three more belonged to the Santos Pereira clan, probably related to an elite family of the same name from Januária. Four of the five owners who specified how they acquired their land received it through inheritance, suggesting that the abandoned fazenda had been occupied for at least two generations.

Moreover, members of prominent local families registered the two most valuable parcels, valued at 125$000 and 120$000. Manoel Alves Pamplona Jr. was the son of a local notable from São Romão. Manoel Ferreira Orsini, of the Conservative Orsini clan of Contendas, was related by marriage to the juiz de direito of São Francisco. Apparently, elites from São Romão and Januária supported the customary rights of their neighbors, which had been formalized through land registration, instead of upholding the claims of strangers holding title to Gameleira. The Serrano threat was neutralized, not by the local authorities, but by the National Guard of the comarca of Paracatú, who possibly had a stake in the Souza Meira claim.

Continuity and Change

The reality that members of the elite used institutions of social control to protect their own interests and to break the law with impunity was hardly a new phenomenon in Brazilian society. Nor was the fact that social class shaped the actions of the judicial and policing systems. Although the imperial criminal code established the precedent that punishment should fit the crime and not the person, it could not guarantee that officials would exert themselves to protect the interests of all social classes. The introduction of new legislation and institutions did not change social custom and hierarchies overnight. Municipal officials continued to use their powers to resolve intraclass disputes, shielding their friends and punishing their enemies. Rarely did they act to protect and serve the interests of the poor. Nor did elite officials go out of their way to target or punish the popular classes prior to 1850.

The expansion of an imperial bureaucracy that was ostensibly designed to promote law and order came to be associated with an increase in violent crime after midcentury. The following chapter demonstrates some of the consequences of the corruption of new institutions of social control. After 1850, the nature of elite impunity changed, being channeled through party more than kinship. Allies received protection, and the opposition suffered potential reprisals, including false arrest, illegal recruitment into the military, beatings, or worse. The "respectable poor," who made up the bulk of the voting population, became drawn into a corrupt judicial system that previously had paid them little heed. Elite authorities had the power forcibly and illegally to impress voters into the military should they vote contrary to the dominant administration. Partisan protectionism and punishment made a travesty of the justice system.

Not surprisingly, more people began to take the law in their own hands. Reports of banditry, murder, and violent assaults increased. And, although it was concerned with social order, the state was more interested in electoral outcomes. Instead of attempting to reform the system, it blamed the marginal poor for much of the social unrest, just as it had targeted the relatively powerless votantes as the agents of electoral upheaval. Yet, for the average voter, lacking reliable protection from either personal patrons or state authorities, survival increasingly involved confrontation with public or private force.

Part 2

CHAPTER 6

The Escalation of Criminality and Political Violence, 1850-89

In the sertão mineiro, official perceptions of social deviance and criminality changed as the Brazilian state became more centralized. The municipal elite reported increased levels of vagrancy, banditry, and violent crime after mid-century. The focus of official concern shifted from intraelite struggles based largely on kinship to a generalized awareness of social disorder that affected all levels of society. To a certain extent, these complaints reflected a growing concern with marginal groups that did not fit neatly into traditional relations of rural dependency. But elite observations did not merely reflect a heightened awareness of an endemic social problem. They also chart a real rise in violent crime associated with elections.

The imperial state, of course, did not invent violence in the sertão mineiro. In rural Brazilian society, masculine honor found expression through personal courage and the willingness to fight in the service of patron-client relations or to reinforce kinship alliances.[1] Violence was an acceptable means to resolve minor disputes over small properties and personal challenges (*desafios*) to one's courage and personal and family honor. The code of the sertão cut across all social strata, binding rich and poor, patrons, clients, and slaves. Individual violence in the defense of one's honor, therefore, was not considered socially threatening but rather was an accepted masculine cultural norm. Over time, local representatives of the state were able to harness this propensity toward violence to affect electoral outcomes.

Yet imperial authorities also depicted endemic violence and banditry as larger threats to the entire social order when they could not be channeled in the interests of party politics. In part, social unrest arose out of the failure of the system of rural patronage to incorporate all members of society. Army deserters, ex-slaves, Indians, criminals, bandits, day laborers, sailors, migrants, vagrants, the unemployed, and the landless fell under the broad category of marginality (*marginalidade*) and represented a constant challenge to the social order. As economic modernization and changing relations of land to labor further weakened the ability of rural patronage to absorb the free poor, the number of people classified as marginals increased. The state was able to turn the existence of marginals to its advantage and had done so since colonial times.[2] It assimilated marginals into the army, urban police contingents, and public works projects.[3] Rural poderosos also contracted dispossessed men as private mercenaries.

Historians who have researched criminality in nineteenth-century Brazil emphasize economic change and the breakdown of patron-client relations as principal explanatory factors. According to this view, rising crime rates became associated with capitalist development, social dislocation, and rising expectations. Community pressures that had inhibited crime in precapitalist face-to-face societies began to break down when confronted with modernization.[4] In the sertão mineiro, economic and ecological factors, the code of personal honor, and a state too weak to control the municipal judicial system it created all contributed to widespread criminality. In order to understand patterns of social deviance fully, however, one must also consider state centralization and machine politics as explanatory factors. Around midcentury, a propensity to engage in violence expanded to serve electoral needs. Violence also became professionalized as some rural dependents made the transition from occasional acts in the service of their patrão to full-time mercenaries.

The Changing Face of Criminality

Criminality in the São Francisco region does not lend itself to precise quantification. Nineteenth-century police statistics are inconsistent and in many cases incomplete. Marked discrepancies exist between municipal reports and figures generated by the provincial police. For example, provincial reports registered between two and three hundred crimes annually for all of Minas Gerais for the years 1850–53. One provincial police chief readily admitted, however, that such reports were incomplete, observing: "Criminality easily conceals itself and passes unnoticed. Evidence disappears before it can be evaluated. . . . Isolation produces egoism, and the imperative of social duty is unknown or supplanted by personal relationships."[5] In comparison, the county prosecutor of Montes Claros related proportionately greater criminal activity for his municipality alone in 1859. He reported twelve murders, numerous assaults, attempts to enslave free children, and twenty cases of rape occurring within six months, painting a vivid and horrific portrait of daily life in Montes Claros:

> *During the day, men wander the streets, armed with large knives, swords swinging at their sides, daggers at their waist, carrying pistols and other offensive weapons. Women walk armed with razors, which they use, not infrequently, to wound and kill. Even the most respectable citizens carry daggers in their vests, rapiers hidden in their canes, and pistols in their pockets to protect themselves. The sound of gunshots is continuous. . . . municipal law is a dead letter. At night, illicit bands meet at every corner. Sinister, cloaked figures ooze out of the alleys or slink along the walls, awaiting their victims. . . . Batuques heat up in the suburbs, boiling over in saturnalia and debauchery of all kinds. . . . Pistols, machetes, clubs, and daggers accompany guitars and bottles of rum. The frightening sounds of gunshots provide a corrupt and dissonant harmony to the clapping and deafening shouts disturbing the peace. This is the state of things that has led to the popular saying, "Viva quem vence." In the past six months, twelve homicides, numerous attempted murders, assaults, and other crimes have been committed.[6]*

Clearly, the perceptions of the county prosecutor of Montes Claros and the annual criminal statistics reported by provincial police chiefs diverged. Incidents reported to the provincial government probably represented only a small portion of the crimes that were actually committed. Municipal authorities, on the other hand, may also have overstated the facts. For example, in 1861, the police delegate of Montes Claros claimed that more than one hundred murders had occurred in the municipality within recent years.[7] Provincial police records do in fact reveal an unusually high number of murders occurring between 1854 and 1864 in Montes Claros but counted only twenty-two deaths.

Municipal officials may also have exaggerated in an effort to obtain more resources or out of frustration over a system of criminal justice that did not function in the interests of law and order. One police delegate of Montes Claros wrote, "If a criminal commits a crime far from the county seat, is not arrested in flagrante, has time to pack his bags, settle his affairs, and retreat under the cover of darkness, he certainly will not be arrested, even if the crime was committed in broad daylight."[8] At trials, witnesses failed to appear, and jurors buckled under intimidation. Two few officials served too large an area. Revealingly, the justice system in Januária was so inefficient that it took three years for the police to capture a blind assassin who had stabbed his victim to death with the help of an accomplice.[9]

Elite complaints reflected in part the social stresses accompanying the demographic growth of the São Francisco region. Montes Claros, in particular, grew markedly during the nineteenth century. As it began to lose its small-town character, municipal authorities became increasingly ignorant of the identities of the poor and disenfranchised. In the 1830s, local magistrates had been able to discuss at length the characteristics of the slaves and free people of color who circulated through the justice system. By the 1860s and 1870s, the poor had become anonymous, identified with the generic tag *de tal* (so-and-so) to describe unruly brawlers or unfortunate murder victims.[10] In contrast, the ports of São Romão and Januária were more accustomed to the presence of migrants and strangers. River merchants and their "turbulent" crews lived up to the stereotyped behavior of sailors in their brawling, drinking, gaming, and womanizing while in town.[11] Outsiders also committed serious crimes, for example, when two Bahian traders murdered a resident Portuguese merchant in São Romão.[12] Drought migrants appeared periodically, and highly mobile bandit gangs frequented the river towns as early as the 1830s.[13]

The municipal elite came to perceive the poor yet mobile population as an amorphous, undifferentiated mass of idle, drunk, unruly brawlers and murderers. Disorderly lower-class women appeared in the police records occasionally, as prostitutes or participants in Afro-Brazilian batuques and overly lively parties.[14] Women were also prosecuted for brawling. In Montes Claros, two women unfittingly named Pacífica and Maria were arrested for fighting in public, tearing at each other's clothes, and pulling out hair.[15] Sometimes even women of higher social status appeared in police records, as in the case of two "respectable" German sisters of São Francisco who were arrested for fistfighting in the streets.[16]

Women most commonly emerged, however, as perpetrators of or victims in crimes of passion and contests of masculine honor. For example, in 1876, Joaquim Ferreira da Silva Faria was prosecuted for attempted bigamy. Faria had married a woman from Gorutuba, frittered away her dowry, tried to poison her, and forced her to prostitute herself. He abandoned her and migrated to São Romão, where he tried to marry a prosperous widow.[17] Husbands enraged over real or imagined infidelities shot their wives and the men who might have cuckolded them. Kin could also suffer, as did the sister of one Januária woman who had given her sibling shelter only to be killed herself when the estranged husband came calling. Women also killed their husbands, often enlisting the aid of their lovers. One estranged spouse even tried to burn his wife alive.[18]

Elite authorities considered the mobile and marginal poor to constitute a social threat for a number of reasons. Generally landless and semiemployed, these folks typically managed to evade the efforts of judges and policemen to bring them to justice by moving on. The only real leverage that authorities had over them was the dubious risk of military conscription. Men classified as truly marginal fell below the minimum income requirements to vote and therefore could not command protection from a political patron unless hired as a private mercenary. Not surprisingly, elite officials tended to blame these rootless elements for most of the crime plaguing the region.

Only in Montes Claros did authorities make any serious attempts to address the problems of disorderly vagrants and violent crime. The Conservative Montesclarense provincial deputy Justino de Andrade Camara battled rival communities in the provincial assembly to secure a trade school to provide training for homeless adolescents and orphaned migrants. During his ten years in the assembly (1870–80), he was one of the principal advocates for an expanded provincial police force, tenaciously fighting against proposed budget cuts that would weaken an already attenuated institution.[19]

Officials recognized a second social category within the nonelite population, the so-called respectable poor. These individuals were small holders, artisans, cowboys, or rural dependents who had access to land or protection from a patron or both. As people who maintained a fixed residence and earned a modest but relatively dependable living, many held voting privileges. The elite sought to discipline this population and the more unruly *marginais* through their domination of institutions of social control. The most effective means of coercion at their disposal was the threat of military recruitment. Moreover, forced conscription proved especially persuasive at election time.

Military Recruitment

Most Brazilians considered military service an ill-paid and dishonorable line of work to be avoided at all costs.[20] The federal army had to resort to forced recruitment to fill its ranks as few volunteers came forth who were willing to endure the rigorous conditions and low pay of army life. Provincial troops and the National Guard bore primary responsibility for carrying out conscription.[21] Single men between the ages of eighteen and thirty-five who did not meet minimum income requirements for the National Guard could be drafted unless their parents depended on them for financial support. Recruitment targeted the colored poor, of whom there was no shortage in the São Francisco region.[22] The comarca, however, and Minas Gerais more generally, was notorious for failing to produce its fair share of recruits.[23]

Prior to 1837, blacks could not be recruited to avoid the entry of slaves and ex-slaves into the armed ranks.[24] This limitation caused one recruitment agent in São Romão to voice considerable regret, claiming that blacks were numerous, robust, and resistant to the fevers that felled whites and racially mixed *pardos* (light-skinned mulattos).[25] Some local slave owners disregarded the formal exclusion of captives. One landowner conditionally freed one of his captives (presumably of lighter color) stipulating that the slave serve five additional years as an army recruit. Another owner protected one of his slaves from criminal prosecution by presenting him as a military volunteer under an assumed name. The slave had killed an assailant in defense of his owner.[26]

A lack of genuine commitment, competing class interests, and the inadequate physical security offered by most municipal jails thwarted recruitment efforts. Typically, word leaked in advance to potential victims, who ran into the bush or fled downriver until the recruitment drive had passed. In one instance, the National Guard commander of São Romão refused to call up a force to help with recruitment unless the government paid for its sustenance. By the time the undisciplined and incompetent guard had assembled for duty, potential draftees had already learned of the draft and had fled. Moreover, guns, chains, iron collars, and padlocks used to transfer recruits to the capital had not been returned by the provincial police chief after a previous sweep, making retention of the reluctant "volunteers" even more difficult.[27]

Personal connections and social status helped avoid conscription. Allegedly, Antonio Teixeira de Carvalho Jr. of Contendas persuaded his father, the parish priest, to register him for the National Guard despite the fact that he lacked the requisite income. Another priest used his office more generally to protect vulnerable parishioners under his care. Recruiters dubbed Padre Antonio Nogueira Duarte of Contendas the number one enemy of the army because of his determination to shield as many young, poor, single men from recruitment as possible. He performed marriages of several couples at once and even married captive recruits inside the town jail. In this instance, the juiz de direito requested that recruitment be suspended because the rash of hasty marriages "benefited neither the couples nor the state."[28]

Property ownership and gainful employment also made a difference in the decisions made by recruitment officials. One hardworking draftee from

Montes Claros was released because he was honorably engaged in the administration of the estates of his elderly widowed father and young sisters. In contrast, Gertrudes Maria do Nascimento was less fortunate. She appealed to the substitute juiz de direito to free her only son, Bernardo, from the clutches of recruitment agents, claiming that she was a widow and that Bernardo provided financial support for her and her daughter. Her case was dismissed when several townspeople testified that Gertrudes was a prostitute and her son a known gambler and vagrant.[29]

National Guardsmen and provincial troops had to capture recruits, confine them in prison until a sufficient number were assembled, and then escort them to the provincial capital. Jailed draftees were housed and fed at municipal expense. Escape from most rural prisons proved relatively easy because of both structural weaknesses and personal negligence or indifference. For example, in 1837, six recruits escaped easily after the soldiers guarding them had a party until dawn and fell into a drunken stupor.[30] In 1843, an escort of six soldiers leading eight recruits from Januária to Montes Claros was no match for a band of forty armed outlaws, who released the draftees by force. The next day, the bandits swaggered into town and gave the soldiers back their guns, clogged with clay and mud.[31] Recruitment agents from Montes Claros also complained of flimsy prisons and the loss of their chains and shackles to other communities who failed to return them.[32]

Although general recruitment drives tended to be relatively unsuccessful, officials could and did target individuals punitively, especially during or near election time. The threat of forced conscription was sufficient to convince most of the poor yet respectable votantes to comply with the wishes of elite officials. In theory, many of them were exempt if they met National Guard eligibility requirements. Yet most were illiterate and faced difficulty making the courts work on their behalf if recruited illegally. Depending on the political climate, their patrons might or might not be able to protect them. Many worked small plots of land and had families. Fleeing to another community to avoid the draft was a less viable option for a poor individual who possessed modest resources worth defending. As a group, this group was more potentially vulnerable to the draft than were the despised marginais.

Criminal Causation

Increasing levels of social disorder cannot be attributed solely to the marginalized poor or to the actions of a few corrupt members of the administra-

Table 9. Criminality in the São Francisco Region, 1832–79

	Murder	Attempted Murder	Assault	Theft	Illegal Slavery	Sex Crime	Corruption & Fraud	Banditry	Vagrancy/ Disorder	Slave Resistance	Election Crimes	Total
1832–47	19	8	4	22	1	0	17	11	3	2	6	93
% interval	20.4	8.6	4.3	23.7	1	0.0	18.3	11.8	3.2	2.1	6.5	100
1848–63	57	2	4	3	5	3	5	8	13	3	21	124
% interval	45.6	1.7	3.2	2.5	4	2.5	4.0	6.5	10.5	2.5	16.9	100
1864–79	33	4	3	3	3	0	13	17	10	1	28	115
% interval	28.7	3.5	2.6	2.6	2.6	0.0	11.3	14.8	8.7	0.9	24.3	100

Sources: APM, SG, *códices* 436–45, SP, *códices* 511, 566, 607–8, 658–59, 707, 709–10, 761–64, 818–19, 877–79, 931–36, 1045–47, 1093–94, 1140–41, 1187, 1251–53, 1304–8, 1362–63, and SP PP 1/18, cxs. 62–66, 118–19, 138–41, 196–97, 232, 237–38, 283–84, 294, 297, 316, 322.

Table 10. Criminality in Montes Claros, 1832–79

	Murder	Attempted Murder	Assault	Theft	Illegal Slavery	Sex Crime	Corruption & Fraud	Banditry	Vagrancy/ Disorder	Slave Resistance	Election Crimes
1832–47	13	5	2	19	2	—	4	4	—	—	3
1848–63	20	—	2	3	2	1	2	2	3	—	9
1864–79	18	1	2	2	1	—	5	5	4	—	13
TOTAL	51	6	6	24	5	1	7	11	7	0	25
%	35.7	4.2	4.2	16.8	3.5	0.7	4.9	7.7	4.9	0.0	17.5

Sources: APM, SG, *códices* 436–45, SP, *códices* 511, 566, 607–8, 658–59, 707, 709–10, 761–64, 818–19, 877–79, 931–36, 1045–47, 1093–94, 1140–41, 1187, 1251–53, 1304–8, 1362–63, and SP PP 1/18, cxs. 62–66, 118–19, 138–41, 196–97, 232, 237–38, 283–84, 294, 297, 316, 322.

tive elite. In order to arrive at a more accurate assessment of criminal patterns in the São Francisco region, I quantified all complaints submitted by municipal authorities from the comarca of São Francisco to the provincial police chief in manuscript and in published provincial reports. These figures may reflect not all criminal occurrences but rather the number of transgressions reported in any given year and preserved in the archives. The data may not be statistically representative but provide information suggestive of categories of social deviance that the local authorities found most disturbing (see tables 9–12).

This sample provides information about 332 crimes that took place in the São Francisco region between 1832 and 1879. Murder, corruption, banditry, and election-related crimes constituted 71.8 percent of all reported crimes. Murder alone accounted for one-third of all recorded crimes. When the data are broken down by fifteen-year intervals, the connections between patronage politics, administrative corruption, and violent crime become obvious. Between 1832 and 1847, theft, murder, and corruption were the most commonly reported crimes. After 1848, corruption became linked to electoral fraud and violence. Complaints of murder and vagrancy also rose dramatically during the period between 1848 and 1863. Election-related crimes demonstrated a steady rise, peaking at 24.3 percent of all crimes reported during the interval 1864–79, when animosities between Liberals and Conservatives were at their height. The frequency of such crimes, incidentally, suggests that national electoral reforms were largely ineffective.

Patterns of criminal behavior differed among the municipalities, yet all three demonstrate remarkably similar timing and rates of election-related corruption and violence, varying between 17.2 and 17.6 percent. Reports of corruption came from local authorities who were in power and from those who had been ousted and were trying to regain control. In other types of crime, the three municipalities diverged. São Romão had the highest percentage of murders, over 43 percent, but low indices of corruption and banditry, both at just 8.6 percent of all crimes. Montes Claros reported the most livestock rustling, a comparatively high number of murders, and the lowest levels of corruption and banditry of the three communities. Januária, in contrast, documented the most corruption, almost twice the number of cases in São Romão and more than three times the amount recorded in Montes Claros.

Regional concern about banditry grew in the late 1840s and reached a peak in the 1870s. Banditry was not social banditry, to use Hobsbawm's term, organized outlaws fighting for class interests. Typically, banditry was

Table 11. Criminality in São Romão, 1832–79

	Murder	Attempted Murder	Assault	Theft	Illegal Slavery	Sex Crime	Corruption & Fraud	Banditry	Vagrancy/ Disorder	Slave Resistance	Election Crimes
1832–47	0	0	0	0	0	0	2	1	1	0	2
1848–63	21	1	0	0	2	1	0	4	2	1	2
1864–79	4	0	1	0	0	0	3	3	3	0	6
TOTAL	25	1	1	0	2	1	5	5	6	2	10
%	43.1	1.7	1.7	0.0	3.4	1.7	8.6	8.6	10.3	3.4	17.2

Sources: APM, SG, *códices* 436–45; SP, *códices* 566, 607–8, 658–59, 707, 709–10, 761–64, 818–19, 877–79, 931–36, 1045–47, 1093–94, 1140–41, 1187, 1251–53, 1304–8, 1362–63, and SP PP 1/18, cxs. 62–66, 118–19, 138–41, 196–97, 232, 237–38, 283–84, 294, 297, 316, 322.

Table 12. Criminality in Januária, 1832–79

	Murder	Attempted Murder	Assault	Theft	Illegal Slavery	Sex Crime	Corruption & Fraud	Banditry	Vagrancy/ Disorder	Slave Resistance	Election Crimes
1832–47	6	3	1	2	—	—	11	6	2	2	3
1848–63	16	2	1	1	2	1	4	3	9	2	7
1864–79	11	3	1	2	1	—	8	8	3	1	14
TOTAL	33	8	3	5	3	1	23	17	14	5	24
%	24.3	5.9	2.2	3.7	2.2	0.7	16.9	12.5	10.3	3.7	17.6

Sources: APM, SG, *códices* 436–45; SP, *códices* 511, 566, 607–8, 658–59, 707, 709–10, 761–64, 818–19, 877–79, 931–36, 1045–47, 1093–94, 1140–41, 1187, 1251–53, 1304–8, 1362–63, and SP PP 1/18, cxs. 62–66, 118–19, 138–41, 196–97, 232, 237–38, 283–84, 294, 297, 316, 322.

practiced by loose bands of marginals operating for personal gain or in the service of a powerful landowner. By the end of the empire, a new type of outlaw emerged. The jagunços, rural dependents willing to engage in temporary violence to uphold their personal honor or that of their patrons, were replaced by the *cangaceiros*, professional mercenaries. Scholars have linked the rise of the cangaceiro with the breakdown of rural patronage and the weakness of the state under the First Republic (1889–1930).[33] The roots of this phenomenon, however, reach back to the emergence of machine politics in the late 1840s, when bandit gangs and murderers began to operate under the auspices of official patrons in the São Francisco region. National Guard commanders and police subdelegates were justly accused of coordinating bandit activities more often than suppressing them.[34]

Electoral Crime

The level of open political conflict on the periphery began to escalate with the elections of 1849. Although only Montes Claros suffered direct military occupation to ensure Conservative victory at the polls, in other electoral districts Liberals were ousted through a variety of public and private means. For example, in three outlying districts of the municipality of Montes Claros, centrally appointed authorities recognized hundreds of unqualified voters out of "party spirit" while excluding qualified landowners and even priests.[35] Authorities from São Romão reported similar manipulation.[36]

In Januária, Liberals put up active resistance to the Conservative takeover by manipulating the size of the electorate. Some Conservative councilmen alleged that, in 1848, the then Liberal-dominated voter registration board had accepted voters who were "proletarian and impoverished with insufficient credit to buy a decent jacket, including in this class day laborers, miserable libertos, and minors under age twenty-one." To prove their point, they revealed that the board had registered 458 voters in the district of Januária, nearly twice the number of National Guardsmen who were subject to the same qualifications. In addition, Conservative-dominated Brejo had lost voters when the board excluded 91 affluent citizens from a list of 286 qualified persons compiled by a Liberal justice of the peace. The Council of State, not surprisingly, ruled in favor of its fellow Conservatives and ruled that a new registration be conducted.[37]

Although a national political turnover had been effected by Dom Pedro II, it had little effect on the locally elected municipal council of Januária, which remained in office. The Liberal-dominated council also attempted to resist the new regime by rejecting the appointment of Conservative Francisco Proença as police delegate, refusing to recognize his credentials and swear him in. Several municipal officials and National Guard officers then circulated a petition claiming that Proença had promised to "recruit and enslave" the people. Proença reported these indignities to the national government, protesting that, aided by a liberto named Ciriaco Lopes da Rocha, the other municipal employees "walked through the streets, convening the infamous, proletarian, and depraved population and gathering boys with horns, rockets, [and] fireworks . . . to vituperate and injure me." He added accusations of treason to strengthen his position, reporting, "Suffice it to say that one disgraceful proletarian said to my attorney these words—the emperor can be cast out, let alone an employee."[38]

According to the Conservative subdelegate Ignacio José do Couto Moreno, Liberals did not limit their insubordination to Proença's appointment but actively opposed demotions of all Liberal National Guard officers and other municipal authorities. Allegedly, preparations for armed revolt proceeded in the districts of Januária and Mucambo. The mastermind behind the presumed revolt was subdelegate Manoel de Souza e Silva, in Couto Moreno's words, "the most bloodthirsty man that this sertão has the shame of holding in its breast." His front man was the municipal Liberal chief, National Guard commander, and president of the town council José Lopes da Rocha.[39]

The election of 1849 represented the first test of the centralized bureaucracy's abilities to manipulate election results. Its success was mixed. Military intervention was required in Montes Claros, and Liberals in Januária used their remaining positions in municipal government to block the ascendancy of Conservative appointees and to manipulate voter registration. By 1851, Conservative authorities had established themselves in key administrative positions, and elections held in that year to select electoral colleges proceeded relatively smoothly, with only a few minor disruptions. In the districts of Coração de Jesus and Montes Claros, election results were voided by the provincial president because of corruption and conflict between Liberal and Conservative factions.[40] Police officers also drew fire in the districts of Montes Claros and Brejo das Almas. Manoel Caetano de Souza e Silva, a Liberal from Januária, attempted to disrupt the elections in the district of Contendas but was unsuccessful. The 1851 campaigns in São Romão and Januária proceeded more peacefully.[41]

The region experienced little political upheaval in the following decade.

This tranquil interim was due largely to a period of stability at the center, ushered in by the Conciliation cabinet, which lasted from 1853 to 1857, followed by a period of Conservative domination in Congress until 1864 (although two Liberal cabinets were appointed between 1859 and 1862). This accord was shattered in 1864 when Dom Pedro II again invoked the moderating power to effect a political turnover favoring the Liberals.

The elections of 7 September 1864 were tumultuous, especially in Montes Claros. The abuses perpetuated by Lieutenant Pacca and his Conservative allies in 1849 may very well have set the stage for the conflict that erupted in the municipality. Conservative juiz de direito Jeronimo Maximo Oliveira e Castro contested the Liberal victory, accusing Liberal police delegate José Rodrigues Prates of election fraud and coercion. In response to a query made by the provincial governor, Prates sent a lengthy defense of his behavior. In so doing, he left a vivid description of the politics and *parentela* (family influence) dominating political life in Montes Claros.

Castro was one of the local Conservative chiefs and a member through marriage of the Versiani clan. Prates was not only an active Liberal but also the nephew of the Liberal patriarch Antonio Gonçalves Chaves Sr. Castro alleged that Prates had exceeded his authority as a police officer and threatened voters with military recruitment in order to gain votes for the Liberal ticket. Prates then disobeyed two of Castro's orders: the first to halt recruitment and release conscripts, the second to dismiss the local police force. Prates denied the allegations, claiming that he had informed voters that they could not carry arms and that he had put the police force at the disposal of the Conservative substitute municipal judge Francisco José Pereira do Amaral. Prates maintained that only sixteen policemen and National Guardsmen had conducted a search for arms to preserve the peace. Both Conservatives and Liberals were searched; pistols and knives were found amid the baggage of some heavily laden mules, and only one slave was arrested. Prates insisted that members of the Conservative Versiani family had been spared such an indignity. He also defended two of Reverend Chaves's adolescent sons, Eusebio Antonio and João Antonio against the charges that they had arrived armed and disrupted the elections.[42]

In addition to denying all charges that he had abused his access to public power, Prates charged that the opposition had resorted to punitive violence. A horde of Conservatives, including the district magistrate's brothers-in-law, nephew, cousin, and niece's husband, had surrounded Prates's house, making violent threats and shouting insults. They acquired powder and shot in the store of Gregorio José Velloso, the Conservative justice of the peace, and subsequently fired into the doors of all homes owned by Liberals. Rumors circulated that the followers of prominent Conservative landowners would show up armed on election day. It was also rumored (falsely) that the Conservatives had secreted sixty or seventy guns in the sacristy.

In response to these public and private shows of force, approximately 70 percent of registered voters did not participate. Only 120 ballots were cast for Liberals and 70 for Conservatives. The limited return suggests that the threat of violence was sufficient to inhibit most voters. Additional data support this observation. Voter turnout figures from 1851 to 1876 show that the majority of eligible votantes did not exercise their right to vote for eleitores, despite the fact that failure to comply brought financial penalties.[43] In most cases, only 25–40 percent of eligible voters actually participated in elections. In some extreme instances, like the election of an electoral college in the district of Coração de Jesus in 1851, only 34 of 338 voters participated.[44] These figures undermine the proposition that local oligarchs exerted almost unlimited control on a mass of ignorant, humble, and dependent votantes. A majority refused to vote at all.

The election of 1864 in Montes Claros reveals ways in which local officials used both public and private power in electoral disputes. Although Prates, a Liberal, controlled the police force as an appointed delegate, the Conservatives had not yet been dislodged from the town council and some judiciary positions that had access to the National Guard. In this instance, however, the Conservatives resorted to private means. Numerous accounts of electoral disputes follow a similar structure in which the party in power was accused of using public force to coerce voters while the party on the "outs" used private mercenaries to disrupt electoral procedures. In addition, Prates stressed repeatedly the links of parentela that bound the district magistrate to the Conservative camp while deemphasizing these same relations when telling his side of the story. Only once, halfway through his defense, did he mention that Antonio Gonçalves Chaves Sr. was his uncle. In the rest of the account, he speaks only of party comrades (*coreligionarios*).

As long as the Conservative-dominated municipal council of Montes Claros remained in office, infighting persisted, despite the Liberal victory at the polls. In 1867, the council again accused the district police officers of illegal and irresponsible army recruitment raids, holding unwarranted searches at night, invading the homes of women and children, and nabbing married men, merchants, ranchers, and even eleitores. The council went so far as to question the masculinity of the substitute delegate, county prosecutor, and

National Guard commander by using feminine grammatical constructions. The exact wording defies translation but is as follows: "Partem elas (as autoridades) para o Arraial a saber: Delegado, Promotor Publico e Comandante Superior (todos colocados no feminino: tal gramatica tal verdade)."[45]

Domingos José Souto, the maligned substitute police delegate, responded by blaming his detractors for irregularities in the recruitment process. He maintained that recruitment errors were inevitable because the municipal council had withheld the qualification lists of both voters and the National Guard, two groups that were exempt from active military service. He further alleged that the council used its influence to shield individuals from recruitment. The police had recruited only two married men, both of whom had abandoned their wives and were known for their criminal, disorderly, and dissolute behavior.

The council also accused Souto of aiding and abetting criminals. It alleged that he had sent three cronies to arrest one Maximo de tal on a frivolous pretext. They then murdered him en route to the local jail in full view of his pregnant wife. In his defense, Souto insisted that he had been framed and that the case of Maximo de tal was based on an "amorous intrigue of the lowest and most infamous sort." The author of the crime was Pepino, a Conservative and former justice of the peace. To further his seduction of Maximo's sister, Pepino hired an assassin who had formerly enjoyed Conservative protection to kill his own wife and Maximo. When the hit man arrived at Maximo's house, he falsely declared to be acting on the orders of the subdelegate. The official investigation that ensued cleared Souto and uncovered no political content other than the Conservative affiliation of the amorous Pepino.[46]

The threat of military recruitment became even more powerful means of political coercion following the outbreak of the War of the Triple Alliance (1865–70). Although the war initially captured the imagination of a few idealistic youths, stalemate was quickly attained, and the war become one of attrition. Recruitment guidelines targeted the marginal poor, but, in the heat of an election, authorities were apt to make mistakes and nab the sons of both elite landowners and the votante class belonging to the opposition. Such fears may well have heightened the level of unrest in the elections of 1868.

In 1868, Dom Pedro II dissolved Congress and called for new elections after appointing a Conservative cabinet. This turnover stimulated a new wave of electoral violence in the São Francisco region. In the district of Boa Vista in the municipality of Montes Claros, the justice of the peace arrived with four hundred armed capangas (bandits) to control the elections. One voter, accused of submitting two ballots, was removed from the scene by the bandit leader and only narrowly escaped the attentions of an angry and drunken mob. Armed rebels from Contendas roamed the municipality, disrupting elections in outlying districts. Later that year, the substitute municipal judge of Montes Claros reported that prominent members of the governista party roamed the streets at night shouting, "Death to the Liberal party."[47]

The 1868 elections also resulted in fraud and violence in sleepy São Romão, where the Liberal municipal council refused to swear in the newly appointed Conservative police delegate until after the elections. In preparation for the electoral race, the municipal judge, in league with the council, requested fifty National Guardsmen to expand an informal armed force of three hundred.[48] A substitute delegate also accused the municipal judge and police delegate of releasing the Conservative Captain Pedro Gonçalves de Abreu (arrested for premeditated murder) as part of their planned electoral takeover.[49] This incident was an exception in São Romão, where covert corruption was more common than open dispute.[50]

Januária remained relatively quiescent during the elections of 1864 and 1868, but problems surfaced in the outlying districts of Morrinhos and Japoré.[51] Throughout the late 1850s and early 1860s, citizens from Morrinhos launched numerous complaints against the municipal council of Januária for deliberately withholding information about scheduled upcoming elections, thereby preventing their participation. The council, in turn, coyly blamed postal delays for the unfortunate incidents.[52] Delaying or diverting the mail was a common strategy to prevent elections from occurring.[53] The electoral college of Januária also annulled elections on the grounds of technicalities; for example, the returns from Morrinhos in 1861 were invalidated because the names and numbers of qualified voters who did not appear after the third roll call had not been recorded in the official minutes. In the same year, in the district of Japoré, a justice of the peace compromised the elections by "seducing" voters with promises to waive any fines incurred for failure to attend.[54] Irregularities and falsified documents also tainted the election proceedings in Januária in 1865.[55]

More active unrest erupted in 1872, when disorderly mobs numbering in the hundreds took to the streets shooting off fireworks, guns, and bombs. Supposedly, the acting police subdelegate and his Liberal allies led this uprising. Many slaves and *quilombolas* (members of fugitive slave communities) also participated. They had run away from their owners, proclaiming themselves free. The slave presence may have resulted from an erroneous understanding of the law of the free womb or resistance against possible sale to coffee regions located to the south. The delegate did not discuss their motives, but he used their presence to invoke the specter of slave uprisings and justify the use of police force to quell the disturbance.[56]

One of the better-publicized examples of electoral collusion in Januária took place in 1875. The legislative assembly had to devote considerable energy to prove that the election had never occurred! The race for provincial deputies had been close, and the returns from Januária were crucial in determining the winner for the seventh district. When the provincial secretary requested an additional copy of the election proceedings, the interim council president responded that he could not comply because the record book had disappeared. Two justices of the peace and four councilmen, all eleitores, then testified that the election had not occurred. Their testimony blamed Luiz Afonso Fernandes for convincing the justice of the peace not to convene the eleitores. In collusion with the local Liberal chief, Luiz falsified the election proceedings in favor of the Liberal candidates. On reading the falsified election returns for Januária in *O diário de Minas*, Eleitor Alvaro José Rodrigues submitted a formal complaint to the juiz de direito. Two parish priests supported Alvaro's account, declaring that they had not been invited to celebrate the electoral mass. Statements issued by notaries and the justice of the peace of Brejo do Amparo also confirmed Alvaro's story. The assembly concluded that Conservative candidate Virgilio de Melo Franco was the legitimate representative of the seventh district.[57]

In 1878, factional tensions again boiled over in Januária. The municipal judge was forced to flee armed forces organized by the police subdelegate. In his words, conditions were "worse than in a village of wild Indians."[58] Violence peaked in 1879 when a Liberal landowner from Jacaré nicknamed "Neco" descended on Januária with his band of jagunços. Reportedly, the juiz de direito panicked, shouting, "Save yourselves if you can!" before fleeing downriver, spreading rumors of death and destruction in his wake. His cowardly behavior earned him considerable derision on the part of the locals.

This partisan conflict originated in a juridical conflict between the Liberal Manoel Caetano Souza e Silva and the Conservative lawyer Pães Landim. Criminal charges had been brought against Manoel Caetano to prevent him from participating in upcoming elections. He hid out until election day and then snuck into the church, where he proceeded to officiate as the head of the election board, taking advantage of a law that prohibited arrests on election day. Another version of the "revolt" claims that the conflict began when

Conservative gunmen disrupted a Liberal wedding reception with gunfire. Tensions rose after they captured one of Neco's followers, trussing him up like a pig and sending him downriver in a flimsy canoe.[59]

Neco set up an armed camp on his estate and captured many of the port hamlets of the Rio São Francisco. The civil engineer Theodoro Sampaio, who passed through Januária during the "revolt," found the tales to be greatly exaggerated and condemned the emotional state of the fugitive judge as "pathetic."[60] The cowardly behavior of the authorities would be long remembered.[61] Ten years later, in response to a rumor that a Conservative planned to attack some prominent Liberals with the help of some of Neco's famed capangas, the juiz de direito called up a volunteer peasant force to confront the danger.[62]

Partisan officials from Januária and Montes Claros also selectively implemented added restrictions to voter registration imposed by the 1875 and 1881 reforms. In 1881, Conservatives accused the judges Clemente Marcondes e Silva (a relative of the minister of the empire) and Antonio Gonçalves Chaves Jr. of showing favoritism to Liberals during the new registration period. Allegedly, they had registered criminals and unqualified voters with Liberal affiliations but had refused Conservative petitions on the basis of bureaucratic minutiae, even requiring that elderly men bring birth certificates to prove that they were of voting age.[63] Chaves retorted that, of the 174 individuals denied registration, 90 were Liberals and only 80 Conservatives. The Conservatives were disgruntled because they still constituted a minority, 208 opposed to 256.[64]

In Januária, in response to the 1881 reform, Liberal bosses developed a scheme in which wealthy notables paid unnecessary taxes on behalf of humbler individuals. These men then presented the tax receipts as proof of eligibility and voted according to the wishes of their benefactors. The county prosecutor who registered this complaint compiled a list of over sixty illegally registered jurors and voters. Most he discounted on grounds of insufficient income. One man earned the prosecutor's special condemnation by attempting to register as a juror, claiming that he qualified by virtue of the salary earned by his wife as a public school teacher. In an unusual defense of female property rights, he denounced the man as a "parasite," declaring, "The salary that his wife can earn is hers alone, her exclusive property, untransferable. Therefore, a third party cannot take advantage of it under these circumstances."[65]

By the end of the imperial period, electoral violence, intimidation, corruption, and fraud had become commonplace. Attempts to refine electoral legislation in order to curb these problems had little or no positive effect. Given that no effort was made to reform the system that made these abuses possible, intensification of electoral upheaval and irregularities should come as no surprise. Consequences, however, were not limited solely to infrequently held elections. As official appointments became more closely linked to partisan identity, treatment in the criminal justice system became linked to party as well. Before midcentury, kinship and class were the keys to one's trajectory through the courts. In the final decades of the empire, party affiliation became crucial as well.

Partisan Imperatives

The paradigm shift from kinship to party in the selection of municipal authorities became evident as early as the 1840s. For example, in 1841, the president of the municipal council of Januária recommended Manoel de Souza e Silva as a candidate for municipal judge because he was of a "political creed compatible with the circumstances of our state and constitution." Souza e Silva tried to avoid the responsibility by relocating to Montes Claros, provoking accusations that he had fled to avoid the risk of offending one political party or the other.[66] Manoel Souza e Silva and his son Manoel Caetano did, in fact, avoid firm partisan alliances in order to manipulate the system to serve their own interests.

Partisan appointments also resulted in the placement of officials who not only exceeded their authority but were also negligent or incompetent. For example, university-educated Justiniano Luiz de Miranda, who served as municipal judge of Montes Claros from 1857 to 1859, was described by his former classmate, the district magistrate Oliveira e Castro, as so "crassly ignorant and supremely stupid" that he required the legal assistance of the layman Antonio Gonçalves Chaves Sr. to fulfill his duties. Allegedly, Miranda also had developed a drinking habit "to the point of falling down drunk in the streets and being carried unconscious to his home."[67] Miranda enjoyed the political patronage of the powerful Liberal Queiroga family of Diamantina, while Castro was a committed Conservative. Yet Castro's objections were not wholly partisan as he included tacit praise for the abilities of Antonio Gonçalves Chaves Sr., a staunch Liberal.

By the 1860s and 1870s, the identification of party affiliation in local denunciations of official corruption had become commonplace. Initiating a paper trail of partisan abuses laid the bases for future dismissal following national political turnovers. One such example is a police delegate of Contendas who made an exceedingly transparent attempt to switch parties in order to retain his post when the Conservatives came to power in 1868. He had received his nomination in 1865 as the protégé of Colonel Prates, the Liberal chief of Montes Claros who had assumed leadership on the death of his kinsman, Antonio Gonçalves Chaves Sr. The subdelegate had harassed Conservatives on the orders of his patron during his administration. When the Conservatives regained power, his enemies retaliated by trying to recruit his brother into the army. In order to save himself, the cornered delegate offered the Conservative chief, Justino de Andrade Camara, allegiance in exchange for protection and patronage. His ploy was unsuccessful.[68]

The importance of party affiliation was made abundantly clear by a substitute municipal judge of the district of Pedras dos Angicos (later São Francisco) when he argued in 1870 that the police delegate and substitute delegate "do not merit one iota of respect on the part of the upstanding citizens of this region to assume the post of police delegate. The former is a red historical Liberal, and the latter broke with the Conservative party over a minor tiff. The third substitute, also a Liberal, makes war against Conservatives." The judge argued that none were to be trusted and that all should be replaced by loyal Conservative candidates.[69]

The role of partisan affiliation in selective law enforcement also became more apparent as the conflict between the radical Liberal chief Manoel Caetano de Souza e Silva and the Conservative faction of Januária shows. When the Conservatives won at the polls in 1868, they took advantage of their rise to power to settle some old scores. Manoel Caetano had been charged with embezzling public and private funds in Bahia, illegally enslaving free people, and attempted murder but had managed to escape the law by illegally calling up the National Guard in his own defense and by assembling a group of armed retainers. Once the political tide turned, newly appointed substitute police delegates decided to freeze Manoel Caetano's assets in order to force payment of his hefty six-conto debt to the state. With the help of the National Guard, they took temporary possession of seven slaves, real estate, promissory notes valued at approximately fifteen contos, and even his wife's household goods, including several pieces of gold and silver jewelry. Whether, in the face of this partisan attack, Manoel Caetano managed to regain his property remains unknown.[70]

Manoel Caetano's story illustrates how, by the mature imperial period, enforcement of the law came to depend on party affiliation. In the first half of the nineteenth century, municipal elites had used the courts selectively to resolve interpersonal conflicts, but these disputes were not defined politically. Social structures defined by kinship and community gave way to party patronage in the mid-nineteenth century. The emergence of this pattern in the rural São Francisco region in the 1840s even predates that observed by Fernando Uricoechea, who writes, "The closer we move toward the periphery and the early periods of the empire, the more kinship defines and stereotypes the chances for the appropriation of office on a traditional, patrimonial basis; conversely, the closer we move to the center and the later periods, the more partisanship defines those same chances for the appropriation of office in a rational, bureaucratic way."[71]

National and provincial government granted positions of municipal authority as rewards to loyal clients who produced favorable election results. The Brazilian nation took advantage of preexisting patronage networks based on kinship and transformed them to serve the needs of the state by linking municipal authority to electoral procedures. As by midcentury the avenues leading to administrative appointments became more centralized, local elites embraced party politics in order to ensure continuation of their monopoly over the mechanisms of social control. Allies of the dominant political party used their control over the police and judicial system to target political adversaries. Municipal clients "on the outs," in turn, began to recruit professional mercenaries from the marginal classes to secure a competitive advantage in the game of electoral intimidation. This choice contributed to the politicization of violent crime.

The Brazilian state managed to graft party politics onto a preexisting system based on kinship ties and personal loyalty. In so doing, the empire did not invent corruption but transformed it to work in the interests of national politics. Partisan politics came to serve as a kind of fictive kinship that superseded localized family loyalties. This transition became increasingly evident by midcentury. Policemen, magistrates, and National Guard officers explicitly invoked party loyalties to defend their actions or to attack their rivals. This dynamic manifested itself in the courts, in the electoral colleges, and in the municipal councils. One police delegate neatly summed up the problem when he observed that complaints addressed to the provincial government about corrupt police were not likely to be effective because they were directed to the people who had appointed the corrupt individuals in the first place.[72]

Maintaining the status quo on the national level thus exacted a high price within the municipal context. State centralization translated into greater levels of localized violence and disorder. Although politically influential members of the landed elite held the advantage when it came to manipulating the less powerful votantes, the "respectable poor" were not entirely passive in this process. Some resisted by refusing to vote at all. Others probably engaged in violent behavior to ensure their own survival. As election conflict intensified and judicial and policing institutions were co-opted to serve party politics, the poor were unable to secure reliable protection. The evidence used here fails to provide a conclusive reconstruction of popular motivations. However, it seems plausible that poor voters might have contributed to electoral violence not necessarily to please their patrões but to reject the electoral pageantry that so patently contradicted liberal ideals.

In any event, politicians and administrators shirked responsibility for rising levels of crime. Discussions about criminality came to bear a striking resemblance to debates concerning electoral reform explored in chapter 4. Votantes, citizens who met the minimal income requirements necessary to participate in municipal elections, were blamed for the problems of the electoral system, just as vagrants who had slipped beyond the reaches of rural patronage were made the scapegoats for the failure of the criminal justice system. The state addressed the symptoms caused by the ills of state centralization rather than their cause. It laid the groundwork for the *política dos governadores* of the First Republic and ensured that abuses inherent to machine politics during the empire would be perpetuated in a republican Brazil.

CHAPTER 7

The Moral Economy of Partisan Identity and Liberal Ideology in the Sertão Mineiro

In 1862, the district judge of the comarca of Rio São Francisco reported to the provincial police chief that second lieutenant Sebastião da Silva Gomes Bittencourt had killed his cousin and *compadre* Josino José Pimenta. The murder, which occurred on 14 December 1860, was grounded in political conflict between members of the Conservative and Liberal parties. According to the judge, the two cousins had always enjoyed a close friendship despite their political differences. The judge commented, "Whenever they met, they would always engage in heated debate about the virtues of the parties that each followed. Josino, a Liberal, and Sebastião, a *saquarema* [Conservative], insulted one another reciprocally during their fervent discussions; however, they always concluded as friends."

On that fateful day in 1860, the two had met at Josino's house and had taken up their customary debate as they got drunk on wine. The insults between them became progressively crude and devolved into threats. Sebastião then drew a dagger and threatened to kill Josino. Josino responded by extending a large machete to his adversary, declaring, "If you want to kill me, do it with this machete and not with that puny knife." Rising to the challenge, Sebastião drove the blade through Josino's body.

The crime took place in full view of Josino's two brothers and his wife. One of the brothers present, the police subdelegate Francisco de Paula Correia, arrested the murderer. Shortly thereafter, Sebastião was released and, according to the district judge, had wandered freely about the district ever since, protected by his influential relatives, who were prominent players in local politics. Only two years later did the district magistrate Jeronimo Maximo Oliveira e Castro finally put aside his political affiliation with Sebastião and request the intervention of federal troops to bring him to justice.[1]

This episode contains a number of now familiar motifs. On the surface, it appears to be a manifestation of the code of the sertão, the customary ethic that required men to defend their personal honor through the public use of violence.[2] Personal courage was an essential ingredient of masculine honor in frontier regions of Brazil and in Latin America more generally.[3] Personal honor derived from two sources: the quality of one's lineage and one's personal virtue. It was also gendered.[4] For women, virtue consisted of guarding their sexual purity before marriage and their fidelity thereafter. Men, on the other hand, defined their honor through safeguarding their female kin from (sexual) danger, keeping their word, and demonstrating virility by refusing to bear insults to self or family.[5] The immediate catalyst of the murderous attack was Josino's challenging Sebastião's masculinity when he ridiculed the size of his weapon. The public nature of the insult apparently required an immediate and violent response.

Kinship and partisan alliances also enabled Sebastião to evade the law. Although he was arrested, he was subsequently released, to be apprehended again only through the efforts of the district magistrate, a university-educated *bacharel* (law graduate) who had been trained to act according to the liberal principles codified in imperial Brazilian law.[6] Judge Oliveira e Castro, however, did his duty only tardily and reluctantly, probably owing to his affiliation through marriage to one of the most influential Conservative families in the comarca.

The Meaning of Partisan Identity

The event took place in the 1860s, when violent political contests in the region had reached an all-time high. Yet more was at stake than initially meets the eye. Up to this point, I have depicted partisan affiliation largely as a strategic choice made to gain access to local power. By the 1860s, however, party identity had come to take on additional layers of meaning in the rural culture of the sertão mineiro. Clearly, partisan identity mattered in the internecine conflict between Josino and Sebastião. Defense of party combined with strong drink escalated into a family tragedy in which Sebastião killed a beloved cousin.

This event challenges a number of scholarly assumptions about the nature of partisan identity in the Brazilian interior. Party identity and family loyalty have frequently been held to be synonymous for rural Brazil, but this example provides an exception to the rule. The long tradition of political debate between the two prior to the assault also suggests that party affiliation meant more than just a convenient label with which to identify separate interest groups or extended family networks. By the 1860s, members of the municipal elite had bought into partisan categories so much that defense of them could provoke murder.

Historians have paid little attention to the meaning that rural, municipal elites assigned to partisan identity. Standard interpretations of imperial political parties tend to adopt a centralist approach, assuming that ideological content diminished the farther one traveled from Brazil's coastal cities. For example, Oliveira Viana characterized the Liberal and Conservative parties as "simple aggregations of clans organized for the common exploitation of the advantages of power."[7] Moreover, nineteenth-century commentators and contemporary scholars also assumed that the subtleties of party affiliations were too sophisticated for humble sertanejos to comprehend. According to Afonso Celso, an absentee imperial congressman from northern Minas Gerais, electoral politics became a form of rustic entertainment: "Politics for the people of the interior is the supreme exercise of the mind, the preferred pastime, the favorite occupation. These are not the politics of ideas and principles but the politics of local power, of petty emulation and of unintelligent conceit, that does not tolerate victory by the opposition, exerting the maximum effort to impede or annul dissent. Politics in these conditions assumes the character of gambling, with all the sensations and excesses of that comparable passion."[8]

Imperial politicians believed that rural populations fell short in their understanding and implementation of liberal ideas and institutions. Therefore members of the elite in Brazil's isolated sertão continued to act according to personalism and customary norms that legitimized violent solutions over due process. Although some appointed district magistrates sought to curb local retrograde tendencies, bureaucrats, politicians, and administrators in the interior appropriated public power to serve private interests.[9] Trained judges and amateur municipal authorities struggled with competing value systems.

These interpretations have much to recommend them. Considerable evidence presented in this study suggests that members of the rural elite did embrace political parties and invoke the language of liberalism in attempts to achieve pragmatic aims. Such a reading is appropriate, but it is also incomplete. As the imperial state matured, and as party identity became grafted onto traditional notions of individual and corporate honor, that identity became intensely meaningful to members of the rural elite. It also came to serve as a kind of fictive kinship that could cement alliances and incorporate nonrelatives. In addition, some members of the local elite adopted the language of liberalism as an idiom through which they defined a moral economy of appropriate political behavior. This terminology was used consistently despite the fact that it yielded few material rewards for interior communities, as demonstrated in chapter 2 above. Upholding modern norms in the absence of tangible benefits suggests that rural peoples genuinely incorporated new ways of thinking about political relationships beyond the level of rhetoric. Finally, municipal notables drew clear distinctions between the two parties in moral terms.

Municipal officials discussed their conceptions of political honor, partisanship, and appropriate boundaries of political behavior in two principal venues. The first was private, consisting of correspondence between municipal authorities and their provincial superiors, including presidents, secretariats, provincial police chiefs, and assemblymen. The second, more public avenue was the partisan press that flourished in Minas Gerais during the final decades of the empire. The development of print media changed the nature and scope of local political contests in which rivals challenged one another's personal honor. As a new and durable venue for debate, the press extended knowledge of dishonorable localized events to a broader audience beyond the immediate witnesses of a heated exchange. Having been recorded in print, such conflicts became permanent, immutable, and available for consumption by a provincial or even national audience. Consistent with Benedict Anderson's analysis of the role of print media in national identity formation, mineiro newspapers were crucial in expanding the field of political honor to a broader socially constructed "imagined community."[10]

The contests detailed here are duels of words, an effete variant of the oral tradition of the *desafio*, or challenge, in which sertanejos questioned each other's honor and that of their families in verse. The desafio tested the participants' stamina, inventiveness, and courage, given that such contests often provoked physical violence, as the example of Josino and Sebastião did. For politicians, the final outcome of a print exchange might be less bloody but was taken no less seriously. As John Chasteen puts it, "Lawyers, pharmacists, doctors, agronomists, notaries, and the townsmen also dueled with verbose thrusts and parries in the public forum provided by local newspapers. Being sensitive matters of honor, these prolix encounters could be unbelievably protracted."[11] The weapons wielded, however, were not knives or machetes but liberal ideals of appropriate political behavior.

When Liberalism Goes Local

Some scholars have understandably viewed the development of liberalism in Brazil with a certain cynicism. It did not develop out of a bourgeois desire to eliminate traditional privilege and enact social reforms; rather, it was adopted strategically by elite interests to preserve their prerogatives following political independence from Portugal.[12] Brazil did adopt many of the classic components of European liberalism, such as a written constitution, division of power into executive, legislative, and judicial branches, relatively broadly based suffrage, the reduction or elimination of trade restrictions, the provision of public education, and formal equality before the law. It sanctioned individualism, competition, and the pursuit of profit, order, and progress. Brazilian statesmen believed that political stability would lead to economic progress, which could be measured scientifically. As the century progressed, social Darwinism and positivism offered competing ideologies that many sought to incorporate into the construction of the modern nation.

In practice, like other liberal nations at the time, Brazil practiced an elitist liberalism underlaid by personalism and patronage.[13] As the historian E. Bradford Burns notes: "In the classical sense, liberalism meant placing individual freedom and material gain over public interest. The elites felt that they shaped their institutions on the latest European models. They ignored the obvious fact that those models did not reflect American experience. As one immediate consequence the European models sired weak and compliant economic structures in the New World. They also favored the strong, wealthy, and resourceful minority over the huge, but weakened majority."[14]

In his perceptive study of state building in imperial Brazil from the perspective of judicial policy and reform, Thomas Flory maintains that the rural elite adopted liberalism purely strategically, arguing, "In frontier areas emerging elites may have favored elective processes and local autonomy as a basis for local institutions since this eased their own ascendancy. But with only socioeconomic motives to sustain it this sort of liberalism could serve, at worst as a euphemism for lawlessness, at best it was self limiting."[15]

Such arguments suggest that the rural elite adopted liberal values as a strategic choice and was unable to imagine ideological possibilities beyond its immediate territorial horizons. Yet, clearly, municipalities could not operate in political isolation following the centralizing reforms of the 1820s–1840s. Municipal officeholders had to choose sides in order to tap into patronage networks. The rationale behind partisan preference in imperial Brazil, however, has remained elusive. Scholars have tried and failed to link party choice to occupation, education, regional identity, relative involvement with the export sector, rural versus urban origins, or bureaucratic tendencies.[16] The parties, however, drew members from heterogeneous backgrounds, and party affiliation cannot be neatly categorized.

At the national level, ideological choice clearly mattered at critical junctures, notably in the 1830s and 1840s and again in the 1860s and 1870s.[17] After the centralizing reforms of the Regresso in the early 1840s, Liberals and Conservatives became more homogeneous in their desire for stability and a strong, effective state. Partisan compromise peaked during the bipartisan Conciliation cabinet (*conciliação*), which lasted from 1853 to 1857.

During the 1860s, ideological debate again deepened.[18] The bipartisan Progressive League, consisting of moderate supporters of the conciliação, began to break down during the War of the Triple Alliance (1865–70). Following a political turnover in favor of the Conservatives in 1868, some members of the Progressive League created the Reform Club, which called for the abolition of slavery, an end to the moderating power, and a parliamentary regime modeled on British lines. Intellectuals belonging to the "Generation of 1870" and the "Recife school" used French and German scientism to critique the monarchy as tyrannical and backward. The military came to see positivism as a viable alternative to liberalism. Finally, in 1870, wealthy but politically marginalized Paulista coffee planters, urban professionals, and some members of the military formed the Republican party. They published a bold antimonarchical, anticlerical manifesto that threatened the socially conservative historical parties. However, the Republicans placed only a few representatives on the national level, and none ever assumed leadership of a cabinet during the empire.

Historians have remained divided over the ideological content of imperial political parties. For example, Richard Graham has argued that the parties were rarely driven by ideology: "First, citizens divided politically not because of party loyalties much less ideological considerations but because of personal ties, making party labels seriously misleading at both the local and the national level."[19] In her study of the Council of State, Lydia Garner qualifies these observations, claiming, "The nature and the level of political discourse between the two parties cannot be ignored. There was deep distrust between Conservatives and Liberals stemming from ideological divisions that had deepened during the Regency."[20] This divide widened as a result of the policy of *derrubadas*, the sacking of high officials from the opposing party at the beginning of every new regime.

If scholars have failed to reach a consensus about the meaning and effect of ideological differences between the Liberal and the Conservative parties on the national level, even less insight exists for regional, provincial, or municipal variants.[21] While the role of statesmen in Rio de Janeiro cannot be ignored, Maria Isaura Pereira de Queiroz's call for an inversion of historical bias to focus on the local also demands a response. In her analysis of First Republic coronelismo, which applies equally well to the empire, she insists: "The importance of family solidarity and the role of municipal conflicts in our politics indicate the necessity to begin research starting from the municipality. Historians must break with the myth that a group of imposing figures at the court or in the federal capital commanded party conflicts, pulling the distant strings that moved the *coronéis* of the interior."[22]

Placing the sertão at the center rather than the periphery permits a historical reorientation of the significance of political culture and how it changed. Municipal officials rarely grappled with weighty policy issues that their respective parties embraced. On the provincial level, the mineiro partisan press did take positions concerning the Paraguayan War (1865–70), electoral reform, the role of the church, and republicanism, and members of the municipal elite, like Josino and Sebastião, no doubt followed these debates. But politically active citizens in the São Francisco region came to see party identity, not in terms of ideology, but according to moral criteria grounded in party loyalty and a form of idealized liberalism. As members of the rural elite internalized new political norms, shifting from kin-based, personalized politics to more formal bureaucratic and partisan alliances, they came to criticize rivals for failing to defend liberal institutions or, worse, using public power for personal gain. Personal honor as manifested in the political press required moral integrity, upholding the law, and maintaining loyalty to one's party.

The Mineiro Political Press

The dissemination of new models of governance to remote regions represented one of the main challenges faced by the Brazilian state. Its ambassadors to the interior were law graduates appointed as juizes de direito to every comarca in the nation.[23] Ideally, these magistrates imposed law and order and spread awareness of new models of governance. To ensure their loyalty to the state, these judges were relocated every few years so that they might avoid getting ensnared by local interests and gain the broad experience that eventually could catapult them into a higher-ranking political or administrative post.

The Brazilian state did not rely solely on these circuit judges to construct a unified, national identity in a former colony that had previously been defined by local identities and loyalties. Newspapers, which began to appear beyond the confines of the coastal cities, contributed to the consolidation of an emerging political culture. In Minas Gerais, official journals became more prevalent following the 1834 Additional Act to the constitution, which established provincial assemblies. In the 1840s and 1850s, government papers informed the literate public about the affairs of the provincial government, publishing laws, presidential reports, and assembly debates.[24] Antonio Gonçalves Chaves Sr. of Montes Claros recognized their importance in 1846, when he advocated sending copies of the *Compiliador* to every municipality in the province, maintaining that popular dissemination (*vulgarização*) of assembly proceedings was essential to good governance.[25]

Some provincial newspapers did articulate clear partisan differences among various political parties and factions. *O Povo* (The people) and *O Bom Senso* (Good sense) were the first overtly partisan mineiro papers that lasted beyond a few issues.[26] *O Povo* was histrionic and allegorical in its rabid attacks on the Liberal party and lasted only until the Conservative victory of 1849. *O Bom Senso* published official news and provided commentary on international issues, religion, and public health. Its editor condemned party intrigue and republicanism. The paper also published paid supplements in which the municipal elite could expound on local conflicts.

The short-lived Conservative *O Compiliador* critiqued Liberals and Republicans as anticlerical, anticonstitutional anarchists and revolutionaries. The paper highlighted the shortcomings of republicanism by linking it with racism in the United States and with the Argentine dictator Juan Manuel Rosas. In contrast, under the Brazilian monarchy, the moral and upright Conservative party had halted the slave trade. Criticism of republicanism came in the form of the regular fictional feature "Monarchist Aurelio and Porphyrio, Young Republican," and in dialogue with other papers.

In the 1860s, 1870s, and 1880s, partisan journals proliferated. In them, official news was supplemented by denunciations of electoral and judicial corruption on the part of the opposition. These papers tended not to address big political or ideological questions on the national level.[27] In the 1870s, re-

gional papers emerged, challenging the journalistic hegemony of the provincial capital, Ouro Preto. Diamantina's *O Jequitinhonha* began as a progressive Liberal paper in 1869 but, in 1871, became the first Republican paper
in Minas Gerais under the editorship of Joaquim Felício dos Santos.[28] In its
pages, Dom Pedro II became the object of overt and sarcastic criticism concerning his Paraguayan war policy, the centralization of government, and
the antidemocratic character of the moderating power. *O Jequitinhonha* also
served as a forum for public responses to slanderous accusations made in the
Conservative press and for mounting counterattacks on the opposition. As
it served northern Minas, letters and commentary from the São Francisco
region appeared frequently. The Conservatives of Montes Claros also produced a newspaper under the editorship of Antonio Augusto Velloso, *O
Correio do Norte* (1884–87). Although it engaged in debate with the Liberals,
it was not stridently partisan and was more concerned with regional economic development.

Although late imperial mineiro papers addressed major policy issues such
as the abolition of slavery and the War of the Triple Alliance, they devoted
much of their space to commentary about the relative merits of the two parties. For example, in the inaugural issue of the *Noticiador de Minas*, the editor declared that the Conservative party "symbolizes economy of public
funds, morality, justice, and respect for the rights guaranteed by the law."[29]
In a subsequent issue, the *Noticiador* printed one mineiro assemblyman's assessment of the Liberals as "a turbulent river, breaking dikes, flooding, and
bringing devastation everywhere" and the Conservative party as "an abundant river [that] flows quietly and peacefully, fertilizing the lands through
which it passes and germinating good seeds."[30]

In addition to indulging in self-congratulatory purple prose upholding
the Conservative party's identity as the "Party of Order," the *Noticiador* also
dealt with more substantive issues. One editorial condemned the Liberal
party for seeking to augment constitutional liberties rather than preserving
the status quo. The paper condemned aspirations for a temporary senate,
provincial autonomy, and the abolition of the Council of State, arguing, "In
this way, the Liberals marched toward a destructive socialism, forgetting
that freedom is not license and that morality does not come from disorder.
Impractical theories are a poison that result in death by anarchy. . . . The
Conservative party is united, compact, patient in adversity, loyal and disciplined in a fight, magnanimous after victory. The Conservative party can
never comprehend freedom without order and progress without respect

[upholding] the prestige of legally constituted authorities and the strength of the beautiful institutions that fortunately govern us."[31]

Partisan papers were guilty not only of hyperbole but of considerable hypocrisy as well. For example, after publishing pages of mass police and judicial dismissals following the Conservative ascendancy in 1868, the *Noticiador de Minas* denied accusations made in the Liberal press of universal demotions and electoral coercion, insisting that the Conservatives had won because of their "superior morality."[32] The *Noticiador* also engaged in considerable mudslinging, routinely accusing adversaries of false posturing, economic mismanagement, and corruption.

For the municipal elite of the São Francisco region, these papers served a different purpose. Local officials did not focus on ideology; instead, they honed new definitions of political honor. Both factions defined themselves in contrast to the behavior of the other side. They constructed a corrupt political enemy in order to justify their own claims to legitimacy. Party loyalty constituted a key element of political honor. Liberals and Conservatives from the São Francisco region vehemently defended their political identity in the press, defining themselves morally in relation to their political "others," that is, members of the opposing party. In so doing, they designated appropriate boundaries of acceptable political patronage.

Municipal notables upheld the ideal of a pure form of liberalism, decrying excessive patronage, nepotism, and favoritism based on partisan affiliation. Of course, these statements should not be taken at face value because considerable evidence demonstrates that these standards were violated routinely by both parties. Each party invoked predictable motifs and shared a common idiom of political honor and dishonor. Discerning whether the details recorded are true, however, is less interesting than decoding the larger meanings embedded in print.[33]

What is most striking, however, is that the majority of these local spokesmen were not *bacharéis*, the law graduates who have been credited with the dissemination of liberal norms during the imperial period. As demonstrated in chapter 5 above, the region boasted few law graduates, and, more often than not, bacharéis appointed to serve from elsewhere failed to assume their posts. Direct or consistent contact with these emissaries of modernizing, national, political norms was the exception rather than the rule.

How, then, did the merchants and fazendeiros who constituted the local political elite come to absorb and embrace these ideal moral standards? Moreover, *why* did they participate in defining moral boundaries to patronage politics? Acquiring municipal administrative posts required partisan affiliation, but no evidence suggests that national and provincial political patrons demanded attitudinal change on the part of local clients. Generally, participation in patronage networks brought material benefits, but, as the next chapter will demonstrate, the rewards that accrued to the São Francisco region were meager. Despite or because of the fact that there was so little at stake, municipal actors persisted in their criticisms. In either case, politically active members of the São Francisco elite did not passively accept abuses that contributed to violence and corruption in their communities. Instead, they attempted to impose their own definitions of appropriate behavioral norms on an evolving discourse about the nature of imperial politics.

Patronage Politics in Print

A decades-long acrimonious exchange that took place from the 1860s to the 1880s between the Liberal Gonçalves Chaves family (both father and son) and their Conservative opponents illustrates how petty municipal officials defined normative standards. Antonio Gonçalves Chaves Sr. (1803–77) was the vicar of Montes Claros and filled various secular positions at both the municipal and the provincial levels. While serving in the provincial assembly in the 1840s, he distinguished himself through his support for education and by redrawing local territorial boundaries in Montes Claros's favor.[34] Chaves Sr. also served one term in the national Chamber of Deputies in 1848–49, but transcripts of the proceedings reveal that he was uncharacteristically silent during his tenure.

Antonio Gonçalves Chaves Jr. (1840–1911), the eldest of ten children, attended secondary school in Diamantina and then the law faculty at São Paulo, graduating in 1863.[35] In the 1860s, he was elected to two terms in the provincial assembly and also served as district magistrate and county prosecutor of Montes Claros. He acted as provincial president of Minas Gerais and Santa Catarina in the mid-1880s. During the Republic, he achieved even greater heights, being elected the first president of the federal Congress. He served as senator and as district judge of Mariana and was one of the authors of the new civil code.[36] Press reports and his personal correspondence reveal that he forged strong ties with the provincial Liberal party directorate. He enjoyed especially close connections with the Liberals of Diamantina from school and through marriage. He also made allies at university.

Father and son played the patronage game sufficiently well to earn them numerous enemies. Their detractors exploited the pages of the Conservative press with a vengeance, producing a series of scathing commentaries about the nepotism and excesses of the Gonçalves Chaves clan. One editorial maintained that politics in Montes Claros were controlled by a *theocracy-oligarchy run by Vicar Chaves*, describing him as "cunning in his present political life, . . . truly a chameleon of the *históricos* [old guard] and *progressistas* [members of the Progressive League] . . . fooling the Afonsos, Silveira Lobos, and Otonis, obtaining what he wants for his *sacred* family." Allegedly, the family controlled the police and the National Guard and, after Chaves Jr. completed his law degree, monopolized the offices of district attorney, municipal judge, and interim district judge. Imperial legislation prohibited the accumulation of multiple offices by an individual or family, a restriction apparently disregarded by the Chaves clan.[37]

Repeated criticisms suggest that the Chaves family used the patronage system to place their kin in formal positions of social control so that they could manipulate election results, notably in 1864, 1867, and 1868. Allegedly, Vicar Chaves used family and party connections to arrest voters, recruit, and intimidate, reprehensible behavior for a man of the cloth.[38] Political rivals accused Chaves Jr. of not attending the sessions of the provincial assembly so that he could fix elections in Montes Claros.[39] They also poked fun at his pretensions when he represented himself as an honest youth of firm character and an upright judge. One detractor accused him of false erudition for citing authoritative works to impress his readership without really understanding them.[40]

After the national Conservative turnover of 1868, the excesses of the Chaves clan came back to haunt them. A major derrubada had occurred in the province, greatly undercutting the family's formal powers. Chaves Jr. characterized the following elections as a recruitment "fury" of the "*mamelucos* [half-breeds] in power," who rounded up elders and youths for military service unless they voted Conservative. Allegedly, the new regime functioned as a "*dictatorship*" guilty of "the most *atrocious persecution*," poised to exterminate Liberals throughout the municipality. Chaves claimed that he, his aged father, and their Liberal allies were forced to flee, insisting, "There are no possible rights for the Liberals of Montes Claros; the law is reduced to the stupid will of a rancorous despot of unspeakable perversity who controls police authority there."[41]

Conservative Montesclarenses combated Chaves Jr.'s purple prose with some biting rejoinders of their own. One police delegate commented that the Chaveses were guilty of translating the word *conscience* into *convenience*, adding that "slander and deceit are the favorite arms of the enemies of the present [authority]; [they lack] clear ideas, deep-rooted beliefs, or fundamental principles with which to erect the walls of their New Babylon."[42] A Conservative police official later emphasized the family ties that had bound the prior Liberal regime: "Chaves Jr., then county prosecutor, and his father, chief of the Liberal party, head an oligarchy composed of father, son, son-in-law (a lieutenant colonel, substitute delegate, and justice of the peace), and his nephew (commander of the National Guard and substitute municipal judge). The Chaves control a band of public employees that are linked through *parentesco* and have left their imprint on every public matter."[43]

Chaves waited out the Conservative interregnum of 1868–78, writing for the radical Liberal papers *O Jequitinhonha* of Diamantina and *A Reforma* of Rio de Janeiro. During his exile, he seems to have become more intensely partisan. Chaves had shown moderation in an editorial written shortly before the Liberal fall, arguing that, although the Liberal and Conservative parties were substantively different, both were acceptable choices. He opposed "unconstitutional" radicalism taken to either extreme, republicanism or absolutism. Chaves did, of course, favor the Liberal party, arguing that it had saved the constitutional monarchy from pro-Portuguese Conservatives. He also criticized Conservative policy on military recruitment and the reform of the National Guard.[44]

Following the Liberal triumph of 1878, Antonio Gonçalves Chaves rose to new heights, being nominated provincial president of Santa Catarina in 1882. Many Conservatives rejoiced at his departure, among them a correspondent from the comarca of Jequitaí (Montes Claros):

> With this step, the imperial government has just provided an incalculable benefit to this unhappy comarca, removing the passionately partisan judge and local chief who never should have been a magistrate in this land. . . . May God (or the government) keep him there for many years, if not always, to satisfy the president's vanity and the tranquility of the Conservative party in these parts, sending us a district magistrate who has neither pretensions to be a party chief here nor cousins, brothers-in-law, uncles, godparents, etc. . . .
>
> It is not appropriate that this segment of the population of Minas continue under a colonial regime in which total authority is concentrated in fact in the hands of a presumptuous kinglet [regulo] who despotically tries to exercise feudal privileges in this small sertaneja captaincy, by right of conquest and birth. . . . His excellency, who was our president . . . who knows how to fix the electorate, to fix elections and grant votes to his friends

seated in the parliaments. He is even presumed to be capable, as it is said, of
nullifying the freedom to vote in the comarca of Diamantina and the twen-
tieth district.[45]

Regrettably for the mineiro Conservatives, Chaves returned to serve two
terms as provincial president of Minas Gerais in 1883 and 1884. During his
tenure, he sustained much criticism both in the press and in the halls of the
provincial assembly, where he was accused of electoral fraud, demoting
competent Conservative municipal employees for petty partisan reasons,
and illegal appropriation of provincial funds to extend the telegraph line to
Montes Claros and to subsidize a privately printed almanac.[46] On the other
side, Chaves did have Liberal allies who praised him for his astute management of provincial funds and his impartiality.[47]

By the 1880s, Chaves seems to have been thoroughly committed to partisan imperatives. Evidence suggests that he lived up to the criticism voiced
by one assemblyman that he "paid more attention to his friends . . . than to
the interests of the province" and that he transformed the assembly into "his
own personal treasury."[48] A table published by *A Província de Minas* revealed that Chaves had managed to employ twenty-five of his relatives in
twenty-eight government jobs and that their combined salaries totaled
more than thirty-one contos.[49]

Accusations made against Chaves demonstrate how politicians defined
appropriate boundaries of patronage. Rewarding political allies was acceptable, but replacing competent and ethical officials with inept substitutes was
not. Using the police and the judiciary to coerce and intimidate, especially
through the mechanism of recruitment, also prompted censure. Members
of both parties violated these standards routinely but on the level of rhetoric
upheld them as honorable ideals and expended considerable time and
money defending them in print.

Specific motifs deserve further analysis. Political rivals sought to discredit
the Chaves clan by depicting them as retrograde throwbacks who had not
kept up with the times. One detractor accused Chaves Sr. of claiming feudal
privileges that had ended with the colonial era, referring to his region of influence as a captaincy, not a province. Excessive nepotism was also depicted
as a regressive and shameful violation of liberal principles and institutions.
The earlier reference to Chaves Sr.'s "sacred family" probably alluded to the
vicar's ten illegitimate children. Interestingly, such slurs concerning the
consensual unions of priests were uncommon, perhaps because this pattern
was so common that it was unworthy of mention. Political adversaries,

however, never went so far as to dishonor Chaves Jr. publically by calling him a bastard in print.

Critics found different grounds to defame Antonio Gonçalves Chaves Jr. In contrast to his backward-looking father, the young lawyer was accused of false pretenses. Rivals represented him as "lacking clear ideas, deep-rooted beliefs, or fundamental principles" and of producing shoddy scholarship, calling into question his bacharel status and intellectual pretensions. Both father and son earned criticism from members of the "Party of Order" for their lack of ideological principles and for their disregard of the law.

Chaves Jr. referred to his political enemies as *mamelucos*, a racial insult signifying an indigenous-European mix. His invocation of a racial epithet was unusual. In general, political commentary in the press avoided the topic of race, despite or perhaps because of the fact that it was a key component of personal honor. Mestiços lacked purity of blood or lineage, rendering them dishonorable by birth. Discriminatory slurs appeared only rarely, perhaps in keeping with the heavily mixed demographic composition of Minas Gerais. In the São Francisco region, negative remarks tended to be cast in terms of Indians or mamelucos, not blacks or mulattos. The juiz de direito of the comarca of São Francisco even alluded metaphorically to "acts of true cannibalism" associated with electoral upheaval in Januária in 1869.[50] Chaves Jr., incidentally, appears *moreno* (brown) in his official portrait.[51]

Another rare exception appeared in a rebuttal written by a group of parishioners from São Romão responding to one aspect of a sustained print exchange between the Liberal Colonel Joaquim Antonio Nunes Brasileiro and the Conservative Teófilo de Sales Peixoto.[52] The townspeople affirmed that Brasileiro's depiction of his rival as a "King of the Congo" (*Rei Congo*) was unworthy and that Peixoto was a "gentleman."[53] It is unclear here whether the term was used to connote race or whether Peixoto served as a patron to the *congados* festivals held by the black brotherhood of Our Lady of the Rosary to crown ritual kings and queens of the Congo. In either case, his detractors implied a connection to an Afro-Brazilian identity.

By the later decades of the empire, race was rarely cited in the press as a factor that affected political aptitude or fitness to serve. Regional attitudes had evolved since the early 1830s as confidential correspondence between local officials from Januária and the provincial president of Minas Gerais suggests. While reporting the details of an aborted nativist conspiracy in 1831, a Portuguese resident of Januária sought to discredit his Brazilian-born neighbors by revealing that they danced the African batuque and practiced the *jogo de búzios*.[54] Another series of documents details the prejudice faced by José dos Santos Pereira, the legitimized son of a slave woman and a prominent landowner.[55] Members of the local elite emphasized his lack of honor by citing his low birth, relative poverty, and menial profession as a tailor whose only professional training had taken place at the "universities of the needle, thimble, iron, scissors, ruler, and tape measure."[56] In this case, objections seem to be grounded more in the fact that he was born a captive and exercised a menial profession than in race per se. The provincial government seems to have discounted local objections as Santos Pereira secured a number of minor official posts.[57]

As represented in the mineiro press, the honorable rural politician or officeholder was a man of means who upheld the liberal institutions that he represented. Although it was expected that he would receive patronage benefits from higher levels and reward his partisan allies, moderation was essential. Rivalry between the two parties intensified as more local appointments were brought under central control. Once a party was in power at the national level, it could remake entire municipal administrations. Political turnovers provided local bureaucrats, judges, and police officers with the opportunity to settle old scores. Unfortunately, many local authorities lacked a sense of proportion and used their offices to humiliate, demean, or endanger their rivals through false arrests, arbitrary military recruitment, or worse. Rare was the municipal officeholder who applied the law impartially and kept partisan favors within reasonable limits.

Such exemplary officials legitimized their ethical reputation and impartiality by seeking endorsements from the political opposition. For example, the political rivals Colonel Brasileiro and Sales Peixoto, from the town of São Francisco, defended the juiz de direito against accusations made by the municipal council. They claimed that he was an impartial judge whose only misdeed was his refusal to protect the criminal clients of his party allies.[58] A former police captain of Montes Claros defended his honor by publishing testaments to his upright behavior from prominent members of both parties.[59] One conservative police commander from São Francisco countered an accusation that he had impeded Liberals from voting by claiming that he previously had been entrusted with military positions during periods of Liberal domination and had the confidence of many members of the local Liberal elite.[60] A kinsman of Antonio Gonçalves Chaves Jr. defended him against accusations of inappropriate handling of provincial funds with documentary evidence from Conservatives of a neighboring town.[61]

Such strategies, however, called into question the party loyalty of the individual involved, another important value highlighted by municipal notables. In a session of the provincial assembly, Colonel Brasileiro of São Francisco claimed to distrust his Liberal compatriots who were defended by Conservatives—an ironic statement given an earlier defense of his own behavior in which he included supporting letters from two Conservative chiefs.[62] A detractor further highlighted Brasileiro's hypocrisy by claiming that he had been Conservative, switching parties only when the Liberals came to power. Moreover, he had arranged nominations for local Conservatives just to cover himself, should the ministry fall. This writer questioned the validity of Brasileiro's identity as a "genuine" Liberal, in contrast to himself and his *companheiros*, who "were nursed on Liberal beliefs."[63]

Such an exchange adds an additional layer to our understanding of partisan commitment in the sertão mineiro. On the one hand, it confirms the belief that some politicians acted strategically to have allies in both camps and changed their political stripes should one or another party gain the advantage. But, on the other hand, Brasileiro's actions also inspired criticism by Liberals for whom party loyalty was an essential part of their identity, apparently since childhood.

The meaning of party identity for politically active citizens in the São Francisco region remains elusive. Distinct partisan differentiation in the São Francisco region became apparent about midcentury. Ideological differences between the two main parties, however, remained blurred. Even when dealing with such important questions as the abolition of slavery, the Liberal and Conservative directorates of Montes Claros alone could not reach a consensus.[64] Local Conservatives reserved most of their ideological criticism for individuals believed to be antimonarchical, often blurring the definition of Liberal and Republican. For example, a letter from the Conservative commander of the National Guard of Januária dating from the 1850s denounced his fellow officers who were Liberals, emphasizing their predilection for red hats, ties, and other garments. Reputedly, Manoel Caetano Souza e Silva, the chimango (Liberal) leader, had imported these offensive scarlet trappings from the Liberal reduct of Diamantina as well as spreading propaganda on republicanism.[65]

The linking of these two tendencies continued in the 1870s, following the publication of the Republican Manifesto. In the 1870s, local Republicans attracted official suspicion as potential antimonarchical subversives or anarchists. In Januária, twenty years after Manoel Caetano distributed his red accessories, rumors circulated that he was trying to organize a Republican club. In Montes Claros, a local official tipped off the provincial police chief that an "international society" was meeting in the church at late hours. The group consisted of "young, intelligent, and robust" men under the direction of the town's radical Liberal chief. The police chief organized an investigation of the suspicious organization, but nothing more was revealed about the group's mysterious activities.[66]

Even if partisanship did not have clear ideological content, it did become a crucial component of personal identity. Party identification was not adopted purely out of convenience, to be abandoned every time a national political turnover took place. Moreover, in the press, politicians questioned the commitment of their fellows if they failed to maintain loyalty to a single party.

An illustrative example of this dynamic comes from a public accusation made in the press by the Pimenta brothers of Januária against the Liberal chief Manoel Caetano Souza e Silva in 1869. The brothers were both Conservative but had been nominated to official positions under both parties. Like many national statesmen who had changed their political affiliation during the Conservative Regresso, they had switched parties a quarter century earlier, following a period of staunch Liberal militarism in their youth. Their charges of partisan unfaithfulness against Manoel Caetano, however, were of a completely different magnitude. The brothers reported that Manoel Caetano and his father had been "Liberal in name" between 1842 and 1860, when they fixed elections in exchange for concessions such as the settlement of large debts in local marketplaces.

By 1860, Manoel Caetano Souza e Silva had become the biggest merchant of the Rio São Francisco, with trade relations in Rio de Janeiro, Bahia, and several towns of the interior. In his ambition to run Januária politically and economically, he began to mediate between Liberals and Conservatives with no commitment to either side.[67] He encouraged crimes and ruthlessly tried to wipe out trade competition. An anonymous contributor to the *Noticiador de Minas* brought home the point that Manoel Caetano had no more legitimacy in Januária, Minas, or Rio, concluding, "He provokes horror among the Conservatives and boredom among the Liberals."[68]

Throughout the region, party switching was viewed with skepticism. Antonio Augusto Velloso criticized his relative Carlos José Versiani, the most influential Conservative to represent Montes Claros, commenting, "In his youth, he was a Liberal; for this reason, he is not an absolutely genuine Conservative."[69] Brasiliano Braz, a local historian from São Francisco, reiterates that flip-flopping between parties was both infrequent and highly dishonorable: "incredible as it might seem, local rule depended not on municipal elections but on the ascension of a particular party. There was more dignity, more security, more stability, in party regimentation. Whoever was Conservative or Liberal remained loyal to the party until the end of his days. Defections were rare, extremely rare, and, for this reason, demoralizing. Whoever switched parties earned the public's disdain."[70]

Those individuals found guilty of party disloyalty were considered unreliable allies and consequently could be turned down for official posts. During a Conservative administration, a substitute municipal judge in São Romão rejected two candidates for the post of police delegate, the first for being a "red liberal" of long standing, the second for having switched from the Liberal to the Conservative camps on the basis of a minor personal altercation. In his eyes, neither was trustworthy.[71] Similarly, a Conservative from Januária sought to discredit the Conservative chief and parish priest of the outlying district of Morrinhos for influencing friends and family to vote for a Liberal candidate of the old guard (histórico). The untrustworthy chief had attempted to justify his behavior on the grounds that the historic Liberals were socially conservative and that he and his allies wanted to retain public jobs, whatever the political complexion of the government.[72]

Conservatives deemed even more suspect individuals who switched to the Republican party, such as the district magistrate Paraiso Cavalcante, who allegedly turned away from the Conservative party on being denied a position.[73] Paraiso Cavalcante was one of three Republican leaders in Januária including the council president and the vicar Levínio José Torres Jatobá. Conservatives condemned the trio on a variety of grounds. One commentator criticized them for the shallowness of their ideological principles, indicating that they were perfectly content to collect salaries and benefits from the monarchical government.[74]

Padre Levinio received special condemnation for his political views, outlandish behavior, and criminal antecedents, all bound together in the minds of his detractors. One Conservative wrote, "This Sr. Levinio is capable of anything, except delivering a sermon or sustaining a serious conversation for five minutes. . . . [He was] Liberal in the beginning, later a Republican, and today a fervent enthusiast of French communism. A socialist priest!" Allegedly, he walked the street at night in a leather hat and fantastic clothing, running the risk of being arrested by the night watchmen.[75] The fanatically Republican Levinio even expressed distaste for preaching before Conservative monarchists.[76] Liberals also attacked his reputation, including one notorious strongman who had bent the law on more than one occasion. He claimed that Padre Levinio had fled Paracatú for Januária after being caught prostituting a thirteen-year-old girl, gaining Conservative protection in Januária for his loyalty during the election of 1868. Allegedly, his crimes in Januária included slander, murdering José Joaquim da Rocha through prescribing an overdose of opium (and then taking the widow as his mistress), and attempting to seduce virgins in the confessional.[77]

The demonization of opposing parties ran the gamut from the immoral to the ridiculous. For example, a Conservative Montesclarense targeted two locals "whom the Liberal party calls honorable and important citizens": a cousin of Antonio Gonçalves Chaves who mysteriously had outlived three wives and despoiled an image of the Virgin Mary by melting it down into gold jewelry and a sergeant who allegedly roamed at night dressed in a wolf pelt to frighten those who believed in werewolves.[78] Some politicians were defined as crooked, not by nature, but because they belonged to a certain party whose defining principle was immoral. One provincial representative accused Antonio Goncalves Chaves Jr. of corruption, not so much out of personal inclination, but because he was a Liberal.[79]

Political identity became so much a part of one's personal honor and legitimacy that it could assume religious overtones. Such commitment appears in a farewell speech to the provincial assembly by Montesclarenese Justino de Andrade Camara. In an eloquent defense of his political identity, he said, "I am Conservative, not only by family tradition, but by conviction. I follow, therefore, the pure ideas of the Conservative Party. . . . I have had no reason to abandon them. With firm conviction, I vow to live and die in their defense if necessary. With respect to religion, I am and always was apostolic Roman Catholic. I equally defend this faith and educate my children to live and die by it."[80] A conservative compatriot and priest from the district of Coração de Jesus expressed similar sentiments, maintaining, "Only God could sway his political beliefs."[81]

One local historian from Montes Claros has even applied the phrase "Liberal by race" (*Liberal de raça*), suggesting that party identity could be passed on through blood.[82] Metaphorically, it could be transmitted through mother's milk, as expressed earlier by the Liberal who was "nursed on Liberal beliefs." During the First Republic (1889–1930), rival political factions throughout Minas Gerais retained their distinctiveness despite the transition to a one-party system. They expressed their identity through the use of intriguing nicknames such as *patos* and *perus* (ducks and turkeys), *luzeiros* and *escureiros* (light and darks), *estrepes* and *pelados* (the boisterous and the naked), and *peludos* and *pelados* (the hairy and the naked). The last example inspired the clever play on words *homen peludo não deve casar-se com mulher pelada* (a hairy man shouldn't marry a naked woman).[83] This saying reinforces the relation between party affiliation and kinship.

Although the mineiro jurist and historian Cid Rebelo Horta has argued that great families could incorporate more than one political faction while retaining harmony among themselves, little evidence from the São Francisco region supports this claim.[84] Political divergence within families was so infrequent that it inevitably inspired comment on the rare occasions that it occurred. Moreover, the murder of Josino by his cousin described at the beginning of this chapter shows that such cleavages could be carried to extremes. The family did represent a key organizing principle of political parties, but it was not the only factor involved. During the decades following independence, local factions increasingly began to define themselves according to partisan affiliation. Family influence continued to shape political careers and intruded into public life, but the extent to which this was considered an appropriate and acceptable strategy became increasingly circumscribed. Political factions such as the Chaves-Prates clan, which organized and distributed patronage along kinship lines, came to be perceived as both inappropriate and retrograde.

The Legitimization of Liberalism

Antonio Gonçalves Chaves Jr. may have been engaging in wishful thinking when he stated, "The parties are not ephemeral creations that depend on the whims of the imagination of some statesman" but were based in ideas.[85] On the municipal and provincial level, Conservatives and Liberals engaged in considerable mudslinging, but their mutual insults focused more on corruption and morality than on ideology. The nature of such accusations depended not so much on partisan affiliation as on which party was in power. Typically, the dominant party accused its opponents of using private force or coercion to subvert institutions and elections, while the party out of power claimed that its adversaries turned the judicial and policing system into instruments of personal control. For example, in the Conservative press, Liberals were alternately implicated for either subverting the electoral process through the use of private mercenaries or using the police and National Guard for that purpose, depending on whether the Liberals were in power. Both types of allegations were probably true.

Obviously, partisan disputes narrated by competing voices present multiple versions of any given event. Even with extensive documentary evidence, it is difficult to tell which version may be the least inaccurate. What is most interesting is not the lengths to which political adversaries resorted to discredit one another but the strategies that they used to do so, strategies that represented a blend of the traditional and the modern. For example, rural elites discredited their enemies by accusing them of dishonoring women. The forced rape, seduction, or prostitution of widows or virginal orphans is a common and probably exaggerated motif. Yet other traditional yardsticks of family honor, such as loyalty to the extended family, underwent subtle transformations. Local elites still channeled influence through extended networks of kin, but flagrant exploitation of public power to benefit one's relatives came to be considered shameful and was condemned as such in print.

The need to legitimize liberal norms also became acute during the final decades of the empire. Political corruption and violence increased steadily, peaking in the years during and following the War of the Triple Alliance (1865–70). Through military impressment and other mechanisms, the level of coercion suffered by the average voter intensified accordingly. Local politicians who voiced their concerns in the political press did not defend the system but rather represented themselves as ethical individuals who rose above it by adhering to liberal norms.

Why local elites felt the need to defend themselves remains a bit of a mystery. One possible hypothesis is that, as imperial politics became increasingly corrupt, officials and politicians could not enforce hegemonic rule. After midcentury, criminality, or, at a minimum, official concern therewith, increased. Municipal authorities lacked sufficient force to quell popular discontent, and law enforcement was also selective, according to partisan affiliation and social class. Corrupt local justice and policing systems lacked both the physical and the moral force necessary to maintain social order. The fact that the rural elite needed to assert its right to power through the discourse of liberalism suggests that these ideals may have gained moral force among the popular classes.[86] Unlike the regional elites discussed by David Nugent in his study of Peru's northern frontier, São Francisco authorities committed themselves to liberal ideals in *public* media as well as private correspondence, thereby signaling their need to attain popular legitimation.[87]

Regardless, liberalism became the moral yardstick by which politicians and bureaucrats were measured. Initially, the use of liberal rhetoric may have been purely instrumental, but over time its values and terminology became internalized. Acceptance of liberal norms and institutions, however, did not mean that rural elites obeyed them. During partisan disputes rural elites concentrated on the ways in which political adversaries transgressed the liberal ideal as well as the ways in which they violated the code of honor of the sertão. Claims to rural authenticity did not carry political clout in Brazil, as they did in Argentina and Uruguay to the south. The supermasculine *caudilho* (regional military leader or local boss) did not become the icon of choice, being supplanted by the refined bacharel.[88]

Elaborate debates in print may have been an improvement over quick, violent solutions (although wading through these verbose wars of words makes the reader nostalgic for the succinct resolution provided by the sword). In addition, through the press and official correspondence, the municipal elite of the sertão mineiro sought out connections with a larger political community. Municipal politicians were not retrograde and isolated, as scholars and contemporaneous statesmen made them out to be. They participated in external patronage systems and sought to shape the terms of that participation through public and private correspondence with provincial authorities. They were neither passive nor indolent but passionately partisan. True, some members of the municipal elite were corrupt, violated liberal norms, and occasionally switched parties for personal convenience. In so doing, however, they were no better or worse than their provincial or national counterparts.

CHAPTER 8

The Limited Benefits of Patronage, 1850 - 89

I don't know why such an important part of the province has been abandoned. It is a place with a prosperous future. Suffice it to say that the great São Francisco, the Brazilian Mississippi, passes through it, yet still we have been forgotten by the powers that be. For fifty years we have been forgotten. Church services have completely disintegrated. The churches no longer look like houses where the people go to offer thanks to God but resemble filthy waste dumps. During the rainy season, the rivers almost always impede the farmers in the harvest and export of their crops. A fertile region where crops are produced in admirable abundance is rendered unimportant because of poor communications and lack of roads. We don't want railroads. We don't have such lofty ambitions. We are content with simple roads by which we can transport our products from here to there. In regard to access to government resources, we have been treated like orphans. —Francisco de Sales Peixoto, provincial assemblyman from São Romão, 1882

By the end of the imperial period, the São Francisco region had undergone profound political changes. A centralized administration subsumed municipal autonomy. Exerting power on the local level required affiliation with national political parties and the willingness to engage in corruption and violence to fix elections. Partisan appointments in the police and judicial system warped institutions of social control and diminished their efficacy. One question remains to be answered: What did rural municipalities gain in return? In the end, did the benefits of political patronage outweigh the considerable social costs?

The words of assemblyman Francisco de Sales Peixoto quoted above suggest that the rewards were meager indeed. Peixoto, however, hailed from São Romão, the municipality that experienced the least growth in the São Francisco region. The provincial government distributed patronage benefits reluctantly prior to midcentury and unevenly thereafter. As foreshadowed in previous chapters, Montes Claros secured the bulk of resources allocated within the region. The municipality's success derived in large measure from its ability to adapt politically.

The municipal council of Montes Claros adopted the rhetoric of liberalism early in its communications with the provincial government. As head of the comarca, it benefited from the presence of a resident, university-educated, and well-connected juiz de direito. Its position as municipal and comarca seat was also secure, freeing it up to lobby for modernizing measures. Montes Claros developed strong local chapters of both the Liberal and the Conservative parties, as early and frequent clashes over elections demonstrate. Finally, Montes Claros produced strong candidates from both parties who were competitive enough to win seats on the provincial assembly in nearly every legislature. Regardless of the party in power at the national level, the municipality was able to get at least one local candidate elected. Provincial delegates formed alliances with representatives from Paracatú to the west and Rio Pardo, Minas Novas, and Grão Mogol to the north and east. Two Montesclarenses even made it to the federal Chamber of Deputies.

By the 1860s, partisan loyalties had become embedded in Januária's social framework as well. The question remains why Januária did not gain more political clout after organizing local chapters of national parties. Only in the 1880s did Januária elect a local son to the provincial assembly. The municipal elite certainly had the financial means to send their sons to law school in order to establish useful political connections, yet it did not. It may be that Montes Claros had such an influential lead that any attempt to catch up would have seemed futile. Or a commitment to localism may have been a conscious choice. Surviving documentation fails to provide a conclusive answer.

Regardless, by midcentury, the key to regional development lay not so much in self-representation as an upstanding civic community but in placing local representatives on the provincial assembly. Municipal strategies changed in response to new political realities. In the 1850s, municipal councils began to direct their proposals, not to the appointed provincial presidents, but to provincial assemblies, where they had elected representatives working on their behalf. Although the chain of command required municipal authorities to appeal to provincial presidents, success required building political relationships with provincial assemblymen. Montes Claros pulled ahead economically through a better adaptation to the new political realities and greater success in the game of political patronage. Its successful drive to establish a textile mill compared to Januária's failure to revive its sugar sector, described earlier, is one case in point. More effective articulation with political parties and networks of patronage translated into greater funding success in the 1860s, 1870s, and 1880s.

Even the relative advantage enjoyed by Montes Claros translated into only modest subsidies to improve the municipality. Modernization efforts made by the three communities, articulated for the most part by their town councils, proceeded slowly and haltingly in many cases. Chances for success increased after midcentury. Initiatives focused on public health and education, urban development, transportation, and communication. The arguments invoked to achieve these objectives were similar to those used prior to 1850. The desire to create an orderly and enlightened society, however, carried more weight if one had partisan allies in the legislature.

Municipal councils expressed deep concern about urban planning and the construction of public buildings. Not only were town halls, churches, and jails necessary for the effective exercise of municipal government, but they had symbolic value as well. By definition, incorporated towns were sites of both civil and ecclesiastical power and as such needed to be formally invested with tangible symbols of their status. The matriz, the mother church of the parish, and the town hall occupied prominent places on the town square. Shoddy jails, deteriorating churches, rented schoolhouses, and nonexistent town halls were more than embarrassing. Such deficiencies could justify demotion in the local hierarchy of cities, towns, parishes, and districts.

Building an Orderly Society

In mineiro towns, the site of legislative authority and that of criminal punishment were generally one and the same. Town halls were subdivided to accommodate prisoners, typically in the basement. When first incorporated as municipal seats, many towns in the São Francisco region lacked the most basic structures to house administrative functions. Januária's county jail was typical, consisting of a tiny rented house flimsily constructed and with an easily excavated dirt floor. Even shackled prisoners had little difficulty escaping. In addition to the jail's architectural defects, it lacked such basic amenities as daily cleaning, lighting, and a jailor. The council suggested that initial improvements should include the provision of a barrel "so the prisoners don't find it necessary to answer calls to nature in the same space where they reside."

Attempts to remedy this situation lagged for decades. In the late 1830s, the council of Januária proposed the construction of a stone and cement jail with separate cells for various categories of criminals. The blueprint submitted to the provincial assembly showed a two-story building, with meeting rooms for the town council, a courtroom, and an archive located on the second floor. Prison cells were placed on the first floor. The two levels would be connected not only by stairs but by trap doors. Presumably, suspects would be charged on the second floor and then dropped down to the "dungeons" below. The council suggested that the jail could be built through contributions, but the wealthiest proprietors, disgruntled over the transfer of the county seat, were unwilling to donate cattle, stone, and wood and to loan carts and slaves.[1]

In the 1840s, the town received a provincial subsidy of 400$000, but the council treasurer embezzled the money by producing fictitious receipts at exorbitant prices for the purchase of materials that had been donated. A second modest subsidy of 50$000 allocated in 1847 for the subsistence of indigent prisoners was stolen by one of the councilmen. Eventually, the council proposed as an interim measure the purchase of a house on the square conveniently located in front of the whipping post.[2]

The municipal council of Montes Claros enjoyed somewhat greater success. It appointed commissions in 1833 and 1837 to research construction costs for a new jail/town hall. Local donors volunteered construction materials, but an additional ten contos were needed to finish the job. The provincial government apportioned three subsidies between 1838 and 1847 amounting to nearly two contos, but funds were slow to arrive in the municipal treasury. As a temporary measure, a new townhouse was purchased with private funds. Only in 1849, the year of the hotly contested Conservative turnover, did Montes Claros finally receive authorization to sell the old town hall and to commence construction on a new building.[3] Additional subsidies materialized in the 1850s in the amount of 2:600$000. The town also managed to secure modest sums to feed and clothe poor prisoners.[4]

The state of São Romão's prisons remained precarious throughout the empire. Its municipal council also commissioned a proposal for consideration by the provincial assembly in the 1830s. After suffering repeated rejections for funding, the council was forced to appropriate money from a bridge subsidy to repair its prison in 1845. By 1853, the jail was so deteriorated that its roof collapsed. São Francisco, São Romão's successor, received funding for a jail in 1880, but, by the end of the decade, prison security was still minimal. The jail was made of mud and soft aroeira boards with four-inch-thick walls that were easily breached.[5]

Jails were not the only decrepit buildings in need of repair. Many churches were not fit for habitation. Churches filled both ecclesiastical and secular functions as the official site of elections. The state required that parish priests participate politically as members of electoral and voter registration boards and by opening and concluding election proceedings with a mass. As repositories of both church and state power, churches needed to be maintained in decent condition. A provincial budgetary law, in fact, specifically set aside funds to aid poor churches.[6]

Churches throughout the region were modest structures that were constantly in need of repair. For example, in 1837, the council of Montes Claros complained, "Speaking without hyperbole, we affirm that the church is presently in a terrible state, more of an affront to religion and an embarrassment for the town than a temple of the living God or a sacred house of moral instruction." It sought four contos to make necessary repairs and requested both provincial subsidies and permission to run a lottery to raise funds. The province granted Montes Claros 600$000 for repairs in 1845 and an additional 1:000$000 in 1851.[7]

The district of Morrinhos in the municipality of Januária possessed a historic church constructed in the mid–eighteenth century that had fallen into disrepair by the 1850s. The church, however, had lost its patrimony in 1846 when, in collusion with some heirs to the church sexton, the municipal judge had sold the church property, including cattle, lands, houses, silver, and artifacts. Subsequently, the parish could no longer afford to maintain the church intact. Although its stone and cement walls were structurally sound, the timbered roof had begun to rot.[8] Rare was the church of N.S. do Bom Sucesso in the district of Barra do Rio das Velhas. Residents described it as "one of the richest and most grandiose monuments to the history of mineiro piety. It was one of the largest and most decorated churches of the province, with five richly gilded, admirably sculpted altars. . . . Its architectonic design inspires admiration in all who are not accustomed to such churches in a region so distant from Rio de Janeiro." Beneath the gilt, however, lay walls constructed of wattle and dab.[9]

With rare exceptions, the province proved unwilling to spare scarce funds on church beautification. Instead, in the 1870s and 1880s, it began to authorize municipalities to conduct lotteries to raise funds to benefit churches and chapels. In 1876, the provincial assembly granted concessions to six districts in Montes Claros as well as one lottery for Januária and Pedras dos Angicos (the new seat of the municipality of São Romão). More lotteries were authorized in the 1880s, with the municipality of Montes Claros retaining an edge over its neighbors.[10]

Churches also did double duty as public schools. Provincial legislation guaranteed schooling for boys in hamlets that boasted more than twenty-four pupils. Incorporated towns were also entitled to secondary schools for boys and segregated primary schools for boys and girls. The province was obligated to provide certified schoolteachers, and interested local candidates could become teachers by passing a civil service exam.[11] In practice, scarce funds limited the number of schools created.

Montes Claros eventually led the uphill struggle to provide elementary and secondary schools for its population. However, all three communities faced difficulties in the early decades following independence. Januária and São Romão were granted primary schools in 1819 and 1820, respectively, but the schools failed to function regularly. São Romão again gained a single primary school in the 1830s but lacked the money to pay the rent on the schoolhouse or to provide school supplies for charity pupils. It lagged behind the other two communities in primary education, gaining only one additional school for boys in the district of Brejo da Passagem and then only in 1880.[12] In Januária, repeated appeals for schools to improve the moral fiber of the contentious community were answered only in 1840, when the province authorized the opening of four new schools in the municipality. Schoolteachers were provided, but materials were not, to the detriment of a large number of indigent pupils who lacked the means to purchase books and supplies.[13] By 1851, the primary schools of Brejo and Porto had been abandoned, unable to attract replacement teachers.[14]

Although Montes Claros enjoyed only marginally greater success in obtaining provincial funding prior to midcentury, it sought to make up the shortfall by drawing on local contributions from the elite. The community did gain a school shortly after it attained municipal status in 1830, but the teacher, Luiz José de Azevedo, who was said to be careless and incompetent, abandoned his classes. He later underwent criminal prosecution for various offenses, including fornication and attempts to reduce free people of color to slavery. In 1837, Montes Claros also gained a secondary school, but, by 1843, the promised teacher had yet to appear.[15] The populous subsidiary districts of Bomfim and Brejo das Almas made repeated appeals in the 1830s and 1840s, but, by 1844, only two primary schools functioned, both attended intermittently by poor children.[16]

Undaunted, the citizens of Montes Claros offered to subsidize the costs of educating its youths. In 1835, several of the town's prominent citizens founded a society for the promotion of public schools. This group reflected the town's developing civic identity in its opinion that only an educated populace was capable of understanding the laws and political system.[17] In 1837, another group of citizens volunteered to assume the costs of repairing a building to serve as a schoolhouse.[18] To stimulate greater provincial commitment, the council of Montes Claros alleged that inadequate public education could lead to political upheaval. It reported that a faction of civil servants opposed to the dominant party in government was spreading subversive doctrines capable of adversely influencing uneducated youths.[19] In the 1850s, Montes Claros did gain four more elementary schools and a chair in Latin, but, by 1853, its schools were so underfunded that the high school teacher, Justino de Andrade Camara, had to supply materials for over half his eighty-seven students out of his own pocket.[20] It may have been this experience that turned Camara into an impassioned advocate of public education.

In 1864, the provincial assembly of Minas Gerais passed a general educational reform that reestablished the right of all parishes to establish schools for boys. Towns and cities were also required to provide classes for girls. A surge in provincial funding for primary education in the 1870s and 1880s suggests that the assembly took this reform seriously. In 1882, one-third of the entire provincial budget went to education. During five successive terms in the provincial assembly from 1870 to 1880, Justino de Andrade Camara of Montes Claros fought unceasingly to improve the educational standards of his region. So too did Montesclarense Antonio Gonçalves Chaves Jr. when he served as provincial president in the 1880s.

Elementary schools proliferated in the 1870s and 1880s, mostly benefiting Montes Claros, which led the region with fifteen new elementary schools for boys.[21] Between 1871 and 1877, Montes Claros gained six schools for girls, compared to Januária's two.[22] Montes Claros also gained funding for new chairs in Latin and French. Januária also received authorization to hire a French and Latin instructor on three separate occasions in the 1870s, suggesting that the town had been unable to find or keep a suitable candidate.[23] Montes Claros retained its lead in the 1880s, with seven new elementary schools, compared to Januária's three and São Francisco's five. In part,

Montes Claros benefited from having a larger population, which enabled it to demand more schools, but efforts of representatives such as Justino de Andrade Camara played a decisive role as well.

Montes Claros also profited from advances in higher education and technical courses. Through the efforts of Assemblyman Camara, it secured one of three provincial trade schools set up to serve underprivileged youths in 1876. Camara cleverly argued that impoverished drought refugees needed training and education to become independent of public subsidies. During a five-to seven-year apprenticeship, youths would learn their three "R's" as well as a trade. The school also offered night courses for adults. When a teacher's college (escola normal) followed in 1880, Camara submitted a project to the assembly that would grant all primary school teachers two year's leave to attend teaching colleges. The province also authorized a night school for workers of the Cedro textile factory in 1882.[24]

These initiatives all related to the liberal goal of social order. However, the provincial government proved reluctant to invest in this intangible ideal in the form of subsidies to construct jails, town halls, churches, and schools. Only in the latter decades of the empire did the province allocate such funds, and it did so selectively—in Montes Claros's favor. Municipalities also made appeals in the interests of economic progress. Transportation and communication limitations hampered the region's ability to expand production. High freight costs ate up profits and curtailed the range of markets. Attempts to squeeze money out of the provincial government for roads, bridges, and innovations such as steamboat lines, however, enjoyed similarly limited success.

Transportation and Communication Initiatives

Montes Claros, São Romão, and Januária faced different challenges in their efforts to improve transportation networks. Montes Claros depended more on land routes and focused its efforts on road building. As river ports, São Romão and Januária emphasized bridges and port facilities. On land, all three communities were vulnerable to flooding as bridges frequently washed out during the rainy season. Even modest proposals to expand trade through transportation improvements were rejected until the three municipalities' provincial representatives interceded on their behalf.

One illustrative example was Januária's thirty-six-year-long campaign to replace a bridge over the river Pandeiros that had been washed out during the flood season in 1836. The council argued that a new bridge would revive commerce with neighboring Urucuia and the distant provinces of Goiás, Paraná, Bahia, and Pernambuco.[25] To sweeten the deal, one petition predicted an increase of traffic passing through the unprofitable customs house of Escuro if the bridge were built.[26] Modest subsidies were promised but not disbursed, and provincial funding remained meager through the 1860s. Only in 1872 did the Januarenses receive four contos to build the bridge. After Januária elected provincial representatives to the assembly in the 1880s, however, the community received the more substantial sum of eighteen contos to modernize its port and to construct two bridges linking it to São Francisco and São José do Gorutuba.[27]

Montes Claros found itself similarly disadvantaged in the early decades of the empire as it lobbied to build bridges along trade routes.[28] In one case, repeated requests made in the 1840s for a bridge over the Rio Verde on the road to Brejo das Almas resulted in approval only in 1852 and did not receive full funding until 1860. Outlying municipal districts acquired a number of modest subsidies to build small wooden bridges in the 1850s.[29] In the 1870s and 1880s, Montes Claros finally benefited from expanded provincial support for transportation, receiving more than ten contos to build bridges over three major rivers that cut through the municipality.[30]

São Romão received almost no funding for transportation improvements whatsoever. Aside from a paltry sum allocated for bridge repair in 1855, the municipality was all but ignored until São Francisco became the county seat in 1870.[31] Shortly thereafter, it began to get locals elected to the provincial assembly. In the 1880s, the municipality secured over twenty contos to build bridges to connect the São Francisco commercially to other districts. Monies released in 1884 benefited both São Francisco and Januária by funding construction of bridges designed to facilitate communications between them.[32] The share received by the municipality of São Romão, however, was insignificant compared to that received by Januária and Montes Claros.

More costly plans to improve the region's transportation networks were imposed from the outside, not generated from within. Throughout the century, politicians had debated the relative merits of the canalization of rivers and the building of railroads to stimulate national economic development.[33] Recognizing the potential of the São Francisco, the imperial government backed several surveying expeditions.[34] The engineer Fernando Halfield surveyed the length of the Rio São Francisco in the 1850s and concluded that the cost of the hydraulic works necessary to free navigation from Barra do Rio das Velhas, Minas Gerais, to Joazeiro, Bahia, came to the prohibitively costly sum of 6,963 contos, a sum many times greater than the entire provincial budget. In 1869, the provincial government estimated that to remove obstructions of the Rio das Velhas and the Rio São Francisco would cost 2,605 and 8,700 contos, respectively.[35] Both imperial and provincial governments offered incentives for investors to exploit Minas Gerais's many rivers, but navigation projects ultimately took second place to railroads after southern Minas Gerais began to cultivate coffee.

Navigation in the São Francisco region remained limited to small and medium-sized craft. The presence of rapids meant that cargo had to be transported overland along some stretches of the river. The largest craft were the picturesque *barcas*, measuring fifteen meters in length and equipped with thatched cabins to carry passengers.[36] In 1878, the provincial government signed a contract with Dr. Aurelio A. Pires de Figueiredo Camargo and Joséfino Vieira Machado to inaugurate an ambitious steamship service. The two entrepreneurs were guaranteed hefty subsidies providing that they completed six annual round-trip voyages between Guaicuí (formerly Barra do Rio das Velhas) and Joazeiro, Bahia. The contract required the vessel *Saldanha Marinho* to explore the navigable channels of the São Francisco, stop at all principal ports, offer free passage to public officials, soldiers, and police officers, and deliver government mail.

From the beginning, the *Saldanha Marinho* suffered misfortune. Its maiden voyage took place during the dry season to avoid malaria. But the level of the river was so low that the boat ran into sandbars, gravel beds, and other obstacles, damaging its hull. The vessel stopped frequently so that its crew could make repairs and cut wood along the river's edge to fuel the burners. The ship did make a profitable side trip along the Rio Corrente in Bahia, but, by the end of 1880, the *Saldanha Marinho* had completed only two round-trip voyages. Aurelio Pires gave various excuses, including the death of his associate, illness among the crew, and a two-month delay in Januária at the arbitrary disposition of police authorities. The provincial president pardoned the fines incurred for failing to complete the requisite number of trips but did not guarantee further payment of subsidies.

The *Saldanha Marinho* completed only four additional voyages between 1881 and 1882, causing the government to request repayment of the subsidy and to deny further payments. The boat had suffered serious damage and was abandoned in 1883, mired somewhere along the São Francisco, stripped of its more valuable fixtures by local thieves. With relief, the provincial government accepted a bid by the Morro Velho British mining company to purchase the damaged vessel. The government decided to cut its losses of thirty-three contos rather than sink more into the boat.[37] During the First Republic, steam navigation eventually succeeded on the Rio São Francisco, but through Bahian initiatives rather than mineiro ones.[38]

The failure of the steamboat company did have some repercussions for Januária and São Romão. The towns remained relatively isolated from overland trade because they could not convince the provincial government to invest in bridges and roads. Although Januária did benefit from the opening of one road from its county seat to the Bahian border, only in the 1880s, when both communities managed to elect representatives to the provincial assembly, did they secure more substantial funding. Montes Claros, in contrast, began to receive funding in the 1860s to build road networks that would link it to other regional markets in all directions, including Diamantina, Bomfim, Grão Mogol, Minas Novas, Rio Pardo, Paracatú, São José do Gorutuba, and Contendas.[39]

Good roads were also necessary to maintain regular communications with the provincial government. A provincial postal service delivered official correspondence, providing a lifeline connecting municipalities to the provincial president and assembly in Ouro Preto. The provincial capital, in turn, provided a tenuous link to the imperial government in Rio de Janeiro. Appointed municipal postal agents contracted mail carriers to carry correspondence both to surrounding villages and back to Ouro Preto. By law, the provincial government reimbursed municipal councils for costs incurred in delivering official mail to outlying districts. Election instructions and protocols constituted an ever more significant part of this correspondence over time. Delays, both involuntary and deliberate, could have political consequences.

In the 1830s, delivery between Januária and Ouro Preto, a distance of roughly 650 kilometers, could easily take over two months, depending on the weather and the number of stops made. The postal service's inefficiency, however, was not due just to bad roads and turbulent rivers. Route changes, inadequate salaries for mail carriers, tardy reimbursement for out-of-pocket costs, and official tampering all contributed to postal delays. The government paid only 1$000 per fifty kilometers traveled when it paid postal carriers at all. A postal agent in Januária resigned in 1844 after not having been paid for six years or reimbursed for expenses.[40] Officials in Montes Claros also complained that carriers could not survive on the meager official salary of 320 réis per day and that, as a result, they dragged out their time on the road to make ends meet. Only persons of the most "useless and incorrigible" class volunteered for the work, and no individuals "of quality" would subject themselves to the dangers of the untamed backlands for so little.[41] The authorities in São Romão even had to resort to hiring a woman (illegally) to deliver official correspondence to outlying districts.[42] Complaints about insufficient resources began to diminish at midcentury.

Reliable and rapid communication with Rio de Janeiro via Ouro Preto was essential to both the economic and the political fortunes of the São Francisco region. Over the course of the empire, rival districts and municipalities competed actively for control over postal routes.[43] Decisions depended not only on the quality of transportation routes in a given area but also on the perceptions of the health risks involved. Riverside communities were considered especially hazardous during the rainy season, when malaria and other fevers struck the region. Municipal authorities argued that health brought prosperity and wrote appeals to fund public hygiene measures as well.

Health and Environment

In the comarca of Rio São Francisco, municipal councils tended to approach public health initiatives as the need arose. Despite the presence of endemic diseases such as malaria, only episodic droughts and epidemics inspired any serious commitment to public health. Municipal councils adopted a few measures, such as a law passed in São Francisco in 1883 that prohibited goats and pigs from wandering the city streets. Given that the law made an exception in the case of those livestock belonging to a prominent landowner, Camilo Lopes de Oliveira, its positive effects on local hygiene must have been limited at best.[44] Municipal health initiatives focused largely on three areas: participation in provincial and national smallpox inoculation programs, lobbying for clean water projects, and petitioning for drought-relief programs.

Smallpox vaccination campaigns encountered considerable resistance on the part of the local population. Even members of the elite believed that the vaccine spread the disease instead of containing it. One petition signed by seventy-three of Januária's leading citizens claimed that its outcome was "to fill the churches with cadavers."[45] Municipal authorities also believed that the vaccine lost its effectiveness during the long, hot journey to the north. Local beliefs were not entirely fanciful. The smallpox vaccine was produced from blood samples taken from victims who had survived the disease. It was then propagated and injected into healthy people. Successive propagation caused the vaccine to become progressively weaker. The vaccine also carried other blood-borne diseases, such as hepatitis and syphilis.[46]

In Januária, popular resistance continued until an epidemic in 1845 carried off more than three hundred victims; the hastily buried corpses were subsequently exhumed by dogs and armadillos.[47] Not until 1887, however, did a provincial hygiene delegate carry out a successful vaccination campaign.[48] The elite of Montes Claros proved more willing to impose the vaccine on its reluctant population. In 1872, Justino de Andrade Camara proposed to the provincial assembly the cost-effective solution of training public school teachers to administer the vaccine. In keeping with their efforts to promote an enlightened image, municipal authorities did not comment on local prejudice against the vaccine and in later decades explicitly denied the existence of such prejudice.[49]

Montes Claros was also the first community in the comarca to offer rudimentary health care. As early as 1847, Montes Claros had a trained resident physician, Dr. Carlos José Versiani, the son of the most progressive farmer of the municipality. Versiani studied medicine in Rio de Janeiro and returned home to practice, teach public school, and politick. Through the combined initiative of Dr. Versiani and the provincial deputy Justino de Andrade Camara, Montes Claros received funding to establish a charity hospital in 1871. Advances in public health coupled with a more favorable disease environment provided Montes Claros with competitive advantages over Januária and São Romão.[50]

Most hamlets and towns had to make do with *curiosos* (learned laymen) and *curandeiros* (traditional healers). A few merchants sold patent medicines to supplement home remedies concocted by locals. Some German physicians of dubious credibility practiced in the sertão mineiro, as did such outright quacks as the Frenchman José Augusto Buchwaller, who performed operations, wrote prescriptions, and called himself "doctor" without credentials, much to the outrage of a provincial health inspector.[51] Few individuals had any accurate understanding of the spread and transmission of disease. For example, the local elite associated malaria epidemics with flooding and "pestilent" waters rather than with breeding mosquitoes. Some authorities from Januária and Montes Claros explained disease resistance according to race and climate, a typical nineteenth-century folk belief.[52]

Some officials did connect the spread of disease to impure water and sought funding to install piped water systems to provide potable drinking water to town dwellers. For decades, the councils of São Romão and Montes Claros made persistent appeals to the provincial government to fund elaborate systems of canals, pipes, and cisterns in the interests of public health. Not surprisingly, Montes Claros proved more successful in achieving its objectives.

The municipal council of São Romão first proposed a piped water system in 1836. The town raised half its estimated budget through local contributions and spent the next nine years petitioning the provincial governor, suggesting that the increased water supply could be used to wash gold-bearing deposits profitably, thereby offering a return in added tax revenues. Despite renewed extravagant promises of fabulous gold mines, the project had yet to meet its goal by 1845. Provincial funding for this project abruptly ceased for more than forty years until 1883, when Francisco Sales Peixoto, an assemblyman from São Romão, negotiated five contos for a water system.[53]

Montes Claros put up an equally lengthy yet ultimately more successful campaign. In 1845, the council built six cisterns at its own expense and was awarded 500$000 to drain a swamp that was said to emit "lethal miasmas." Over twenty years after submitting a complete proposal in 1848, the province issued a contract in 1869 to João Antonio Maria Versiani. The government then rescinded the contract after the municipal council vetoed Versiani's choice of a water source. The province awarded additional monies in 1875, but the project languished.[54] Various members of the politically influential Liberal Prates family took over the project from the Conservative Versiani but abandoned it in 1887. In 1888, the Conservative newspaper *Correio do norte* initiated a piped water campaign calling for a company to raise fifteen contos. Enthusiasm ran high until the pledges came due. The provincial government made up the balance, and, by 1893, the system was in place. Regrettably, however, owing to engineering errors, it did not function. Water spilled out into the streets instead of arriving in the tanks and cisterns. The system was finally up and running in 1898 but functioned only intermittently for the next twenty years.[55]

Drought conditions also posed potential health risks. During droughts, massive influxes of starving migrants crowded into the small cities and towns of the São Francisco region. Heightened demand for limited foodstuffs caused shortages, which led to inflation in the price of basic supplies. For example, during the drought of 1860, prices in Januária rose 500–800 percent over the course of weeks.[56] Migrants often brought disease from other areas, and, weakened by hunger, they and the local poor were vulnerable.

Municipal councils attempted to combat these problems by manipulating market forces.[57] During the drought of 1833, the municipal council of Montes Claros sent its National Guard to the Gorutubas to seize stores of manioc held by food speculators.[58] The councils of Montes Claros and São Romão also unilaterally suspended a provincial tax on beef because it pushed the price of already scarce meat beyond the means of the poor.[59] During the drought of 1860, Januária's council attempted to regulate the town market by imposing prohibitive taxes and fines on merchants who tried to export large quantities of food to drought-stricken Bahia.[60]

Municipal councils, however, lacked the resources and the will to implement long-term strategies to deal with drought. They tended to focus on temporary drought-relief programs rather than initiate flood control projects or irrigation systems. By addressing the symptoms of ecological fragility rather than its causes, communities in the São Francisco region instituted few long-term initiatives to manage the environment. They relied largely on episodic handouts. Yet, even during the "Great Drought" of 1877–80, national and provincial subsidies were inadequate at best and did little to alleviate widespread hunger and disease.[61]

Municipalities faced financial and technological barriers in their efforts to improve public health. The inability to combat disease, however, had political and economic consequences. Rival communities invoked health dangers to explain the rise or decline of certain centers or to justify the transfer of the municipal seat from one place to another. Regional authorities claimed that endemic malaria contributed to the commercial and demographic decline of Barra do Rio das Velhas and São Romão. On the other hand, during droughts, river communities proved less vulnerable than upland towns such as Montes Claros. Insufficient resources and knowledge created more dangerous disease environments and contributed to the underdevelopment of the region.

The Price of Regional Hegemony

By the 1860s, Montes Claros dominated the São Francisco region politically and economically. Moreover, by maintaining an almost constant presence in the provincial legislature, it was able to challenge other urban centers like Diamantina, Paracatú, and Minas Novas for scarce resources such as permanently stationed infantry regiments.[62] Diamantina, which boasted a viable mining economy, seminary, preparatory schools, and newspapers and was a Liberal party stronghold, battled for position with Montes Claros in the halls of the provincial assembly. Representatives from Diamantina praised their city as "the capital of northern Minas" or "the most important city of the north." They tried to discredit Montes Claros by citing the sins of its officials, singling out one municipal tax collector who used his position on the emancipation board to undervalue slaves and then purchase them cheaply from "rustic proprietors." In 1878, the assemblyman Candido de Oliveira criticized the newly created Santa Casa da Misericórdia of Montes Claros, claiming that even the Montesclarenses preferred to undergo medical treatment in Diamantina. It was a slap in the face to Carlos José Versiani and Justino de Andrade Camara, who had spent decades lobbying and fund-raising for the charity hospital to become reality. Montes Claros also competed successfully with Diamantina over the location of a regional trade school.[63] Its autonomy stands in sharp contrast to the neighboring towns in the São Francisco region.

Yet getting local sons elected, participating in a broader political system based on patronage, and espousing the principles of liberalism remained insufficient selling points, even for Montes Claros. Although it was more successful than its neighbors in securing provincial funding, it had to compete with other municipalities in regions that commanded greater government interest. Local representatives had to struggle against negative stereotypes and cope with the economic disadvantages of a nonexport economy in an export-oriented society.

Montes Claros sought to overcome negative images and achieve legitimacy in the imperial order by observing the norms promulgated by the center. The Montesclarenses entered into party politics early and with enthusiasm. Being the administrative head of the comarca may have provided some advantage. A centrally appointed, university-educated district magistrate, Jeronimo Maximo Oliveira e Castro, resided in the comarca seat for decades. He became active in provincial politics and may have given Montes Claros an initial competitive advantage. The municipality also developed strong Liberal and Conservative parties and rapidly began to stress partisanship over personalities in local disputes. The Prates, Gonçalves Chaves, Velloso, and Versiani families provided political leadership and forged extramunicipal relationships. External connections and sound municipal management were key to Montes Claros's credibility.

In contrast, Januária remained too embroiled in local intrigue to be taken seriously. The elite could not get beyond its personal conflicts to work together for the good of the municipality. Municipal authorities reported much higher levels of corruption in Januária than did their counterparts in Montes Claros and São Romão. Although Januária actively engaged in agriculture and trade, it was less successful in collecting tax revenues and customs duties. The flagrant violation of basic administrative procedure probably eroded Januária's position as well. Only José Ignacio Couto Moreno and Padre José Antonio Marinho developed any long-lasting political connections beyond the municipality. Both died in the early 1850s, at just the moment when extramunicipal ties became more crucial. Although local branches of the Liberal and Conservative parties participated actively in elections, they did not elect local candidates to the provincial assembly until the 1880s. São Romão remained politically passive until the municipal seat passed to Pedras dos Angicos in 1870. The new vila subsequently produced local politicians who became active at the provincial level.

Members of the elite in the sertão mineiro had to create a positive, modernizing image in order to be taken seriously by the provincial presidents and assemblies, who allocated municipal funding. By invoking the language, if not the substance, of liberalism, constitutionalism, and transplanted European norms of order and progress, the municipal elite built up political capital. Committing oneself to the party system brought tangible rewards. The São Francisco region could not overcome its marginal environment or comparative isolation, but its elites could present themselves as capable of adaption and innovation. The citizenry of Montes Claros adapted most quickly to new political norms and put up a strong modern front. This strategy contributed to its growth into the informal capital of the São Francisco region.

Yet, in the end, the rewards were meager, given the social costs. Despite local willingness to play the game of patronage politics and subscribe to liberal ideals, the provincial and federal governments remained unwilling to invest heavily in the sertão for a number of reasons. First and foremost, it represented a poor financial risk with little possibility of any returns in the form of increased revenues for the state. In addition, the sertão provided an uncomfortable reminder that the Brazilian reality did not correspond to the European ideal. The "barbaric" backlands did not produce an ideal hierarchical society based on the harmonious, well-ordered, extended family. Instead, violence and disorder continually bubbled up from underneath. Despite the fact that much of this upheaval was connected to electoral politics engineered by the center, the interior was expected to conform to ideal, modern expectations of behavior. The rewards received were far less dramatic than those earned by export-oriented regions. Instead of railroads and lighting and water systems, sertanejo communities gained wooden bridges, dirt roads, and roof repairs to the town hall. Patterns of electoral corruption and violence established during the empire persisted in the São Francisco region well into the twentieth century.

CHAPTER 9

The Continuity of Political Violence in the Sertão Mineiro

On 6 February 1930, Dr. Fernandes Melo Viana, vice president of the Federal Republic of Brazil, arrived in Montes Claros to deliver a speech. As night fell, a crowd gathered in front of the newly constructed train station. Following the speech, shots rang out, and Melo Viana fell wounded by a bullet to the head. In the ensuing melee, two rival factions, one supporting Júlio Prestes and the other Getúlio Vargas, killed half a dozen people, including women and children. Violent outbursts continued during the revolution led and won by Getúlio Vargas.[1] The year 1930 signified the culmination of forty years of endemic violence in Montes Claros, punctuated by the murders of police officers, judges, and prominent fazendeiros.

By the end of the First Republic (1889–1930), Montes Claros undisputably had become the regional political and economic capital of northern Minas Gerais. It boasted a railroad station, banks, newspapers, a teacher's training school, piped potable water, a telegraph service, telephones, and many other trappings of modernity. In large measure, Montes Claros owed its relative success during this period to three prominent politicians: Antonio Gonçalves Chaves Jr., Camilo Filinto Prates, and Antonio Augusto Velloso.[2] Each had become active in mineiro politics in the final decades of the empire. Prates was first elected to the provincial assembly of Minas Gerais at the tender age of twenty-two. He served as provincial deputy from 1883 to 1889, was nominated intendant of Montes Claros in 1889 after the declaration of the republic, and served several terms in the federal Senate and House between 1905 and 1917. Antonio Augusto Velloso also served as provincial assemblyman from 1882 to 1889. He traveled widely, forging connections in

Rio de Janeiro and São Paulo. Antonio Gonçalves Chaves Jr. continued to grow in stature during the republic. He was nominated to the constituent assembly that wrote the constitution of 1891 and was also one of the authors of the new civil code. Chaves served as a federal senator from 1893 to 1903 and as a director of the Ouro Preto law school. He died in 1911.

In the republic, as during the empire, political success rested on patronage, electoral machinery, and localized violence. The political restructuring introduced with the constitution of 1891 granted broader autonomy to the former provinces. States exerted greater control over their own revenues, could dictate independent foreign policy, and could organize militias. Brazil moved to a single-party system in an attempt to get past the excessive bickering and factionalism that characterized late imperial politics. The Republican party assumed a decentralized organization built around state chapters. Elected governors replaced appointed provincial presidents. These governors supported candidates and factions on the federal level by fixing elections on the municipal level, distributing rewards such as bureaucratic posts and funding for public works to their municipal allies. After 1895, state governors nominated the presidents of the town councils, subsequently called intendants (*intendentes*) and later prefects (*prefeitos*).

This system, known as the politics of the governors (*política dos governadores*), changed the balance of power at the state level. Wealthy states such as São Paulo benefited from greater fiscal autonomy and channeled funding into economic diversification and industrialization. Minas Gerais, on the other hand, drew its strength from numbers. It enjoyed a congressional and electoral majority until 1930 that enabled it to place its people in key administrative positions. Representatives from Minas Gerais held the Ministries of Finance, Justice, and Public Works 70 percent of the time. Mineiros usually headed the federal lottery, channeling most of its revenues to schools and public works in their home state. Minas Gerais played an important role as federal president maker during the republic. Demographically, it was also able to influence political outcomes. By presenting a stable and united provincial front in Rio de Janeiro, Minas Gerais secured impressive levels of federal funding for railroads, telegraphs, and postal systems, thereby overcoming the drawback of the state's relative economic weakness.[3] The cost at the municipal level remained high as local oligarchs engaged in corruption and violence to manipulate the electoral system.

Political patronage under the First Republic has been characterized as a product of government decentralization. This interpretation focuses largely on the federal/state nexus. From the municipal perspective, however, little had changed except that local appointments were made at the state instead of the federal level. Municipalities still depended on state governments for funding. The constitution of 1891 granted only meager municipal funding, tightening the system of political patronage and personal distribution of rewards in exchange for votes. By adding a literacy requirement, suffrage fell to just 1–3 percent of the population, but electoral conflict continued or even escalated. During the republic, the excesses of local boss rule and endemic banditry, especially in the sertão, became legendary.

Montes Claros adapted to the new political criteria of the republic as it had acculturated to the political exigencies of the empire. It also underwent socioeconomic change. During the early decades of the twentieth century, Montes Claros experienced rapid demographic growth, especially of its black population, which increased from 15.72 percent of the total in 1890 to 24.1 percent in 1940. Migrants from drought-stricken Bahia seeking free lands continued to arrive. In 1920, Montes Claros was one of only five cities in Minas Gerais with a population that exceeded ten thousand. Its municipal population surpassed sixty-eight thousand.

Land distribution and labor relations also changed. Between 1920 and 1940, the number of small family farms measuring from one to forty hectares increased from 37,375 to 177,893. In 1920, these small holders constituted 32.3 percent of the total number of landowners; by 1940, this number had swelled to 62.5 percent. As more small holders slipped into landlessness, some were reincorporated into large commercial estates as tenants and sharecroppers. In the early twentieth century, new taxes had been levied on agricultural production. These taxes had to be paid in cash by estate owners. The landed elite responded by requiring traditional rural retainers (agregados), who had formerly enjoyed access to land in exchange for occasional labor services to work as sharecroppers, to provide additional income for estate owners.[4] In addition, dependent tenants could be persuaded to vote for their patron's candidate of choice.

The political stature of Montes Claros was reflected in its steadily rising municipal budget. Despite Montes Claros's modest tax base (providing less than 1 percent of all state revenues), it commanded an impressive proportion of government subsidies. In 1891, the municipal budget stood at a meager 5:300$000. By 1897, it had expanded to 30:000$000; by 1919, 42:000$000; by 1921, 73:000$000; and, by 1928, 169:400$000.[5] Sons of the São Francisco region secured funds by virtue of their political positions. For example, as minister of transportation, Dr. Francisco Sá wheedled enough funds to push the railroad to Montes Claros by 1926.

The municipality continued to lead the region in economic and urban development and maintained its political dominance of the São Francisco region. Electoral violence persisted or even accelerated.[6] According to the historian John Wirth, Montes Claros was "divided into two armed camps . . . each with its own marching band, its own newspaper, its hired thugs and allies . . . spanning two worlds, that of respectable elite society and that of crude backlands politics."[7] Although correctly depicting the factionalism that divided Montes Claros, Wirth falls into the misconception that the politics of the interior were retrograde and backward.[8] The municipal elite of Montes Claros, however, had shown itself to be capable of a high level of political sophistication. If anything, geographic isolation and relative poverty required a more astute understanding of national politics if benefits were to be gained from the state.

Montes Claros demonstrated more political continuity with the imperial past than it reflected changes associated with the republican era. The roots of coronelismo in the sertão mineiro were not due to the weakness of the republican state but reached deep into the imperial soil. Although some scholars have suggested this possibility, they have not been able to ground this hypothesis empirically at the local level for the imperial period.[9] This study permits some reinterpretation of the origins and timing of patronage politics in Brazil. It documents the presence of the ingredients for the política dos governadores of the First Republic as early as 1850.

At midcentury, local authorities had already begun to report oligarchs who intimidated votantes or purchased their votes with glasses of cachaça.[10] By the 1860s, the political press attested to the devastating effects of machine politics, partisan divisions, vote buying, electoral violence, intimidation, and a pattern of wholesale replacement of municipal officials following electoral upsets. Although the electoral "reforms" of the 1880s and 1890s greatly reduced the number of eligible voters, the dynamics of machine politics remained remarkably similar. The política dos governadores represented not a break with the imperial past but rather the continuation of the power and privilege of local oligarchs, who were bound to provincial and national political networks. The key to this system was not the relative degree of centralization existing between province or state and the national government but rather the degree of centralized control affecting the municipality.

The stereotypical elements of rural republican society all have imperial antecedents. Omnipotent colonels, corrupt oligarchies, and ruthless bandits who hired themselves out to fix elections or settle old scores appear frequently in the pages of nineteenth-century manuscripts. Institutionalized impunity, paternalism, and patronage bound, and continued to bind, the disparate classes of sertanejo society in a complex web of interdependent, albeit unequal, social relations. As the population increased and some estates became increasingly subdivided, struggling patrons became less able to respond to the needs of their dependents, and ties between client and patron were loosened. As the numbers of the landless and unemployed increased, these men hired themselves out to the few expansionist landowners with capital who wished to augment their personal force of loyal retainers with hired bandits.

The participation of the "respectable poor" was essential to municipal political life. In order to retain power at the local level, the landed elite had to exert firm control over voters at the polls. To secure their position, they enlisted the services of men excluded from the electoral system, agregados and bandits willing to engage in violence on behalf of their patrons. Unfortunately, the role of these voters and bandits as active agents in the electoral process remains somewhat obscure. Members of the elite drew fine social or cultural distinctions only with reference to members of their own class. They elaborated their colleagues' behavior, character, or family at length but lumped nonelites together in an undifferentiated mass. Poor individuals were identified by the ubiquitous and anonymous marker *de tal* (so-and-so). Either the intricacies of the social life of the *povo* (the masses) were closed off to them, or they simply did not care to investigate. Slaves, vagrants, and the respectable poor usually did not represent a direct threat to elite personal status. Only when they threatened class interests did authorities stir themselves.

Yet this study also shows that neither the humble votantes nor the more privileged eleitores conformed to the stereotypes or prejudices voiced by the national elite in charge of electoral legislation and reform. The notion that a tiny group of oligarchs exerted unchallenged control over misguided, ignorant, and weak voters was not entirely untrue but certainly exaggerated. High rates of turnover in local elected offices suggest that some "freedom to vote" was possible. Some votantes risked the possibility of violent conflict in order to vote for the candidate of their choice. Others resisted by refusing to vote, despite the risk of incurring financial or social penalties.

Partisan control over local municipal councils did not always mirror national trends, again suggesting that rural communities exercised some autonomy to resist partisan imperatives. For example, in Montes Claros, the Liberals controlled the municipal council during the 1840s, while the Liberals dominated the national scene. After the crucial 1849 election, the Conservatives, led by the Versianis, won the municipal elections in 1853 and managed to control local government until 1880 despite the fact that, on the national level, the Liberal and Conservative parties alternated. Liberals regained control of the municipal council with the help of Antonio Gonçalves Chaves Jr. after he was nominated provincial president of Minas Gerais in 1879. Control of the municipality then alternated between the two parties during the final years of the empire.[11] Patterns of party dominance in Montes Claros reveal that a perfect fit did not exist between national and local trends.

Changes in Regional Identity and Political Culture

This book has also documented subtle changes in the ways that rural elites perceived themselves, their political identities, and their region. A close reading of various kinds of political discourse, both public and private, suggests that the political culture of liberalism ran more than skin deep. The imperial political elite of the São Francisco region waged an uphill battle to gain political respectability and legitimacy. Not only did they face ecological and economic limitations, but they also had to combat pejorative stereotypes of the sertão that were thrust on them. Contemporaneous observers and modern scholars alike perceived the sertão as a static, subsistence-based economy and society, erroneously equating economic stagnation with intellectual torpidity. Underdevelopment, isolation, and a harsh environment that inhibited regular communication did represent barriers, but not impenetrable ones. Had those barriers been so insurmountable, the imperial goal of state centralization would never have succeeded so well in Brazil.

In the nineteenth century, the São Francisco elite attempted to create positive images of the sertão and its inhabitants on the basis of its capacity for modernization. In the provincial assemblies, its representatives tried to convince their colleagues that the people of the region were ready and eager for progress but were hindered by official neglect and lack of infrastructure. Election correspondence and police reports, however, revealed a very different picture, one of a maddeningly mobile populace ready, willing, and able to commit violence and unwilling to subject themselves to disciplined labor. The povo fell short of the standard of liberalism that some members of the elite held dear. These sentiments, expressed by a justice of the peace from São Romão in 1826, changed little over the course of the nineteenth century: "The majority of the people who inhabit the fertile margins of the São Francisco river vegetate in sloth. . . . It would be very interesting if a well regulated and very energetic police force were to come and repress idleness and oblige the people to work. Thereby, base customs would be transformed, and the dissolution, libertinism, and drunkenness that define the character of nearly the entire population of these backlands would be eliminated."[12]

The elite observed popular resistance bubbling up from underneath but rarely examined such behavior in detail. Nineteenth-century police documentation contains abundant references to a large, fluctuating, uncontrollable population of unruly boatmen, swaggering cowboys, mobile and occasionally rebellious slaves, and army deserters. These marginals lived beyond the patronage system, and their mobility enabled them to resist military recruitment, modern work discipline, the judicial system, and taxes. Such "outlaws" formed communities deep in the Bahian sertão and swept down into the São Francisco region when opportunities for their violent services arose. During the First Republic, as the "respectable poor" became reduced to greater unemployment and landless status, banditry increased. Although the elite piously complained about the excesses of outlaws, typically focusing on those in the employ of their rivals, they nonetheless depended on the services of these mercenaries to win elections.

The sertão mineiro faced challenges that would dampen the enthusiasm of its most ardent, modernizing politicians and administrators. Underdevelopment was one of the principal constraints to ideological and political change. A liberal system of government required a minimum level of infrastructure to function. Dependable systems of communication and decent transportation conditions were needed in order for jurors and voters to participate regularly in juridical and political life. Mass political socialization required the expansion of the public educational system. Improved access to higher education also broadened the pool of competent candidates available to serve in administration and politics.

Although the extent to which the povo assimilated new ideas of governance remains unclear, the elite demonstrated in multiple ways that it was capable of internalizing new political ideologies. The pace of political acculturation varied from the rapid assimilation of Montes Claros, to a delayed reaction in Januária, to inertia in São Romão. Although little is known about modes of transmission of ideas to the interior, this book has shown that Brazilians at the far reaches of the empire internalized liberal ideas. Overall, political developments in the sertão reflected what was happening in the political center of Rio de Janeiro and the more dynamic export sectors with a slight time lag. The initial euphoria and uncertainty following independence in the 1820s were succeeded by the emergence of political societies and parties in the late 1830s. News of the many regional revolts of the 1830s and 1840s quickly spread to the sertão mineiro. After parties began to form, political life in the sertão took on a life of its own. Justices of the peace, police officers, councilmen, and officers of the National Guard educated themselves about the constitution and kept informed about new legislation. They also vied with increasing determination and ruthlessness to win elected and appointed offices.

Municipalities that failed to adapt to new ideas and institutions suffered real consequences. Adopting the tenets of liberalism to establish political legitimacy was the first step taken by many transitional elites who had come of age prior to, or during, independence. The relative tumult of the regency (1831–40) and a brief flirtation with decentralized institutions were followed by centralizing measures that demanded that isolated rural elites integrate themselves politically beyond the municipal or regional level. Party loyalty brought access to a network of patronage stretching from the distant sertão all the way to Rio de Janeiro. The price of participation was judicial impunity and electoral violence at the municipal level.

Liberalism and Modernity

Municipal authorities also underwent important and complex ideological shifts. The language used in their official correspondence with provincial presidents underwent subtle linguistic changes over time. Many members of the first postindependence generation seem to have bought into liberal discourse quite readily yet on one level were slow to internalize new ideas about the relation of citizens to the state. This dynamic becomes clear in official correspondence, which did not separate bureaucratic duties or politics into distinct and professionalized realms. Provincial superiors learned about the weather, the year's crop, conditions of trade, local intrigue, drunken brawls, a murder or two, and who was sleeping with whom. Municipal authorities prattled about their families and their slaves, their physical ailments, and the social conflicts that led to violence in the backlands.[13] This blurring of public and private extended even to the physical body. José Ignacio do Couto Moreno of Januária began one missive to the provincial governor by describing how a tick had embedded itself in his right testicle and had caused such swelling as to prevent him from mounting a horse and carrying out his duties.[14] Likewise, the district judge of the comarca once wrote about the discomfort and treatment of his syphilitic ulcers before launching into the details of municipal administration.[15]

The undifferentiated manner with which early nineteenth-century rural officials communicated to their superiors brings a sense of intimacy with the teller not commonly associated with official documentation. Clearly, first-generation notables such as the Portuguese rancher and military commander from Januária José Ignacio do Couto Moreno, the juiz de direito Jeronimo Maximo de Oliveira e Castro, the model fazendeiro and commander of the National Guard Pedro José Versiani, and the priest and Liberal party chief Antonio Gonçalves Chaves Sr. had not thoroughly internalized new ideas about the relation of citizens to the state, even if they embedded their stories in a constitutional, liberal framework.[16]

During the period lasting from 1822 to 1850, the rural elite indulged in considerable introspection as its members sought to assert their right to authority in a changing world. They drew on traditional categories of power and prestige as well as new concepts of liberal government and modernity. In this process of self-affirmation, the municipal elite of the sertão mineiro discussed issues that fell beyond the confines of their bureaucratic offices and incorporated highly personalized information in their claims to moral and political legitimacy. Postindependence municipal leaders told stories about themselves and their worlds in order to reinforce their right to power. These personalized narratives defined their own sense of status and social worth.[17]

The first generation blended traditional concepts with modern categories. For example, José Ignacio do Couto Moreno of Januária demonstrates this ambiguity between colonial and imperial values.[18] His letters reflect a premodern ethos that did not compartmentalize the public and the private yet invoked the "modern" and "liberal" terminology of constitutional government. His understanding of his relationship to the monarch remained one of submissive vassal to paternal sovereign, but he also imagined Brazil as a civilized, Europeanized nation that embraced the principles of liberal government and economic progress. His version of liberalism emphasized the right to private property and the maintenance of order, not the extension of democratizing reforms to the popular classes.

A generational shift in municipal politics took place around midcentury. This transfer of power coincided with the consolidation of the centralized Brazilian state, which demanded an educated elite capable of forging alliances with emerging national political parties. Second-generation municipal politicians with no direct experience of the colonial era adopted a decidedly more professional and modern tone. Traditional patriarchs sent their sons to the coastal cities to acquire university degrees. These young men adopted a veneer of "civilization" quite distinct from the manner of their rustic fathers. They also made the mental shift from a local understanding of politics based on kinship and personal relationships to a more bureaucratic notion grounded in national patronage defined through partisan affiliation. They became citizens of a modern state, not subjects of a patriarchal emperor.

Both the first and the second generation affirmed their beliefs in a new venue, the partisan press of Minas Gerais. In heated exchanges designed to defend one's political honor and defame one's enemies, local politicians and bureaucrats revealed the internalization of a kind of liberal moral economy. Although most of the individuals in question were probably guilty of violating the standards that they defended in print, their words should not be dismissed as mere hypocrisy. Certainly, both hypocrisy and hyperbole were present in equal measure, but ideal boundaries of political behavior were also drawn in the process. Members of the rural elite also came to embrace partisan affiliation as an integral component of their personal identity and liberalism as a yardstick of honorable behavior.

Revisiting the Sertão

The force of political change in imperial Brazil is perhaps most evident the farther one moves from the center. Patronage politics make sense when the rewards are immediate and obvious. Yet the São Francisco region garnered only modest benefits in exchange for its participation in a political system that facilitated, and in many cases encouraged, the use of violence and coercion. Machine politics corrupted institutions of social control, rendering social protection of individual security ever more precarious. Despite the fact that the system gave little in return, municipal elites felt compelled to play the game and paid the social costs involved. Although Montes Claros benefited the most and continued to reap rewards into the First Republic, it also inherited a legacy of social and political unrest that lasted for decades.

The sertão mineiro did not reflect just one reality; rather, it encompassed many. Two of the most famous works about the sertão, João Guimarães Rosa's *The Devil to Pay in the Backlands* (*Grandes sertões: Veredas*) and Euclides da Cunha's *Rebellion in the Backlands* (*Os sertões*), use the plural when speaking of the vast stretches of semiarid plains and mountain ranges that constitute Brazil's vast northeastern interior. In the São Francisco region, the sertão meant different things to different people. The Portuguese-born military officer José Ignacio do Couto Moreno of Januária was so moved by the landscape that he felt compelled to write poetry and inscribe his thoughts in the margin of a district census:

Fertil campo florescente
Junto de montes coroados
D'arvoredo: verdes prados
Bordando mansa corrente:
Canais, por arte da gente
Saem de um, e de outro lado
Vê um e outro povoado
No meio alegre verdura:
Eis esta fiel pintura
É do Brejo do Salgado.[19]

Flourishing fertile fields
Alongside mountains crowned
with arbors; green meadows
Bordered by gentle streams:
Canals, of our own making,
Emerge in every direction:
Settlements visible in the midst
of this exuberant greenness:
This portrait, faithful and true,
is of Brejo do Salgado.

For Couto Moreno, the sertões of the São Francisco region were not dry, barren wastes. He depicted his home, which bore the unfortunate name of Brejo do Salgado, or brackish swamp, as a region blessed by nature yet tamed and improved by man's industry. Handcrafted irrigation systems and densely settled rural estates rendered his sertão richly productive. In his mind, his patch of sertão had the potential to evolve into an orderly, hierarchical society defined by thrift, temperance, piety, respect for the constitution, liberal institutions, and the empire.

For less privileged members of society, the sertão might represent either danger or opportunity. For hapless army recruits, desertion into the sertões represented escape from an unpleasant, ill-paid military existence. For poor women of color, it often meant single motherhood and eking out a humble existence from the fruits of the land, by spinning and weaving, processing castor oil or soap, or working as a prostitute. For elite women, it signified a circumscribed existence defined by male relatives and the confines of home and church. Masculine honor, legitimized violence, and social deference based on a hierarchy of class, gender, race, and wealth bound all levels of sertanejo society.

The sertão also serves as an apt metaphor for imperial politics in all its complexity. The interior inspires strong emotions, be they the condescension of smug coastal dwellers or the parochial pride and poetry of a coronel of the interior. The sertão inspired impassioned imagery from the pen of Euclides da Cunha as he penetrated the interior for the first time. He wrote, "Upon leaving behind . . . the majestic perspectives which unfold to the south and exchanging them here for the moving sight of Nature in torment, one cannot but have the persisting impression of treading the newly upraised bed of a sea long extinct, which still preserves, stereotyped in its rigid folds, the agitation of the waves and the stormy deeps."[20]

Euclides da Cunha captures not only the arresting nature of the landscape but also the social texture of politics in the interior. The melding of rooted traditionalism with the capacity for violent upheaval exerts an enduring fascination, making the study of sertanejo society and politics such a captivating subject. Moving beyond the coastal areas of Rio, São Paulo, and Bahia also provides rich rewards for the scholar far beyond a sense of regional intrigue. Study of the periphery has demonstrated that political history has multiple layers, like the fossilized sea depicted above by Da Cunha. To define political events according to their significance in urban centers results in an incomplete understanding of the whole. The interconnectedness of coast to interior and the state to the municipality demands further reevaluation, work that I hope this book has inspired.

Abbreviations

AN	Arquivo Nacional (Rio de Janeiro)
Anais	*Anais da Assembléia Legislativa de Minas Gerais*
APM	Arquivo Público Mineiro (Belo Horizonte, Minas Gerais)
CEDEPLAR	Centro de Desenvolvimento e Planejamento Regional (Belo Horizonte, Minas Gerais)
CJ	Coração de Jesus
CM	*câmara municipal* (municipal council)
CMJ	municipal council of Januária
CMMC	municipal council of Montes Claros
CMSR	municipal council of São Romão
cx.	*caixa* (box)
del.	*delegado* (police delegate)
JD	*juiz de direito* (district magistrate)
JM	*juiz municipal* (municipal judge)
JMOC	Jeronimo Maximo Oliveira e Castro
JP	*juiz de paz* (justice of the peace)
LM	*lei mineira* (provincial law of Minas Gerais)
MC	Montes Claros
p.	(ps. [pl.]) *pasta* (folder)
PP	*presidente da província* (provincial president)
PPMG	provincial president of Minas Gerais
Rel. PPMG	*Relatórios dos Presidentes da Província de Minas Gerais*

Res.	Resolução (resolution)
RIHGB	*Revista do Instituto Histórico e Geográfico Brasileiro*
SG	Seção do Governo
SP	Seção da Província
SR	São Romão

Notes

Introduction

1. Foreign nations delayed recognition of Brazilian sovereignty until Great Britain negotiated peace between Portugal and Brazil in 1825.

2. See Chasteen, "Cabanos and Farrapos"; and Kraay, "As Terrifying as Unexpected."

3. See Queiroz, *Mandonismo;* and Leal, *Coronelismo.*

4. Richard Graham's important work (see, e.g., his *Patronage and Politics*) stresses the role of national elites in controlling election results. Linda Lewin's study of family-based oligarchies, *Politics and Parentela in Paraiba*, places greater emphasis on municipal dynamics and sources. *Politics and Parentela in Paraiba* is the most recent contribution to a series about regional oligarchies in the First Republic that began with Joseph Love's *Brazilian Regionalism.* An ambitious comparative history project followed that yielded Love, *São Paulo and the Brazilian Federation;* Levine, *Pernambuco in the Brazilian Federation;* and Wirth, *Minas Gerais in the Brazilian Federation.* See also Graham, "Comparing Regional Elites"; and Pang, *Bahia in the First Brazilian Republic.*

5. In placing this study at the margins of the state, I am following Latin American Subaltern Studies Group, "Founding Statement." On the centrality of municipality, see Bastos, *Província*, and *Os males do presente;* Maia, *O município.*

6. Flory, *Judge and Jury*, xii.

7. Queiroz, *Mandonismo*, 25.

8. Zemella, *Abastecimento.*

9. See Martins and Martins, "Slavery in a Non-Export Economy"; "Notes and Comments: Comments on "Slavery in a Non-Export Economy"; and Martins and Martins, "Notes and Comments: 'Slavery in a Non-Export Economy': A Reply."

10. Freitas, "Slavery and Social Life."

11. An exception is colonial and preindustrial São Paulo, studied by Nazarri (*Disappearance of the Dowry*) and Metcalf (*Family and Frontier*). For Minas Gerais, see

Libby, "Reconsidering Textile Production," and "Proto-Industrialisation in a Slave Society"; and Martins and Martins, "As exportações de Minas Gerais no século XIX."

12. On sertão geography and climate, see Andrade, *Land and People*, esp. 6–40, 141–77.

13. Dean, "Frontier"; Hall, *Drought and Irrigation*.

14. See Dean, "Frontier," 23; Andrade, *Land and People*, 26, 142.

15. Russell-Wood, "Frontiers in Colonial Brazil," 36–37.

16. Metcalf, *Family and Frontier;* Chandler, *The Feitosas and the Sertão dos Inhumans.*

17. Burns, *Poverty of Progress.*

18. Dias, "The Establishment of the Royal Court in Brazil."

19. Paulino José Soares de Sousa, *Relatório do ministro da justiça, 1841*, 19, cited in Mattos, *Tempo saquarema*, 34.

20. See Pratt, *Imperial Eyes*, 151.

21. See Cunha, *Rebellion in the Backlands.*

22. See Abreu, *Capítulos de história colonial;* and also Lombardi, "The Frontier in Brazilian History."

23. Simonsen, *História econômica.*

24. Cardoso, *Margem da história*, 3–7, 19, 37.

25. Amado, "The Frontier in Comparative Perspective."

26. Vianna, *Monographia*, 20. To brave the labyrinth, try Fundação João Pinheiro, *O vale do São Francisco.*

27. The best of these works are Velloso, "Chorographia mineira"; Vianna, *Monographia;* and Paula, *Montes Claros.* See also Vianna, *Efemérides montesclarenses;* Brasil, *História e desenvolvimento de Montes Claros;* Braz, *São Francisco;* Brasil, *De Contendas a Brasília de Minas;* and Prefeitura Municipal de Januária, *Primeiro centenário.* In *Sertão noroeste*, Mata-Machado has provided a general portrait of the mineiro northwest, from the Rio São Francisco to Paracatú.

28. *Everyday Forms of State Formation*, ed. Joseph and Nugent, demonstrates that, by decentering the study of the Mexican Revolution, multiple, alternative interpretations arise. What is defined by the center as chaotic or anarchic may be seen by local communities as a time of peace, stability, and freedom from the demands of the state.

29. Guha, "Methodology," 35.

30. Spivak cautions against depicting subaltern peoples as homogeneous in "Subaltern Studies."

31. These prescriptions are borrowed from Mallon, "Promise and Dilemma." Other Latin Americanists who discuss subaltern and postmodern approaches include Joseph, "On the Trail of Latin American Bandits"; and the historians and literary critics who engaged in a heated exchange inspired by Seed, "Colonial and Postcolonial Discourse": Vidal, "The Concept of Colonial and Postcolonial Discourse"; and Mignolo, "Colonial and Post Colonial Discourse."

32. Subaltern approaches inform a number of recent studies of Mexico and Peru: Stern, *Secret History of Gender;* Alonso, *Thread of Blood;* Thurner, *From Two Republics;* and Mallon, *Peasant and Nation.*

33. Antonio Gramsci, "Notes on Italian History," 55, cited in Mallon, "Promise and Dilemma," 1497.

34. Mallon, "Promise and Dilemma," 1507.

35. Success or failure should not be the criterion of historical significance, as Guha ("The Prose of Counterinsurgency") points out.

36. In addition to studies cited in nn. 31–32 above, see Guardino, *Guerrero;* and Nugent, *Modernity.*

1. The Development of Minas Gerais

1. An early proposal to reorganize Minas Gerais and Espírito Santo into four new provinces can be found in Biblioteca Nacional (Rio de Janeiro), II-36, 8, 6, 9 July 1843. See also Biblioteca Nacional, II-36, 9, 22, no. 15, n.d. (ca. 1850s).

2. Simonsen, *História econômica*, 150–57.

3. Braz, *São Francisco*, 44–47; Vasconcelos, *História antiga*, 1:5–36, 105–9; and Lima, *A capitania das Minas Gerais*, 22–52.

4. On regional markets, see Zemella, *Abastecimento*. For an overview of the gold boom, see Boxer, *The Golden Age of Brazil*.

5. Vasconcelos, *História média*, 101.

6. Vasconcelos, *História antiga*, 2:15–88, passim.

7. Cardoso, *Margem da história*, 13.

8. Anastacia, "Potentados e bandidos."

9. Iglesias, *Política econômica;* Prado, *Colonial Roots;* Leff, "Economic Retardation."

10. Libby, *Transformação e trabalho;* Slenes, "Os múltiplos de porcos e diamantes."

11. Martins and Martins, "Slavery in a Non-Export Economy."

12. On the late colonial period, see Libby, "Reconsidering Textile Production."

13. Silveira, *O algodoeiro em Minas Gerais;* and Carvalho, *Notícia historica sobre o algodão em Minas*.

14. Blasenheim, "Regional History of the Zona da Mata."

15. Lenharo, *As tropas de moderação*.

16. Libby, *Transformação e trabalho*, 122, 347–48.

17. Mata-Machado, *Sertão noroeste*, 28.

18. See two accounts describing neighboring municipalities by Antonio da Silva Neves: "Chorographia do município de Boa Vista do Tremendal" and "Chorographia do município do Rio Pardo."

19. Franco, *Homens livres*.

20. Jacob, *Minas Gerais no XXo. século*, 5–26.

21. APM, SP 612, CMSR to PPMG, 16 Jan., 4 Feb. 1856.

22. APM, SP PP 1/18, cx. 302, p. 5, 2 Feb. 1832, and SP PP 1/18, cx. 138, 2 Dec. 1833.

23. APM, SP PP 1/33, cx. 288, p. 7, 27 May 1835, p. 8, 2 June 1835, and p. 9, 2 June 1835, and SP PP 1/33, cx. 289, p. 2, 9 Jan. 1838, and p. 6, 10 Mar. 1838.

24. APM, SG 533, del. of MC to PPMG, 17 July 1875.

25. Wells, *Exploring*, 1:364.

26. Manchester, *British Preeminence in Brazil;* Rippy, "British Investment in Brazil"; and Graham, *The Onset of Modernization*.

27. Eakin, *British Enterprise in Brazil;* Libby, *Trabalho escravo e capital estrangeiro*.

28. *Rel.* PPMG, *1835*, 6; *Rel.* PPMG, *1836*, 16; *Rel.* PPMG, *1837*, 20, 24, 43; *Rel.* PPMG, *1838*, 22–23.

29. Iglesias, *Política econômica*, 112.

30. Iglesias, *Política econômica*, passim.

31. The comarca consisted of the former julgados of São Romão and Januária, removed from the comarca of Paracatú, and of the julgado of Barra, formerly of the comarca of Serro Frio. This should not be confused with the comarca of Rio São Francisco created in 1720, which was a large territory to the north of the Rio Carinhanha, formerly part of Pernambuco.

32. LM 32, 14 Mar. 1836; LM 288, 12 Mar. 1846; LM 291, 26 Mar. 1846; LM 515, 10 Sept. 1851; LM 763, 2 May 1856; LM 974, 2 June 1859; LM 1200 and LM 1201, 9 Aug. 1864; LM 1663, 16 Sept. 1870; and LM 1717, 5 Oct. 1870. Each of these laws had multiple clauses dealing with boundary changes. See also Barbosa, *Dicionário histórico-geográfico*.

33. *Rel.* PPMG, *1837*, 20; Matos, *Corografia*, 1:41, 169–81; *Recenseamento de 1872*, 9:364–66, 373–75, 886–88.

34. The comarca was subdivided many times during the 1860s, 1870s, and 1880s. In 1861, the julgado of Barra do Rio das Velhas was elevated to municipal status and renamed Guaicuí. Guaicuí and Montes Claros were removed from the comarca of Rio São Francisco to form the comarca of Jequitaí in 1866. Grão Mogol was added on two years later. In 1870, Guaicuí was transferred to the comarca of Rio São Francisco and Januária to the comarca of Jequitaí. Later that year, the comarcas were again reorganized, Jequitaí to consist of Montes Claros and Januária and the Rio São Francisco to include São Romão and Guaicuí. In 1872, the termo of Januária became the comarca of Itapirassaba, its name changing to Januária in 1884. In 1876, the comarca of Rio São Francisco was redefined as the termo of Pedras dos Angicos (the former São Romão). Jequitaí incorporated Montes Claros and Jequitaí (the former Guaicuí). Itapirassaba remained unchanged, consisting of the termo of Januária. The comarca of Montes Claros was created in 1886. (LM 1112, 16 Oct. 1861; LM 1389, 14 Nov. 1866; LM 1507, 20 July 1868; LM 1679, 21 Sept. 1870; LM 1740, 8 Oct. 1870; LM 1868, 15 July 1872; LM 3194, 23 Sept. 1884; LM 2273, 8 July 1876; LM 3451, 1 Oct. 1886.)

35. Martins, "Revistando a província"; *Recenseamento de 1872*, 9:364–66, 373–75, 886–88.

36. Dean, "Latifundia and Land Policy."

37. Costa, *Brazilian Empire*, 78–93.

38. At the time, the parish of Montes Claros consisted of the districts of Montes Claros and Brejo das Almas, São Romão the districts of São Romão, São Sebastião das Lages, Brejo da Passagem, and Bomfim, and Nossa Senhora do Amparo the districts of Januária, Brejo do Salgado, Japoré, and Mucambo (APM, RP [registro paroquial (land register)] 106, 107, 128, 129, 130, 208, 209).

39. Matos (*Corografia*) indicates average households of three to six persons. Paiva and Martins ("Minas Gerais em 1831," 71) show two-to four-person households. Data on the free population were obtained from APM, SP 609, population map of Montes Claros, 1856.

40. For example, the *Rel.* PPMG, *1854*, 55, claims that Januária had a municipal population of 15,000 free and 1,500 slave, a total that exceeded its 1872 population. Figures from 1855 seem more consistent with other data, giving a total population of 9,659.

São Romão's population for 1855 was listed as 3,805, but its municipal population was 6,828 in 1838. (*Rel. PPMG, 1855*, 37.)

41. APM, SP PP 1/33, cx. 103, p. 16, 30 Sept. 1834.

42. Wells, *Exploring*, 2:4; see also 1:127.

43. APM, SP PP 1/18, cx. 138, 10 Nov. 1834, and SP PP 1/18, cx. 335, p. 31, 16 June 1826.

44. Wirth, *Minas Gerais in the Brazilian Federation*, 9.

45. APM, SP 657, Manoel Souza e Silva to PPMG, 1 Jan. 1857.

46. APM, SP 657, Teófilo de Sales Peixoto to PPMG, 6 Feb. 1857.

47. APM, SP 1055, CMSR to PPMG, 16 Apr. 1854.

48. Burton, *Explorations*, 2:268–69.

49. Social and economic linkages between the free poor, the enslaved, and the elite deserve further clarification but are beyond the scope of this work. For colonial Minas Gerais, see Souza, *Desclassificados de ouro*. Castro (*Ao sul da história*) provides a comparative case for rural Rio de Janeiro. For São Paulo, see Franco, *Homens livres*.

50. Minas Gerais was the home of nearly 40 percent of all Brazilian captives (Conrad, *World of Sorrow*, 22).

51. Libby, *Transformação e trabalho*, 54.

52. Libby, *Transformação e trabalho*, 47; Botelho, "Demografia," 2–3, and "Famílias e escravarias."

53. Freitas, "Slavery and Social Life."

54. Godoy, "Posse de escravos."

55. Spix and Martius, *Viagem*, 2:173–98; Pohl, *Viagem no interior do Brasil*, 319–25; Saint-Hilaire, *Viagem*, 307–61.

56. Term borrowed from Pratt, *Imperial Eyes*.

57. Spix and Martius, *Viagem*, 2:198.

58. Costa, *A cana-de-açúcar em Minas Gerais*, 192. An engenhoca was a technologically primitive sugar mill, a less capitalized and smaller-scale operation than an engenho.

59. APM, SP PP 1/6, cx. 4, p. 19, 24 July 1836, cx. 5, p. 18, n.d. (but ca. 1836), and cx. 5, p. 49, 19 Aug. 1836.

60. APM, SP 832, atas da CMJ, 2 Apr. 1860, CMJ to PPMG, 31 May 1860, exchequer (*fiscal*) to PPMG, 9 Oct. 1860, and Dr. Francisco Fogaça de Bittencourt to PPMG, 15 Oct. 1860.

61. APM, SP PP 1/6, cx. 8, p. 21, 26 June 1846, and SP 225, CMJ to PPMG, 27 Aug. 1839.

62. APM, SP PP 1/33, cx. 106, p. 53, Aug. 1841, SP 570, João Bernardo de Vasconcelos Coimbra to PPMG, 25 Jan. 1855, and SP 1007, CMJ to PPMG, 23 July 1863.

63. APM, SP 569, CMJ to PPMG, 27 Mar. 1854. Januária did not get funding for an agricultural school until 1885. An *alquiere* was the rough equivalent of an English bushel or eight gallons.

64. APM, SP PP 1/33, cx. 103, p. 13, 9 Aug. 1834, SP PP 1/33, cx. 105, p. 11, 1 Dec. 1837, and SP 657, Manoel de Souza e Silva to PPMG, 1 Jan. 1857. An *arroba* was the equivalent of fifteen kilograms.

65. APM, SP 657, Carlos Ashley to Manoel Souza e Silva, JM of Januária, 1 Jan. 1857, and SP 1055, José Antônio de Almeida Saraiva to PPMG, 22 Oct. 1854.

66. APM, SP 570, João Martins do Hugo to PPMG, Curvelo, 10 Jan. 1858, 570, João Bernardo de Vasconcelos Coimbra to PPMG, 25 Jan. 1855, SP PP 1/33, cx. 109, p. 43, 18 Aug. 1852, and SP 657, Manoel Souza e Silva to PPMG, 1 Jan. 1857; *Rel. PPMG, 1854*, 49.

67. Ottoni, "Da Diamantina a São Francisco," 671−81.

68. See, for example, Wells, *Exploring*, 1:358, 374, 390.

69. Wells, *Exploring*, 1:406−7.

70. APM, SP AL (Assembléia Legislativa) 1/8, cx. 2, p. 23, 22 Aug. 1877.

71. Iglesias, *Política econômica*, 112.

72. Gardner, *Travels*, 412.

73. See Paiva, "Engenhos e casas de négocios."

74. APM, SP 657, Teófilo de Sales Peixoto to PPMG, 6 Feb. 1857.

75. APM, SP PP 1/45, cx. 1, p. 17, n.d.

76. APM, SP 657, Teófilo de Sales Peixoto to PPMG, 6 Feb. 1857, and SP 570, Jan. 2, 1855.

77. APM, SP PP 1/6, cx. 1, p. 44, 2 Nov. 1834, and SP PP 1/6, cx. 7, p. 41, 27 Jan. 1845.

78. APM, SP PP 1/18, cx. 196, p. 2, 3 July 1831, and SP PP 1/33, cx. 289, p. 13, 23 Aug. 1838.

79. APM, SP 656, CMJ to PPMG, 13 Mar. 1857 and 27 Apr. 1857, and CMSR to PPMG, 24 Mar. 1857, and SP 1007, CMSR to PPMG, 28 Jan. 1868, JM of SR to PPMG, 21 Aug. 1863 and 2 Dec. 1863, and vicar of SR to PPMG, 22 Aug. 1863.

80. APM, SP PP 1/33, cx. 287, p. 41, 4 Dec. 1833, p. 46, 13 Jan. 1833, and p. 63, 15 July 1834. SP 223, CMSR to PPMG, May 6, 1839.

81. APM, SP PP 1/33, cx. 290, p. 15, 30 Dec. 1845.

82. Burton, *Explorations*, 2:189, 244.

83. Ottoni, "Da Diamantina a São Francisco."

84. APM, SG 531, CMSR to PPMG, 13 Jan. 1874 and 14 Apr. 1874.

85. Spix and Martius, *Viagem*, 2:177.

86. Saint-Hilaire, *Viagem*, 333.

87. Gardner, *Travels*, 428.

88. APM, SP PP 1/6, cx. 8, p. 25, 12 June 1846.

89. Pohl, *Viagem no interior do Brasil*, 325.

90. Saint-Hilaire, *Viagem*, 323.

91. Instituto Histórico e Geográfico Brasileiro (Rio de Janeiro), DL 178.2−4, 6−12, 14−15; *lata* 188, 64−67.

92. Saint-Hilaire, *Viagem*, 323; Gardner, *Travels*, 433; APM, SP PP 1/18, cx. 66, p. 2, 2 June 1846.

93. Spix and Martius, *Viagem*, 2:178−80; APM, SP 609, del. of MC to PPMG, 10 Jan. 1856, and SP 612, CMMC to PPMG, 23 Dec. 1856.

94. *Rel. PPMG, 1862*, 11.

95. Martins, *Almanack*, 358−75.

96. APM, SP 1157, CM of Guaicuí, 9 July 1866, and SP 1158, João Francisco da Mota to PPMG, 11 Aug. 1866.

97. APM, SP PP 1/18, cx. 232, p. 1, 31 Dec. 1863; and Araujo, "Relatório," 96−97.

98. *Rel. PPMG, 1854*, 49; APM, SP 657, Jeronimo Martins do Hugo to PPMG, Curvelo, 10 Jan. 1857, Brejo das Almas, 10 Aug. 1866, and Contendas, 12 Aug. 1866.

99. APM, SG 27, provincial treasury of Minas Gerais, 8 June 1879, contract dated 21 Jan. 1878, and balance, 12 Apr. 1881.

100. APM, SG 27, description of factory by Gregorio José Velloso, 10 July 1883.

101. Mata-Machado, *Sertão noroeste*, 74; Carneiro, *Pirapora a Joazeiro*, 11−13.

102. Velloso, "Chorographia mineira," 587.

103. Paula, *Montes Claros*, 1:290.

104. Velloso, "Chorographia mineira"; Vianna, *Monographia*, passim; *Serviço de inspecção e defesa agricola*, 255–58.

105. Mattoso, *Bahia século XIX*.

106. Araujo, "Relatório."

107. Carneiro, *Pirapora a Joazeiro*, 9–13; Mata-Machado, *Sertão noroeste*, 116–26.

108. Brasil, *História de Montes Claros*, 60.

2. Marginalization of the Municipality

1. Classic overviews of the empire include Haring, *Empire in Brasil;* Torres, *A democracia coroada;* Holanda, ed., *História geral da civilização brasileira;* and Costa, *Da monarquia à república.* See also Stein, "The Historiography of Brazil." More recent works on imperial politics include Barman, *Forging of a Nation;* Mattos, *Tempo saquarema;* and Graham, *Patronage and Politics.*

2. This literature emphasizes the ethnic, racial, and class makeup of participants (see Chasteen, "Cabanos and Farrapos"; Kraay, "As Terrifying as Unexpected"; Carvalho, "Hegemony and Rebellion"; and Reis, *Slave Rebellion in Brazil*).

3. Carvalho, *A construção da ordem*, "Elite and State Building," and "Political Elites and State Building"; Barman and Barman, "Prosopography."

4. This point has been persuasively argued by Costa (*Brazilian Empire*, 53–77).

5. The generation of Marxist scholars trained at the University of São Paulo in the 1960s asserts that independence had little revolutionary content and reflected a rupture between the mercantile colonial pact and an emerging capitalist ideology (see Costa, "Introdução ao estudo da emancipação política do Brasil"; and Novais, *Portugal e Brasil*).

6. Burns, *Poverty of Progress.*

7. Graham, *Patronage and Politics*, 108.

8. Garner, "In Pursuit of Order."

9. Historians disagree about the periodization of partisan differentiation. Costa (*Brazilian Empire*, 62) dates the emergence of loosely defined Liberal and Conservative parties by the 1820s, while Barman (*Forging of a Nation*, 224) more conservatively places their definitive origin at 1844.

10. Palmer, "Momentous Decade."

11. One of the earliest proponents of this thesis was Percy Alvin Martin (see his classic essay "Federalism in Brazil").

12. Flory, *Judge and Jury*, 158.

13. Two municipal studies that deal with the coffee elite are Stein, *Vassouras;* and Dean, *Rio Claro.*

14. Boxer, *Portuguese Society in the Tropics;* Raymundo Faoro, *Os donos do poder*, 144–248; Mourão, "Municípios."

15. The câmaras differed from the Spanish-American *cabildos* in their selection of aldermen. Purchase of offices never extended to the council level in Portuguese America, nor could positions on the council be passed down to one's heirs.

16. Zenha, *O município no Brasil;* Russell-Wood, "Local Government."

17. Schwartz, "Magistracy and Society," and *Sovereignty and Society.*

18. *Leis do império*, 1 Oct. 1828, 79–88.

19. Leal, *Coronelismo*, 74–75.

20. Mourão, "Municípios," 314.

21. See Garner, "In Pursuit of Order."

22. Flory, *Judge and Jury*, 143.

23. Palmer, "Momentous Decade," 210.

24. Leal, *Coronelismo*, 196.

25. LM 210, 7 Apr. 1841; LM 240, 30 Nov. 1842; LM 243, 2 July 1843; LM 266, 13 Apr. 1844; LM 277, 11 Apr. 1845; LM 299, 28 Mar. 1846; LM 336, 3 Apr. 1847; LM 417, 14 Oct. 1848; Res. 456, 20 Oct. 1849; Res. 504, 4 July 1850; Res 2447, 14 Nov. 1877; Res. 2896, 7 Nov. 1882; Res. 3126, 18 Oct. 1883; Res. 3286, 30 Oct. 1884; *Anais, 1876*, 212; *Anais, 1878*, 142; *Anais, 1879*, 167; *Anais, 1881*, 316; *Anais, 1883*, 232; *Anais, 1884*, 385.

26. For a brief study of the mineiro provincial government, see Martins, "Anotações sobre a organização administrativa."

27. Anderson, *Imagined Communities*.

28. LM 54, 9 Apr. 1836; LM 279, 11 Apr. 1845; LM 472, 31 May 1850; LM 654, 17 June 1853; LM 1814, 30 Sept. 1871; LM 3297, 27 Aug. 1885.

29. APM, SP PP 1/33, cx. 103, p. 9, 2 June 1834.

30. APM, MP03, n.d., and SP PP 1/10, cx. 15, p. 3, 1838.

31. Burton, *Explorations*, 2:257.

32. APM, SP PP 1/33, cx. 103, p. 9, 2 June 1834.

33. APM, SP PP 1/33, cx. 108, p. 15, 22 Mar. 1848.

34. APM, SP PP 1/9, cx. 6, p. 30, 28 Oct. 1850.

35. APM, SP PP 1/18, cx. 63, p. 18, 25 Jan. 1835, SP PP 1/18, cx. 306, 1 Aug. 1835, and SP PP 1/18, cx. 237, p. 13, 1 May 1836.

36. APM, SP PP 1/33, cx. 105, p. 8, 30 Sept. 1837.

37. APM, SP PP 1/33, cx. 105, p. 37, 24 Nov. 1838.

38. APM, SP PP 1/33, cx. 108, p. 7, 26, 27, 29 June 1847, 11 July 1846, and p. 15, 22 Mar. 1848.

39. APM, SP 482, CMJ to PPMG, 28 Jan. 1853.

40. *O correio oficial de Minas*, 2 July 1857, 1–4.

41. LM 1814, 30 Sept. 1871; LM 2705, 30 Nov. 1880; LM 3297, 27 Aug. 1885; LM 3358, 10 Oct. 1885.

42. APM, SP PP 1/33, cx. 107, p. 69, 10 Oct. 1845, 4 Apr. 1847, 13, 15, 17 (three documents), 18 Feb. 1849.

43. APM, SP 1115, secretary of the CMJ to PPMG, 10 Jan. 10, 1865, and acts of CMJ, 7 Jan. 1865.

44. APM, SP 221, CMJ to PPMG, 7 Feb. 1839.

45. APM, SP PP 1/33, cx. 109, p. 46, 26 Oct. 1852.

46. APM, SP PP 1/33, cx. 108, p. 7, 15 July 1846, p. 54, 23 Apr. 1850, and cx. 109, p. 41, 10 May 1852.

47. APM, SP PP 1/33, cx. 105, p. 40, 24, 31 Jan. 1839, and cx. 106, p. 29, 23 Nov. 1840, and p. 53, Aug. 1841.

48. APM, SP PP 1/33, cx. 106, p. 60, 6 Feb. 1842.

49. LM 703, 15 May 1855.

50. APM, SP PP 1/33, cx. 108, p. 11, 13 Oct. 1846, 17 Oct. 1847, 8 Apr. 1848.

51. APM, SP PP 1/33, cx. 108, p. 11, 13 Oct. 1846, and p. 13, 1 Dec. 1847.

52. APM, SP PP 1/33, CX. 109, p. 39, 5 May 1852.

53. During the 1850s, Montes Claros accrued in taxes 52:815$315, Januária 27:283$245, and São Romão 9:453$612 (*Rel. PPMG, 1862*, II; APM, SP 609, del. of MC to PPMG, 10 Jan. 1856, SP 609, population map, 7 Feb. 1856, and SP 612, Simeão Ribeiro da Silva to PPMG, 23 Dec. 1856.

54. APM, SP 945, CMJ and CMMC, n.d.

55. APM, SP PP 1/33, CX. 104, p. 46, CMJ to PPMG, 2 Jan. 1837.

56. This privilege was granted under LM Res. 790, 31 May 1856.

57. APM, SP 212, Domingos Pereira da Silva to PPMG, 12 Aug. 1839, SP 224, CMMC to PPMG, 12 July 1839, SP 244, José Ignacio do Couto Moreno to PPMG, 1 Aug. 1839, and SP 225, CMJ to PPMG, 27 Aug. 1839.

58. APM, SP PP 1/33, CX. 107, p. 11, 28 Aug. 1843.

59. APM, SP PP 1/33, CX. 105, p. 7, 30 Sept. 1837.

60. APM, SP PP 1/33, CX. 106, p. 7, series of letters dated 12 Mar. 1840, and p. 10, 13, 31 Mar., 13 Apr., 16 Apr. 1840.

61. APM, SP PP 1/33, CX. 106, p. 16, 21 June 1840, p. 26, 30 Sept. 1840, and p. 36, 4 Jan. 1841.

62. APM, SP PP 1/33, CX. 106, p. 36, 12 Dec. 1840, 9 Jan. 1841, p. 37, 27 Jan. 1841, p. 39, 28 Jan., 19 July 1841, and p. 59, 20 Nov. 1841.

63. APM, SP PP 1/33, CX. 106, p. 14, 4 Aug. 1840, p. 17, 27 Aug. 1840, and CX. 107, p. 84, 14 Oct. 1846.

64. APM, SP PP 1/33, CX. 108, p. 10, 11 Oct. 1847.

65. APM, SP PP 1/33, CX. 108, p. 49, 17 Jan. 1850.

66. APM, SP SeP 1/3, p. 63, 31 Aug. 1888, and p. 70, JD of São Francisco, 24 Sept. 1888.

67. Burns, *Poverty of Progress*.

68. The councilman and vicar Antonio Gonçalves Chaves reiterated these ideals in the provincial assembly in his appeals to expand school funding (*O compiliador*, 27 Feb. 1846, 3; 8 Mar. 1846, 4; 29 Mar. 1846, 2; and 16 Apr. 1846, 2).

69. APM, SP PP 1/33, CX. 143, p. 32, 1 Jan. 1834; the social pact was also invoked in SP PP 1/33, CX. 146, p. 4, 13 Jan. 1838.

70. APM, SP PP 1/18, CX. 138, p. 3, 8 Aug. 1831.

71. APM, SP PP 1/33, CX. 143, p. 71, 29 Mar. 1836.

72. APM, SP PP 1/33, CX. 147, p. 57, 20 Apr. 1843, p. 20, 3 Feb. 1845, and p. 29, 31 May 1845.

73. APM, SP PP 1/33, CX. 143, p. 68, 26 June 1834.

74. APM, SP PP 1/33, CX. 143, p. 23, 11 Sept. 1833; and Freitas, "Marginal Elites," 130–32.

75. The council of Montes Claros was not perfect, failing to submit annual reports from 1857 to 1862, but was markedly more forthcoming than competing municipalities.

76. APM, SP PP 1/33, CX. 144, p. 35, 25 Oct. 1835, p. 54, 26 Jan. 1836, p. 82, 11 Aug. 1836, CX. 146, p. 1, 2 Jan. 1838, CX. 146, p. 17, 16 Aug. 1838, p. 27, 15 Oct. 1838, and p. 35, 14 Jan. 1839.

77. APM, SP PP 1/33, CX. 146, p. 71, 7 May 1841, CX. 147, p. 9, 13 July 1841, CX. 148, p. 21, 7 Nov. 1843, CX. 149, p. 12, 14 Dec. 1844, CX. 150, p. 30, 20 Oct. 1847, and CX. 151, p. 55, 26 Oct. 1850.

78. APM, SP PP 1/33, CX. 146, p. 27, 15 Oct. 1838, p. 28, 20 Dec. 1838, p. 29, 20 Dec. 1838, p. 33, 14 Jan. 1840, p. 34, 14 Jan. 1840, and CX. 147, p. 14, 8 Jan. 1842, p. 60, 21 Apr. 1843;

LM 198, art. 25, 1841; Res. 212, art. 10, 7 Apr. 1841; Res. 241, art. 11, 11 July 1843; Res. 267, art. 12, 15 Apr. 1844; Res. 300, art. 19, 28 Mar. 1846.

79. Res. 341, 20 Sept. 1848.

80. Res. 1345, 5 Nov. 1866; LM 2422, 5 Nov. 1877; Res. 2504, 13 Nov. 1878; Res. 3225, 10 Oct. 1884.

81. *Anais, 1872*, 366–70.

82. Res. 3401, 22 July 1886; Paula, *Montes Claros*, 1:291.

83. Queiroz, *Mandonismo*, 69.

3. From Kinship to Party Politics

1. Analogous to the use of the term *pátria* as discussed by Barman (*Forging of a Nation*, 25).

2. APM, SP PP 1/11, cx. 146, ps. 8–12, 15–29, 31, 33–37 (justifications dated 1824).

3. APM, SP PP 1/11, cx. 146, p. 43, 4 Mar. 1828, and p. 58, 7 Feb. 1829.

4. APM, SP PP 1/11, cx. 146, p. 47, 11 Nov. 1828.

5. APM, SP PP 1/11, cx. 146, p. 31, 23 Feb. 1828.

6. Subsequent details about Montes Claros come from Paula, *Montes Claros*, 1:151–56, 162, 180.

7. APM, SP PP 1/15, cx. 13, p. 1, 19, 25, 26, 28 May 1831, and incomplete fragment, n.d., p. 2, 31 May, 24 Mar. 1831, p. 3, 3 Oct., 11, 25 Sept. 1831, and p. 4, 22 Oct. 1831.

8. APM, SP PP 1/11, cx. 147, p. 32, 20 Mar. 1833. Proença and Silva Gomes later became members of the Conservative party.

9. See Francisco Iglesias's introduction to Marinho, *História do movimento político*, 13–36.

10. APM, SP PP 1/7, cx. 1, p. 20, 24 Sept. 1832, p. 29, 3 Feb. 1833, and p. 43, 30 June 1833.

11. APM, SP PP 1/18, cx. 119, p. 27, 1 Nov. 1838.

12. APM, SP PP 1/18, cx. 196, p. 22, 28 Aug. 1833.

13. APM, SP PP 1/33, cx. 287, p. 65, 27 Oct. 1834, cx. 289, p. 37, 19 June 1841, and cx. 147, p. 10, 15 Oct. 1841.

14. APM, SP PP 1/33, cx. 106, p. 32, 27 Jan. 1841.

15. APM, SP PP 1/33, cx. 105, ps. 26–27, 26 May 1838; Vianna, *Monographia*, 346–47.

16. Paula, *Montes Claros*, 1:15–17; APM, SP PP 1/17, cx. 4, p. 10, 4 Oct. 1842, and p. 33, 17 Dec. 1842.

17. APM, SP PP 1/16, cx. 43, p. 48, 23 Jan. 1853.

18. Ramos, "Marriage and the Family," and "City and Country." Imperial household censuses reveal an average household size of five coresident individuals, with female-headed households attaining proportions of more than 40 percent of the total in some communities (see Martins, "Revisitando a província").

19. Unfortunately, this source is nearly useless for determining patterns of land tenure because the data are inconsistent and ambiguous. Only 10–20 percent of the entries recorded dimensions, and these measurements are dubious. A similar percentage recorded assessed value, and only about 5 percent recorded both.

20. Figures on the distribution of owners among estates were all derived from the following land registers: APM, RP 106–7, 128–30, 208–9.

21. The following kin relations have been reconstructed from land registers APM, RP 128–30.

22. APM, RP 208–9.

23. Paula, *Montes Claros*, 2:54–55, 200–214.

24. Paula, *Montes Claros*, 2:19, 110, 210–14.

25. Paula, *Montes Claros*, 2:37–38, 140–46.

26. APM, registro paroquial 106–7, and SP PP 1/10, cx. 15, p. 8, census from Brejo, 1838.

27. APM, SP PP 1/11, cx. 147, p. 33, 23 Mar. 1833, and p. 34, 23 Mar. 1833.

28. Here, I cross-registered data from the land registers APM, RP 208 and 209, with sources on local office cited in n. 31 below.

29. Paula, *Montes Claros*, 2:16–18, 37–38.

30. Horta, "Famílias governamentáis," 80–81.

31. I located returns for 27 elections for municipal councils, 101 for justices of the peace, 57 for members of electoral colleges, and 48 for special electoral colleges convened to vote for senators. Most of these elections date from the 1840s to the 1870s. (APM, SP PP 1/11, cxs. 12–13, 21–27, 37, 47, 64, 66, 72–73, 75–76, SP PP 1/33, cxs. 103, 106, 109, 148–51, 287, SP 603, 663, 665, 712, 909, and SG 116–19, 121–23, 125, 127–28, 130, 132, 134–35, 137, 139–40, 400, 408, 414, 781.)

32. Stein and Stein, *Colonial Heritage*, 171; Costa, *Brazilian Empire*, 60.

33. Graham, *Patronage and Politics*, 108.

34. *Constituição política do Império do Brasil*, chap. 6, arts. 90–97.

35. Voter registration lists, National Guard registries, and juror lists provide a partial demographic reconstruction of the São Francisco electorate. For a more extensive discussion of these sources and the methodology used, see Freitas, "Marginal Elites," 195–210.

36. According to several articles in the official newspaper, *O compiliador*, the huge leaps in numbers of voters from 1842 to 1844 were due to electoral fraud (see the issues for 5, 12, and 14 Mar. 1845). The equation of male heads of household to the adult male population is approximate only. Male adults residing with their parents would be excluded from the general sample. Sons residing with their fathers were also ineligible to vote.

37. We have no complete sources documenting the pace of inflation in nineteenth-century Minas, and inflation probably varied across regions. Scattered references dating from the 1830s to the 1870s report local interest rates of 2.5–3 percent per month. If loans were tagged to inflation, these rates would represent inflation's outer limit.

38. *Recenseamento de* 1872, 9:364–66, 373–75, 886–88.

39. *Rel. PPMG, 1881*, 10. In 1872, São Francisco had an adult free male population nearly double that of São Romão (1,449 and 763, respectively), but, unfortunately, pre-1881 voter registration data from São Francisco have not been found.

40. APM, SP PP 1/11, cx. 16, p. 16, 23 Jan. 1847, p. 18, 23 Jan. 1847, p. 22, 24 Jan. 1847, cx. 17, p. 15, 31 Jan. 1847, and cx. 18, p. 8, 4 Feb. 1847, p. 12, 6 Feb. 1847.

41. APM, SP PP 1/11, cx. 17, p. 15, 31 Jan. 1847.

42. APM, SP PP 1/11, cx. 33, p. 19, 24 Jan. 1850, p. 20, 24 Jan. 1850, cx. 34, p. 20, 3 Feb. 1850, p. 22, 3 Feb. 1850, p. 24, 4 Feb. 1850, cx. 35, p. 24, 26 Feb. 1850, cx. 36, p. 1, 28 Feb. 1850, cx. 37, p. 23, 10 July 1850, cx. 40, p. 8, 19 Jan. 1851, p. 21, 24 Jan. 1851, cx. 41, p. 3, 26 Jan. 1851, p. 9, 29 Jan. 1851, p. 16, 30 Jan. 1851, p. 18, 31 Jan. 1851, and cx. 43, p. 21, 1 Mar. 1851, p. 34,

9 Mar. 1851; AN, cx. 538, pacote 2, doc. 12, 3 Apr. 1865, and cx. 549, pacote 2, doc. 18, 5 Nov. 1870; Arquivo da Prefeitura de Montes Claros, voter qualification lists for Montes Claros parish, 1848, 1862, 1876, uncataloged.

43. APM, SP 609, population map, 1856; and *Rel. PPMG, 1855*, 60.

44. *Relatório do ministerio do Império, 1871*, 8; and *Relatório do ministerio do Império, 1874*, 16 (*parte estatística*).

45. Pinto, ed., *Reforma eleitoral*, 19–26.

46. APM, SP PP I/II, cx. 77, p. 29, 21 Nov. 1834.

47. APM, SP PP I/II, cx. 77, p. 7, 17 Nov. 1834.

48. APM, SP PP I/II, cx. 79, p. 1, 15 Oct. 1838.

49. APM, SP PP I/II, cx. 79, p. 1, 15 Oct. 1838, p. 2, 15 Oct. 1838, p. 14, 17 Nov. 1840, p. 16, 17 Nov. 1840, p. 28, 24 Nov. 1840, cx. 80, p. 11, 28 Nov. 1842, p. 30, 28 Nov. 1842, p. 36, 29 Nov. 1842, cx. 81, p. 5, 14 Oct. 1844, p. 34, 4 Oct. 1846, and cx. 82, p. 26, 9 Dec. 1847, p. 43, 11 Dec. 1847.

50. APM, SP PP I/II, cx. 83, p. 25, 7 July 1849, and SP PP I/9, cx. 14, p. 63, 12 Aug. 1849, p. 64, 4 Sept. 1849; Vianna, *Monographia*, 73–74.

51. APM, SP PP I/II, cx. 84, p. 27, 7 Dec. 1851, p. 43, 8 Dec. 1851, p. 51, 8 Dec. 1851, and cx. 85, p. 7, 9 Dec. 1851, p. 15, 10 Dec. 1851.

52. APM, SP PP I/II, cx. 86, p. 22, 5 Nov. 1855, and SG 117, election for CM and JP, Januária, 1853.

53. APM, SP Assembléia Legislativa I/4, cx. 10, election returns for provincial assembly, 6 Nov. 1855.

54. I derived the following conclusions about the relative importance of party identity and occupation of candidates from the election returns from eight elections for national deputies, eighteen for provincial deputies, and five for senators. In most cases, returns for two or all three municipalities were preserved. This sample yielded a total of 1,368 elected candidates. Because of the small number of returns after 1876, these figures were excluded from the occupational analysis of 1,050 candidates. My sources were APM, SP PP I/II, cxs. 77, 79–87, 89, 93, 98, 100–101, 103–11, 156, SP AL I/4, cx. 10, and SP 664–65, 765–66, 835, 891, 1001, 1003, 1058.

55. Many of these undefined individuals used the title *doutor*, which most likely meant that they were lawyers. Whether that implied professional training is difficult to say. The honorific could also be applied to physicians and teachers. Rather than make false assumptions about the occupations of these "doutores," I have placed them in the category *no information*.

56. Election "irregularities" were reported in the districts of Bomfim, Extrema, and Morrinhos in APM, SP PP I/II, cx. 143, p. 28, 27 Oct. 1833, p. 55, 24 May 1834, and cx. 145, p. 80, 17 Oct. 1837. For Januária, see APM, SP PP I/II cx. 72, p. 12, 24 Sept. 1836.

57. APM, SP PP I/18, cx. 302, p. 8, 30 Mar. 1833.

58. APM, SP PP I/II, cx. 148, p. 42, 26 Feb. 1844.

59. APM, SP PP I/18, cx. 119, p. 19, 1 Mar. 1838.

60. APM, SP 204, JMOC to PPMG, 10 July 1839, and SP 206, JMOC to PPMG, 6 Sept. 1839, CMMC to PPMG, 22 July 1839, and JMOC to PPMG, 22 July 1839; Paula, *Montes Claros*, 1:163.

4. Centralized Bureaucracies

1. APM, SP PP I/9, cx. 14, p. 63, 12 Aug. 1849, and p. 64, 4 Sept. 1849. See also Vianna, *Monographia*, 73–74.

2. A local history of the region claims that he resigned because the juiz de direito informed him that his ecclesiastical duties were legally incompatible with political office (Vianna, *Efemérides montesclarenses*, 218).

3. Flory, *Judge and Jury*.

4. Rezende, "Policia administrativa," 410.

5. Galvão, "Poder judiciária no império"; and Mello, "O poder judiciário no Brasil."

6. Leal, "O ato adicional."

7. See Holloway, "The Brazilian 'Judicial Police,'" and *Policing Rio de Janeiro;* and Barman, *Forging of a Nation*.

8. Holloway, "The Brazilian 'Judicial Police,'" 737.

9. See tables 6–8 in chap. 5.

10. Castro, "Milícias nacionais."

11. *Lei do Império 602*, 19 Sept. 1850.

12. Carvalho, "Elite and State Building," 376; Faria, "Guarda nacional."

13. *Lei do Império 602*, 19 Sept. 1850.

14. *Lei do Império, 2395*, 10 Sept. 1873.

15. Iglesias, *Política econômica*, 41.

16. Souza, *Reforma eleitoral*, 5.

17. Garner, "In Pursuit of Order," 283–352.

18. Pinto, ed., *Reforma eleitoral;* Souza, *Sistema eleitoral*.

19. Pinto, ed., *Reforma eleitoral*, 43–44.

20. See Pinto, ed., *Reforma eleitoral*, 19–61.

21. Pinto, ed., *Reforma eleitoral*, 148.

22. *Lei do Império, 387*, 19 Aug. 1846.

23. Almeida, *Estudo e comentários*, 1–93.

24. Pinto, ed., *Reforma eleitoral*, 173–79.

25. Pinto, ed., *Reforma eleitoral*, 181–223.

26. Pinto, ed., *Reforma eleitoral*, 200–201.

27. Pinto, ed., *Reforma eleitoral*, 242–71.

28. Pinto, ed., *Reforma eleitoral*, 312–27.

29. *Relatório do ministro do Império, 1877*, 15.

30. Graham, *Patronage and Politics*, 180–206.

31. *Relatório do ministro do Império, 1881*, 12.

5. Criminality and Impunity

1. APM, SP 204, JMOC to PPMG, 10 July 1839.

2. APM, SP 211, interim JM, João Pereira da Costa, to PPMG, 3 Apr. 1839. See also APM, SP 210, juiz de orfãos of Januária to PPMG, 27 Apr. 1839, SP 215, JP of Januária to PPMG, 10 Apr. 1839, JP of SR to PPMG, 3 Apr. 1839, SP 222, CMJ to PPMG, 10 Apr. 1839, CMMC to PPMG, 30 Mar. 1839, CMSR to PPMG, 4 Apr. 1839, and SP 242, National Guard of MC to PPMG, 30 Mar. 1839.

3. APM, SP 242, petition of the parishioners of Contendas, 22 Apr. 1839.

4. APM, SG 396, *matrícula de juizes municipais, juizes de direito, promotores públicos e chefes de polícia, 1853–66*, and SP 925, JMOC to PPMG, 13 Mar. 1862.

5. APM, SP PP 1/18, cx. 66, p. 2, 2 June 1846.

6. APM, SP PP 1/18, cx. 66, p. 16, 20 Feb. 1850.

7. APM, SP 608, Joaquim Manoel de Carvalho to PPMG, 25 Aug. 1856.

8. Instituto Histórico e Geográfico Brasileiro (Rio de Janeiro), DL 178.2–4, 6–12, 14–15; *lata* 188, 64–67.

9. Schwartz, *Sovereignty and Society*.

10. As for evidence of literacy, numerous signatures were barely legible, and some signed with a notarized *x*.

11. *Rel. PPMG, 1844*, 17.

12. APM, SG 395, *matrícula de juizes de direito e promotores públicos, 1843–50*, SG 392, 67, 67v, 69, 69v, 71, 17v, SG 395, SG 396, SG 397, SG 401, SG 404, SG 405, SG 406, SG 409.

13. APM, SP PP 1/33, cx. 287, p. 37, 22 Aug. 1833, cx. 287, p. 61, 15 July 1834, cx. 288, p. 31, 14 July 1836, p. 46, 20 Mar. 1837, p. 49, 20 Mar. 1837, cx. 289, p. 15, 22 Aug. 1838, p. 40, 3 Nov. 1841, SP 223, 6 May 1839, and SP 225, 26 Aug. 1839, 6 Sept. 1839.

14. APM, SP PP 1/33, cx. 103, p. 36, 25 Aug. 1835, cx. 104, p. 42, 17 Dec. 1836, cx. 105, p. 10, 29 Nov. 1837, p. 37, 19 Sept. 1838, p. 39, 15 Dec. 1838, cx. 106, p. 33, 14 Jan. 1841, p. 55, 20 Oct. 1841, cx. 106, p. 31, 9 Jan. 1841, and SP 225, 26 Sept. 1839.

15. APM, SP PP 1/33, cx. 143, p. 18, 25 June 1833, cx. 145, p. 18, 22 Oct. 1836, cx. 146, p. 5, 15 Jan. 1838, cx. 144, p. 63, 2 May 1836, p. 73, 20 July 1836, cx. 146, p. 17, 16 Aug. 1838, p. 63, 16 Feb. 1841, p. 68, 27 Apr. 1841, and cx. 147, p. 24, 30 Apr. 1842.

16. Paula, *Montes Claros*, 1:163–65, 180, 182.

17. APM, SG 392, *matrícula dos juizes municipais e orfãos da provincia, 1842–57*, SG 398, *juizes municipais substitutos, 1857–69*. SG 443, first substitute JM to PPMG, 24 Feb. 1874.

18. Brandão, Mattos, and Carvalho, *Polícia*, 90.

19. APM, SP PP 1/33, cx. 145, p. 60, 12 July 1837, and p. 69, 7 Sept. 1837.

20. APM, SP 205, JD to PPMG, 29 Aug. 1839, SP 223, JD to PPMG, 25 Apr. 1839.

21. APM, SP PP 1/33, cx. 287, p. 37, 22 Aug. 1833, SP PP 1/33, cx. 288, p. 41, 3 Jan. 1837, p. 44, 4 Jan. 1837, and cx. 289, p. 18, 8 Mar. 1840.

22. APM, SG 510, SG 511, SG 512, SG 513, SG 520, SG 524, *matriculas* of the police.

23. APM, SP PP 1/18, cx. 196, p. 21, 7 June 1833, SP PP 1/33, cx. 287, p. 28, 29 May 1833, cx. 287, p. 32, 4 June 1833, p. 33, 4 June 1833, cx. 287, p. 43, 7 Dec. 1833, cx. 287, p. 58, 24 Apr. 1834, and cx. 289, p. 33, 1 Dec. 1840.

24. APM, SP PP 1/33, cx. 103, p. 15, 25 Aug. 1834, cx. 106, p. 30, 1840, p. 73, 23 Oct. 1842, cx. 107, p. 7, 6 July 1843, SP PP 1/18, cx. 119, p. 59, 18 Aug. 1845, SP 244, José Ignacio do Couto Moreno to PPMG, 1 Aug. 1839, and SP 246, José Ignacio do Couto Moreno to PPMG, 2 Dec. 1839.

25. APM, SP PP 1/33, cx. 145, p. 79, 10 Oct. 1837, cx. 147, p. 43, 13 Oct. 1842, cx. 148, p. 34, 13 Jan. 1844, SP PP 1/18, cx. 140, p. 65, 10 July 1844, and SP PP 1/17, cx. 4, p. 10, 4 Oct. 1842, p. 33, 17 Dec. 1842.

26. Faria, "Guarda nacional," 44, 49–52.

27. Faria, "Guarda nacional," 66–67.

28. Uricoechea (*Patrimonial Foundations*) has claimed that the National Guard retained a democratic flavor until the reform of 1850. Castro ("Milícias nacionais") disagrees, emphasizing the hierarchical nature of the guard.

29. Faria, "Guarda nacional," 1–10, 12–13. Faria characterizes the guard as a paramilitary force that ended up protecting local interests. Uricoechea (*Patrimonial Foundations*), in contrast, argues that the guard met the needs of the centralized state

by serving as a cheap alternative to a salaried bureaucracy to supervise rural clans that dominated municipal government. Brandão, Mattos, and Carvalho (*Polícia*) also emphasize state needs served by the guard.

30. Bastos, *Província*, passim. Bastos was a prolific publicist who inveighed against the shortcomings of centralized government and favored a return to decentralized institutions.

31. APM, SP PP 1/15, cx. 86, p. 9, 15 Mar. 1841.

32. APM, SP 1045, del. of SR to PPMG 8 May 1864.

33. APM, SP PP 1/24, cx. 147, p. 10, 20 July 1843, SP PP 1/18, cx. 237, p. 50, 23 Dec. 1843, cx. 322, 5 July 1847, SP 937, del. of Januária to PPMG, 29 Nov. 1862, SP 1252, Ricardo Rodrigues Horta to del. of SR, 8 Sept. 1868, and SG 437, substitute JM of SR to provincial police chief, July 4, 1871.

34. APM, SP PP 1/18, cx. 63, p. 23, 9 Mar. 1835, and SP PP 1/24, cx. 126, p. 19, 8 July 1847.

35. APM, SP 986, del. of SR to provincial police chief, 20 Dec. 1862, and del. of SR to Mesa das Rendas, 9 Feb. 1863.

36. *Rel. PPMG, 1835*, 10; LM 8, 28 Mar. 1835; APM, SP PP 3/1, cx. 1, p. 8, 17 Feb. 1836.

37. See APM, SP PP 1/24, cx. 100, p. 7, 29 Nov. 1842, SP 933, del. of Januária to PPMG, 12 Apr. 1862, SP 1046, Antonio Gonçalves Chaves to PPMG, 22 July 1864, SP 1094, report of provincial police secretary, 1865, SP 1304, report of provincial police secretary, 29 Apr. 1869, SG 439, del. of Guaicuí to PPMG, 2 Feb. 1872, provincial police chief to PPMG, 23 Mar. 1872, and SG 441, del. of SR to PPMG, 19 Feb. 1873, third subdelegado (police subdelegate) of Pedras dos Angicos to PPMG, 22 Apr. 1873, provincial police chief to PPMG, 29 Sept. 1873, del. of SR to provincial police chief, 28 July 1873.

38. On Januária: APM, SP PP 1/18, cx. 63, p. 53, 20 Oct. 1835, SP 710, del. of Januária to PPMG, 6 Dec. 1858, 11 Dec. 1858, SP 937, João Elisberio de Souza to provincial police chief, 29 Nov. 1862, SP 987, Bertoldo José Pimenta to PPMG, 9 May 1863, and SG 436, provincial police chief to PPMG, 18 Feb. 1871. On Montes Claros: SP PP 1/18, cx. 322, p. 23, PP of MC to PPMG, 27 May 1846, SP 1306, provincial police secretary to PPMG, 20 July 1869, and SG 439, provincial police chief to PPMG, 19 Jan. 1872.

39. APM, SP PP 1/33, cx. 106, p. 33, 14 Jan. 1841.

40. APM, SP PP 1/33, cx. 143, p. 71, 25 June 1836, 29 Mar. 1836.

41. APM, SP PP 1/18, cx. 63, p. 10, 10 Jan. 1835.

42. APM, SP PP 1/9, cx. 20, p. 49, 10 Nov. 1831.

43. APM, SP PP 1/18, cx. 196, p. 1, 6 Nov. 1830.

44. APM, SP PP 1/33, cx. 144, p. 31, 10 Oct. 1835, p. 47, 2 Jan. 1836, p. 48, 2 Jan. 1836, p. 49, 2 Jan. 1836, p. 51, 4 Jan. 1836, and p. 55, 28 Jan. 1836.

45. APM, SP 214, Felipe José de Santana to PPMG, 1 Feb. 1839.

46. APM, SP PP 1/33, cx. 106, p. 33, 14 Jan. 1841.

47. APM, SP PP 1/33, cx. 144, p. 28, 25 July 1835.

48. *O conciliador*, 24 Nov. 1866, 1–2.

49. APM, SP PP 1/18, cx. 66, p. 2, 2 June 1846.

50. APM, SP PP 1/45, cx. 1, p. 25, 27 Mar. 1852.

51. APM, SP PP 1/33, cx. 109, p. 14, 10 Jan. 1851.

52. APM, SP PP 1/18, cx. 63, p. 37, 2 June 1835, and cx. 63, p. 26, 11 Mar. 1835.

53. APM, SP PP 1/33, cx. 143, p. 54, 14 May 1834.

54. Duarte's scientific curiosity and enlightened learning earned praise from Saint-Hilaire (*Viagem*, 332) and Spix and Martius (*Viagem*, 182).

55. APM, SP PP 1/33, cx. 145, p. 16, 21 Oct. 1836, cx. 146, p. 36, 15 Jan. 1839, p. 53, 13 Nov. 1840, and cx. 147, p. 54, 16 Feb. 1843.

56. APM, SP PP 1/33, cx. 143, p. 68, 26 June 1834.

57. APM, SP PP 1/18, cx. 63, p. 3, 1, 31 Aug. 1834.

58. APM, SP PP 1/18, cx. 63, p. 4, 8 May 1836, cx. 65, 5 Dec. 1836, and cx. 138, p. 60, 6 Aug. 1835.

59. APM, SP PP 1/18, cx. 64, p. 61, 20 May 1837.

60. APM, SP PP 1/9, cx. 20, p. 48, 13 Nov. 1829, SP PP 1/18, cx. 63, p. 16, 24 Jan. 1835, p. 33, 7 May 1835, p. 49, June 1835.

61. APM, SP PP 1/9, cx. 20, p. 47, 21 Apr. 1824.

62. APM, SP 214, Felipe José de Santana to PPMG, 1 Feb. 1839.

63. APM, SP PP 1/24, cx. 147, p. 10, 20 July 1843, SP PP 1/18, cx. 237, p. 37, Pedro Antonio Correia Bittancourt to PPMG, 24 Apr. 1843, p. 38, 2 Mar. 1843, p. 40, 19 July 1843, p. 50, 23 Dec. 1843, SP PP 1/23, cx. 1, p. 1, 4 Apr. 1843, and SP PP 1/33, cx. 63, p. 18, 30 Apr. 1848.

64. APM, SP 933, del. of Januária to PPMG, 12 Apr. 1862, SP 828, JMOC to PPMG, 28 Feb. 1860, Vicar Francisco Xavier da Silva to JMOC, 20 Feb. 1860, and SP 1046, Antonio Gonçalves Chaves Jr. to vice provincial president of Minas Gerais, 12 June 1864.

65. APM, SP PP 1/15, cx. 86, p. 6, 13 Feb. 1838, p. 9, 15 Mar. 1841, p. 13, 28 Dec. 1841, p. 14, 11 Mar. 1844, p. 15, 14 Apr. 1844, and SP 1187, José da Silva Moura to PPMG, 13 May 1867.

66. APM, SP PP 1/15, cx. 86, p. 15, 14 Apr. 1844.

67. APM, SP PP 1/15, cx. 23, p. 1, 2 Oct. 1831.

68. APM, SP PP 1/18, cx. 196, p. 6, 26 Jan., 3 Feb. 1832, and cx. 62, p. 20, 20 Aug. 1836, 26 May 1835, 22 Aug. 1836.

69. APM, SP PP 1/18, cx. 62, p. 20, 13 June 1832.

70. APM, SP 480, JMOC to PPMG, 1 Mar. 1853, SP 482, soldier of the third company to PPMG, 11 Nov. 1853, SP 505, JMOC to PPMG 18 Jan. 1854, and SP 511, 30 Nov., 6, 8, 9, 10 Dec. 1854 (a series of letters written to the provincial police chief about Cesar).

71. APM, SP 877, 6 Apr. 1861, del. of SR to provincial police chief, and SP 1307, provincial police secretary to PPMG, 28 Sept. 1869.

72. APM, SP 877, del. of Januária to provincial police chief, 16 Apr. 1861, and SP 878, del. of Januária to provincial police chief, 15 May 1861. *Tres Bundas* is a nickname meaning "three backsides," his, his wife's, and his lover's.

73. *O bom senso*, 30 Apr. 1855, special supplement; 5 July 1855, 4; 9 July 1855, 4; 3 Dec. 1855, 4; 18 Feb. 1856; 28 Feb. 1856, 4; 14 July 1856, 4.

74. APM, SP 877, PP to CMSR, 28 Jan. 1861.

75. APM, SP 932, subdelegado of Morrinhos to PPMG, 26, 27 Feb. 1862, JD of Paracatú to PPMG, 6 Mar. 1862, del. of Paracatú to PPMG, 7 Mar. 1862, José Augusto Palentino to PPMG, 7 Mar. 1862, Francisco de Paula Carneiro Franco to PPMG, 7 Mar. 1862, del. of SR to PPMG, 31 Mar. 1862, Joaquim Pedro de Melo to PPMG, 8 Mar. 1862, SP 933, subdelegado of Morrinhos to del. of Paracatú, 27 Feb. 1862, Francisco de Paula Carneiro Franco to PPMG, n.d., Ludgero Goncalves da Silva to PPMG, 1 Apr. 1862, Luiz Martins Canabrava to PPMG, 2 Mar. 1862, Pedro Antonio Roquete Franco to PPMG, 7 Mar. 1862, Pedro Gonçalves de Abreu to João Antonio Rodrigues, 17 Mar. 1862, Joaquim José de Almeida to João Antonio Rodrigues, 17 Mar. 1862, Antonio Martins Al-

varo to del. of SR, 18 Mar. 1862, Pedro Gonçalves de Abreu to del. of SR, 26 Mar. 1862, Pedro Gonçalves de Abreu to del. of SR, 29 Mar. 1862, provincial police secretary to provincial police chief, 12 Apr. 1862, chief of police to PPMG, 12 Apr. 1862, Ricardo Rodrigues Horta to PPMG, 17 Apr. 1862, Pedro Gonçalves de Abreu to PPMG, 30 Apr. 1862, SP 934, provincial police secretary to PPMG, 5 May 1862, SP 935, Joaquim José de Almeida to Joaquim Pedro Vellaça, 22, 27 June 1862, report of the provincial police secretary, July 1862, Joaquim Pedro Vellaça to PPMG, 14 July 1862, Antonio Martins de Amorim Rangel to PPMG, 26 July 1862, 1 Aug. 1862, Joaquim José de Almeida to JD of Paracatú, 17 Aug. 1862, and SP 936, Commander Rangel to vice provincial president of Minas Gerais, 27 Sept. 1862.

6. Escalation of Criminality

1. Franco, *Homens livres*, passim.
2. Souza, *Desclassificados do ouro*.
3. Aufderheide, "Order and Violence."
4. Huggins, *From Slavery to Vagrancy*.
5. *Rel. PPMG, 1850*; *Rel. PPMG, 1851*; *Rel. PPMG, 1852*; *Rel. PPMG, 1853*; APM, SP 566, report of the provincial police chief, Mar. 1855.
6. APM, SP 762, Luiz Gomes Ribeiro to PPMG, 1 June 1859.
7. APM, SP 932, Francisco José Pereira Correia to PPMG, 18 Mar. 1862.
8. APM, SG 529, del. of MC to PPMG, 20 Mar. 1873.
9. APM, SP 937, Joaquim Ferreira Carneiro to vice provincial president of Minas Gerais, 4 Dec. 1862.
10. APM, SP PP 1/18, cx. 1, p. 35, 9 July 1879.
11. APM, SP 707, del. of Januária, February 1858, and SP 761, del. of Januária, 28 Dec. 1859.
12. APM, SP 511, del. of SR to PPMG, 28 Apr. 1854.
13. APM, SP PP 1/18, cx. 63, p. 23, 9 Mar. 1835, and cx. 64, p. 49, 3 Feb. 1837.
14. APM, SP PP 1/18, cx. 63, p. 4, 8 May 1836.
15. APM, SP PP 1/18, cx. 138, p. 1, 15 Mar. 1830.
16. APM, SP SeP 1/3, p. 64, 31 Aug. 1888.
17. APM, SP SeP 1/5, cx. 2, p. 5, 6 Aug. 1876.
18. APM, SP 877, del. of SR to police secretary, 18 Jan. 1861, SG 437, memos from the provincial police chief to PPMG, 8 May, 7 July 1871, and SG 438, memos from the provincial police chief to PPMG, 12 Sept., 9 Nov. 1871.
19. *Anais, 1876*, 94, 116–20, 200–210; *Anais, 1879*, 569.
20. McBeth, "The Brazilian Recruit"; and Beattie, "Transforming Enlisted Army Service."
21. Brandão, Mattos, and Carvalho (*Polícia*, passim) highlight the role of the guard in disciplining the dishonorable poor by recruiting them into the military. Aufderheide ("Order and Violence," 139–43) concurs, suggesting that recruitment into the police force acted as a sort of dole that kept marginals off the street. Chaloub (*Visões de liberdade*) has also emphasized the humble social origins of the police and petty bureaucracy in Rio de Janeiro.
22. APM, SP PP 1/15, cx. 23, p. 4, 3 Mar. 1836.
23. Beattie, "Transforming Enlisted Army Service," 72, 132–34.

24. *Leis do império*, decisão 560, 3 Nov. 1837.

25. APM, SP PP 1/15, cx. 86, p. 2 Feb. 17, 1836; p. 3, Apr. 25, 1836.

26. APM, SP PP 1/15, cx. 23, p. 9, 29 Dec. 1835, p. 10, 15 June 1836, p. 13, 3 July 1836, p. 21, 26 Mar. 1841, and SP 756, JD to PPMG, 3 Sept. 1859.

27. APM, SP PP 1/24, cx. 126, p. 1, 20 Nov. 1842, p. 5, 20 Feb., 7 Mar. 1843, p. 6, 10 May 1843, p. 13, 1 Feb. 1845, p. 15, 20 Sept. 1845, and p. 16, 16 Oct. 1845.

28. Paula, *Montes Claros*, 1:18; APM, SP PP 1/18, cx. 65, p. 2, 12 Feb. 1838, and SP 219, JP of Contendas to PPMG, 13 Sept. 1839.

29. APM, SP PP 1/18, cx. 64, p. 15, 12 Apr. 1836.

30. APM, SP PP 1/18, cx. 64, p. 62, 2 Sept. 1837.

31. APM, SP 481, JM of Januária to PPMG, 12 Oct. 1853.

32. APM, SP 199, JD to PPMG, 26 Feb. 1839, SP 200, JD to PPMG, 14 Mar. 1839, SP 203, JD to PPMG, 5 June 1839, and SP PP 1/15, cx. 23, p. 23, 6 June 1841, p. 24, 8 June 1841, p. 25, 25 Sept. 1841, p. 26, 5 Oct. 1842, p. 30, 28 May 1846, p. 31, 2 Sept. 1846.

33. Souza, "The Politics of Violence"; Hobsbawm, *Primitive Rebels*, and *Bandits*. Queiroz (*Os cangaceiros*) examines contrasting images of the cangaceiro, from the mythical to the Marxist.

34. APM, SP PP 1/24, cx. 156, p. 60, 6 Mar. 1845, and SP PP 1/18, cx. 1, p. 34, 28 July 1878.

35. APM, SP PP 1/11, cx. 161, p. 1, 19 Apr. 1849, p. 2, 19 Apr. 1849, p. 3, 19 Apr. 1849. The districts were Coração de Jesus, Bomfim, and Brejo das Almas.

36. APM, SP PP 1/11, cx. 150, p. 60, 7 July 1848.

37. AN, cx. 510, pacote 4, p. 84, letter from Candido José Pimenta, F. P. P. Proença, and Joaquim Lopes Pereira da Rocha to the Conselho do Estado, 10 Oct. 1848.

38. AN, AP07, cx. 8, pacote 1, no. 1, copy of letter from Francisco Proença to PPMG, 18 Feb. 1849.

39. AN, AP07, cx. 8, pacote 1, no. 1, copy of letter from Ignacio José do Couto Moreno to PPMG, 26 Jan. 1849.

40. APM, SP PP 1/11, cx. 38, p. 29, 12 Jan. 1851, and cx. 40, p. 26, 12 Jan. 1851.

41. APM, SP PP 1/18, cx. 66, p. 35, 5 Apr. 1851, p. 36, 24 May 1851.

42. APM, SP 1093, José Rodrigues Prates to PPMG, 30 Jan. 1865.

43. Freitas, "Marginal Elites," 226–30. Election proceedings for senator, CJ, Contendas, MC, Itacambira, Januária, Morrinhos, SR, 1851 (APM, SG 116); senator, MC, Bomfim, Contendas, CJ, Januária, Morrinhos, SR, 1856 (APM, SG 116); JP and CM, SR, Porto do Salgado, Morrinhos, MC, 1856 (APM, SG 117); CM and JP, MC, SR, Januária, 1856 (APM, SG 118); chamber of deputies, Januária, Morrinhos, SR, MC, Bomfim, Contendas, CJ, and Bom Sucesso, 1856 (APM, SG 118); senator, Januária, Morrinhos, SR, MC, Bomfim, Contendas, CJ, Bom Sucesso, 1860 (APM, SG 118); chamber of deputies, Guaicuí, Januária, Morrinhos, SR, 1863 (APM, SG 119); senator, Guaicuí, Januária, Morrinhos, SR, MC, Bomfim, Contendas, 1863 (APM, SG 119); senator, Bomfim, Guaicuí, MC, CJ, Boa Vista, SR, Morrinhos, Januária, 1868 (APM, SG 121); chamber of deputies, MC, CJ, Guaicuí, Bomfim, Boa Vista, Itacambira, Januária, Morrinhos, Mucambo, SR, 1868 (APM, SG 122); CM, MC, Guaicuí, SR, 1869 (APM, SG 123); senator, Januária, Morrinhos, 1870 (APM, SG 125); chamber of deputies, MC, CJ, Januária, Morrinhos, Bomfim, Contendas, SR, 1872 (APM, SG 127); senator, MC, Contendas, Januária, CJ, Bomfim, Morrinhos, 1872 (APM, SG 128); CM, Januária, SR, Guaicuí, 1873 (APM, SG 130); eleitores, SR, Bomfim, 1876–78 (APM, SG 132); chamber of deputies,

Pedras dos Angicos, SR, 18// (APM, SG 134); JP and CM, Pedras dos Angicos, 1877 (APM, SG 134); chamber of deputies for SR, 1877 (APM, SG 135); CM, Pedras dos Angicos, MC, 1877 (APM, SG 137); chamber of deputies, Januária, Morrinhos, Pedras dos Angicos, MC, SR, CJ, Contendas, Bomfim, Brejo das Almas, 1878 (APM, SG 139); senator, Januária, SR, Morrinhos, MC, Contendas, CJ, Brejo das Almas, 1878 (APM, SG 140).

44. APM, SG 116, election for senator, proceedings for Coração de Jesus, 1851.

45. APM, SP 1187, CMMC to PPMG, 28 Jan. 1867.

46. APM, SP 1187, Domingos José Souto to PPMG, 21 June 1867.

47. APM, SP 1251, report of the secretary of the provincial police, 26 Apr. 1868, report of the police secretary, 1 July 1868, and JD of Jequitaí to provincial police chief, 2 June 1868.

48. APM, SP 1252, substitute JM of MC to PPMG, 2 Sept. 1868, del. of SR to PPMG, 10 Sept. 1868, Anacleto de Magalhães Rois to PPMG, 8 Oct. 1868, and Ricardo Rodrigues Horta to del. of SR, 8 Sept. 1868.

49. APM, SP 1253, João Antônio Rodrigues to PPMG, 12 Nov. 1868.

50. APM, SG 440, Pedro Gonçalves de Abreu to PPMG, 5 May 1872, SP 999, SR elections, 28 Aug. 1863, and SP 1000, justice of the peace of São Sebastião das Lages to PPMG, 17 Aug. 1863.

51. APM, SP 1001, Manoel do Carmo Barbosa to PPMG, 31 Aug. 1863, and SP 1253, Francisco Manoel Paraiso Cavalcanti to PPMG, confidential, 26 Dec. 1868.

52. APM, SP 765, electoral college of Morrinhos to PPMG, 24 Aug. 1859, and SP 835, JM of Januária to PPMG, 7 Jan. 1860, JP of Morrinhos to PPMG, 6 Aug. 1860.

53. APM, SP 898, Antonio de Paula Pereira to PPMG, 25 Jan. 1861.

54. APM, SP 890, electoral board of Januária, 11 July 1861, and SP 891, elections, 27 Aug. 1861.

55. APM, SP 1115, Alvaro José Rodrigues to PPMG, 17 Jan. 1865.

56. APM, SG 440, João de Paulo Pereira to PPMG, 24 Apr. 1872.

57. *Anais, 1876*, 441–46.

58. APM, SP PP 1/18, cx. 1, p. 34, 28 July 1878.

59. Sampaio, *Rio São Francisco*, 116; Prefeitura Municipal de Januária, *Primeiro centenário*, 52–53.

60. Sampaio, *Rio São Francisco*, 111–16.

61. Rosa (*The Devil to Pay*) refers to Neco's notoriety in his account of jagunço life in the sertão.

62. APM, SP PP 1/18, cx. 1, p. 33, n.d. (late 1870s).

63. *Provincia de Minas*, 10 July 1881, 2–3; *Provincia de Minas*, 28 Aug. 1881, 4.

64. APM, SG 550, Clemente Marcondes e Silva to João Florentino Meira de Vasconcelos, 25 June 1881, Antonio Gonçalves Chaves Jr. to PPMG, 25 June, 1 July 1881.

65. APM, SP PP 1/18, cx. 1, p. 32, 31 Dec. 1888.

66. APM, SP PP 1/33, cx. 106, p. 31, 9 Jan. 1841, cx. 106, p. 33, 14 Jan. 1841, cx. 106, p. 56, 9 Aug., 20 Oct. 1841.

67. APM, SP 817, JMOC to PPMG, 16 Feb. 1860, and SP 929, JMOC to PPMG, 8 Mar. 1862.

68. APM, SP 1367, Victoriano Lopes da Cruz to Justino de Andrade Camara, 27 Nov. 1868, JD of Rio São Francisco to PPMG, 20 Jan. 1870, Antonio Francisco dos Santos to del. of MC, 9 Jan. 1870.

69. APM, SP 1363, del. of SR to PPMG, 1 Oct. 1870, and SP 1367, José Augusto de Magalhães to PPMG, 4 June 1870.

70. APM, SP 1252, Paulino de Andrade Faria to PPMG, 30 Sept. 1868, Francisco de Sá Pereira to PPMG, 11 Sept. 1868, Francisco de Sá Pereira to PPMG, 20 Sept. 1868, SP 1253, Lúcio José da Rocha to PPMG, 20 Dec. 1868, and SP 1305, Anna Luisa de Souza Meneses to PPMG, 12 Dec. 1868, Francisco de Sá Pereira to provincial police chief, 31 Mar. 1869, *autos de penhora* drawn up by Sabino da Silva Mattos, 11, 12 Dec. 1868.

71. Uricoechea, *Patrimonial Foundations*, 57.

72. APM, SP 937, del. of Januária to PPMG, 29 Nov. 1862.

7. The Moral Economy of Partisan Identity

1. APM, SP 935, JMOC to PPMG, 12 July 1962. Sebastião was arrested in late 1863 (SP 989, Manoel do Carmo Barbosa to PPMG, 2 Nov. 1863).

2. Franco (*Homens livres*) coined the phrase *código do sertão*.

3. In Brazil, male violence and the frontier have been associated since early colonial times, as demonstrated in Russell-Wood, "Frontiers in Colonial Brazil." During the First Republic (1889–1930), frontier violence became romanticized in the figure of the bandit king Lampião and other cangaceiros (see Chandler, *The Bandit King;* Lewin, "The Limitations of Social Banditry"; and Queiroz, *Os cangaceiros*). On the Brazil-Uruguay frontier, see Chasteen, *Heroes on Horseback*.

4. See Julian Pitt-Rivers's classic essay "Honour and Social Status."

5. On female honor in Spanish America, see Seed, *To Love, Honor and Obey;* Socolow, "Acceptable Partners"; Gutiérrez, *When Jesus Came;* and Stern, *Secret History of Gender*. For Brazil, see Dias, *Power and Everyday Life;* and Graham, *House and Street*.

6. On the political socialization and cultural formation of Brazilian law graduates, see Adorno, *Aprendizes*.

7. Vianna, *O ocaso do império*, 19.

8. Celso, *Oito anos de parlamento*, cited in Queiroz, *Mandonismo*, 82.

9. Franco, *Homens livres*.

10. See Anderson, *Imagined Communities*, esp. 30–39.

11. Chasteen, "Violence for Show," 56.

12. See Costa, *Brazilian Empire*, 53–77.

13. Costa, *Brazilian Empire*, 59.

14. Burns, *Poverty of Progress*, 8.

15. Flory, *Judge and Jury*, 11.

16. For example, Faoro (*Os donos do poder*) has argued that Conservatives favored the development of a modernizing bureaucracy while Liberals supported retrograde bosses.

17. See Holub, "Liberal Movement"; Melo, *Os programas dos partidos e o segundo império;* Barman, *Forging of a Nation;* and Mattos, *Tempo saquarema*. Research in progress on the Conservative party by Jeffrey Needell promises to provide a more nuanced understanding of partisan motivations and ideology, especially for the post-1850 period.

18. On Liberal and Republican partisan objectives, see Evanson, "Reform in Brazil." Colson ("The Destruction of a Revolution") highlights the strategies of an "establishment" of prominent families. On Liberal policies regarding abolition and land reform, see Graham, "The Overthrow of the Empire," and "Joaquim Nabuco."

19. Graham, *Patronage and Politics*, 148.

20. Garner, "In Pursuit of Order," 158.

21. One exception is Filler, "Liberalism in Imperial Brazil."

22. Queiroz, *Mandonismo*, 25.

23. Barman and Barman, "The Law Graduate."

24. Such papers included *O Correio de Minas* (1841–42), *O Compiliador* (1843–47), *O Povo* (1849), *O Bom Senso* (1852–56), and *O Correio Oficial de Minas* (1857–60).

25. *O Compiliador*, 14 Mar. 1846, 1.

26. See "A imprensa em Minas Gerais, 1807–1897."

27. The Conservative vanguard included *O Constitucional* (1866–68, 1878), *O Noticiador de Minas* (1868–73), *Conservador de Minas* (1870), *O Correio de Minas* (1878), *A Província de Minas* (1880–89), *O Vinte de Agosto* (1885–86), and *A União* (1886–89). Liberal papers included *O Diário de Minas* (1866–68), renamed *Liberal de Minas* (1868–70), *Liberal Mineiro* (1882–89), and *Opinião Liberal*. The proceedings of the provincial assembly also began to be published regularly in serial form or bound as the *Anais*. I include the *Anais* as part of the political press.

28. Santos, *Memórias do distrito diamantino*, 28.

29. *Noticiador de Minas*, 19 Aug. 1868, 1.

30. *Anais, 1881*, 564.

31. *Noticiador de Minas*, 31 Aug. 1868, 1.

32. *Noticiador de Minas*, editorials of 19 Aug. 1868, 1; 17 Sept. 1868, 1; 22 Sept. 1868, 1; 26 Sept. 1868, 1; 3 Oct. 1868, 1; 8 Jan. 1869, 1; 10 Feb. 1869, 1.

33. My approach is similar to that of Greenberg's attempt (in *Honor and Slavery*) to translate the language of men of honor in the Old South.

34. *O Compiliador*, 25 Feb. 1846, 3; 4 Apr. 1846, 1.

35. AN, 001 16, *graus de bacharéis e doutores, 1831–83*.

36. Vianna, *Monographia*, 150–56.

37. *O Conciliador*, 24 Nov. 1866, 1–2.

38. *O Conciliador*, 24 Nov. 1866, 1–2.

39. *O Conciliador*, 24 Nov. 1866, 1–2.

40. *O Constitucional*, 1 June 1867, 2–3; 28 Mar. 1868, 3.

41. *Opinião Liberal*, 3 Dec. 1868, 3.

42. APM, SP 1304, Antônio Francisco Barbosa to José Fernandes Periera Correia, 9 Jan. 1869.

43. APM, SP 1304, Francisco Freire de Fonseca to PPMG, 16 Jan. 1869.

44. *O Diário de Minas*, 23 Jan. 1868, 3.

45. *Província de Minas*, 26 Aug. 1882, 3.

46. *Anais, 1883*, 87, 343, 360, 379, 695–96, 698, 702; *Anais, 1884*, 154–59, 565, 672–73.

47. *Anais, 1884*, 162–63, 702–3, 726–27.

48. *Anais, 1884*, 672–73.

49. *Província de Minas*, 10 May 1883, 2.

50. APM, SP 1304, JD to PPMG, 29 Jan. 1869.

51. See Torres, *História de Minas Gerais*, 4:932.

52. For the exchange between Nunes Brasileiro and Sales Peixoto, see *Província de Minas*, 21 Aug. 1881, 3; 2 Oct. 1881, 3; 17 Aug. 1882, 3; 5 Oct. 1882, 4; 6 Apr. 1883, 3–4; 10 July 1884, 3–4; 7 Aug. 1884, 3–4; 9 Oct. 1884, 4; 27 Nov. 1884, 3; 21 May 1885, 3. For Neco's comment, see *Província de Minas*, 1 Jan. 1883, 3.

53. *Província de Minas*, 10 July 1884, 3.

54. Bieber, "Postmodern Ethnographer," 57–59.

55. APM, SP PP 1/33, CX. 103, p. 19, 7 Sept. 1834.

56. APM, SP PP 1/33, CX. 103, p. 27, 14 Nov. 1834, p. 28, 18 Nov. 1834.

57. APM, SP PP 1/33, CX. 105, p. 36, 15 Oct. 1838, CX. 106, p. 19, 26 Sept. 1840, p. 47, 20 July 1840, CX. 107, p. 26, 16 Apr. 1844.

58. *Anais, 1884*, 536.

59. *Província de Minas*, 1 Jan. 1882, 3.

60. *O Vinte de Agosto*, 19 Mar. 1886, 3.

61. *Anais, 1884*, 702–3.

62. *Anais, 1884*, 536; *Província de Minas*, 21 Aug. 1881, 3.

63. *Província de Minas*, 2 Oct. 1881, 3; 6 Apr. 1883, 3.

64. Paula, *Montes Claros*, 1:19–21; *Anais, 1884*, 267–70.

65. APM, SP PP 1/16, CX. 43, p. 48, 23 Jan. 1853.

66. APM, SG 441, Paulino de Andrade Faria to PPMG, 30 Mar. 1873, and SG 442, José Joaquim Bento Neves to PPMG, 25 July 1873.

67. *Noticiador de Minas*, 8 Mar. 1869, 3–4.

68. *Noticiador de Minas*, 15 Oct. 1869, 3.

69. *Província de Minas*, 18 June 1882, 4.

70. Braz, *São Francisco*, 72.

71. APM, SP 1362, José Augusto de Magalhães to PPMG, 4 June 1870.

72. *O Diário de Minas*, "Januária," 4 May 1867, 2.

73. *Noticiador de Minas*, 14 Mar. 1871, 3–4.

74. *Noticiador de Minas*, 27 Sept. 1870, 3.

75. *Noticiador de Minas*, 29 June 1871, 3.

76. *Noticiador de Minas*, 14 Mar. 1871, 3–4.

77. *Província de Minas*, 11 Sept. 1881, 4.

78. *Noticiador de Minas*, 17 Mar. 1869, 2–3.

79. *Anais, 1883*, 87.

80. *Anais, 1879*, 574.

81. *O Vinte de Agosto*, 26 June 1886, 3.

82. Paula, *Montes Claros*, 1:155.

83. Carvalho, "Os partidos políticos em Minas Gerais," 27–28.

84. Horta, "Famílias governamentáis," 53.

85. *O Diário de Minas*, 23 Jan. 1868, 3.

86. The hypothesis that the rural poor may have participated more actively in the creation of political ideologies such as liberalism has been demonstrated in other regions of Latin America (see Mallon, *Peasant and Nation;* Guardino, *Guerrero;* Joseph and Nugent, eds., *Everyday Forms of State Formation;* and Nugent, *Modernity*).

87. Nugent, *Modernity*, 20.

88. For a counterexample, see Chasteen, *Heroes on Horseback*, esp. chaps. 13, 17.

8. Limited Benefits of Patronage

1. APM, SP PP 1/33, CX. 104, p. 11, 5 Mar. 1836, p. 38, 12 Dec. 1836, and SP 224, CMJ to PPMG, 11 July 1839.

2. APM, SP PP 1/33, CX. 104, p. 11, 5 Mar. 1836, CX. 105, p. 5, 30 Sept. 1837, CX. 106, p. 14, 4

Aug. 1840, p. 17, 27 Aug. 1840, cx. 106, p. 35, 27 Jan. 1841, cx. 107, p. 84, 14 Oct. 1846, cx. 108, p. 10, 11 Oct. 1847, p. 49, 17 Jan. 1850, cx. 109, p. 1, 24 May 1850, p. 2, 25 May 1850, p. 6, 13 July 1850, p. 8, 24 Oct. 1850, p. 38, 27 Jan. 1852.

3. APM, SP PP 1/18, cx. 138, p. 10, 5 Mar. 1833, SP 206, JMOC to PPMG, 7 Sept. 1839, SP PP 1/33, cx. 143, p. 10, 22, 25 Jan. 1833, p. 69, 15 Oct. 1834, cx. 144, p. 53, 26 Jan. 1836, p. 64, 2 May 1836, cx. 146, p. 2, 2 Jan. 1838, p. 14, 16 July 1838, p. 70, 7 May 1841, cx. 149, p. 12, 14 Dec. 1844, p. 42, 12 Sept. 1845, cx. 150, p. 30, 20 Oct. 1847, cx. 151, p. 55, 26 Oct. 1850; LM 951, 6 June 1858; APM, SP PP 1/46, cx. 3, p. 47, 15 July 1837; LM 441, 6 Oct. 1849.

4. APM, SP PP 1/33, cx. 147, p. 9, 13 July 1841, p. 62, 25 Apr. 1843, p. 72, 26 June 1843, cx. 148, p. 21, 7 Nov. 1843, p. 37, 29 Jan. 1844, p. 43, 26 Feb. 1844.

5. APM, SP PP 1/33, cx. 288, p. 40, 6 Dec. 1836, p. 63, 31 Oct. 1837, cx. 289, p. 10, 19 May 1838, p. 11, 23 Aug. 1838, p. 13, 23 Aug. 1838, p. 19, 2 July 1840, p. 43, 21 Feb. 1842, p. 74, 28 Feb. 1844, cx. 290, p. 2, 21 Mar. 1845, SP PP 1/24, cx. 126, p. 20, 24 Nov. 1853; LM 2720, 18 Dec. 1880; APM, SP SeP 1/3, cx. 16, p. 15, 5 Mar. 1887.

6. APM, SP PP 1/46, cx. 1, p. 58, 28 May 1834, and SP PP 1/33, cx. 143, p. 52, 28 Apr. 1834.

7. APM, SP PP 1/33, cx. 145, p. 61, 13 July 1837, cx. 146, p. 59, 19 Dec. 1840, cx. 151, p. 71, 12 July 1851; LM 281, 12 Apr. 1845.

8. APM, SP PP 1/9, cx. 6, p. 31, 15 Aug. 1853, p. 32, 8 Jan. 1863.

9. APM, SP OP (Obras Públicas) 3/6, cx. 29, 20 June 1854, 2 June 1862.

10. APM, SP OP 1/2, cx. 2, 14 July 1871; LM 2277, 8 July 1876; LM 3249, 30 Oct. 1884; LM 3460, 4 Oct. 1887.

11. LM 13, 28 Mar. 1835. For provincial debates on education, see Torres, *História de Minas Gerais*, 5:1027–47.

12. *Leis do império*, lei 29, 14 Aug. 1819; *Leis do império*, lei 27, 17 Apr. 1820, p. 29; APM, SP PP 1/33, cx. 289, p. 3, 15 Jan. 1838; LM 2721, 18 Dec. 1880.

13. APM, SP PP 1/33, cx. 103, p. 6, 27 May 1834, p. 39, 1 Sept. 1835, cx. 105, p. 21, 8 Feb. 1838, p. 36, 15 Oct. 1838, cx. 106, p. 11, 29 Feb. 1840, p. 24, 20 Oct. 1840.

14. APM, SP PP 1/33, cx. 109, p. 24, 6 Aug. 1851, p. 25, 11 Aug. 1851.

15. APM, SP PP 1/33, cx. 143, p. 10, 23 Jan. 1833, p. 47, 28 Apr. 1834, p. 75, 25 Oct. 1834, cx. 145, p. 78, 6 Oct. 1837, cx. 146, p. 6, 28 Sept. 1837, 15 Jan. 1838, cx. 147, p. 63, 26 Apr. 1843.

16. APM, SP PP 1/33, cx. 144, p. 37, 26 Oct. 1835, cx. 147, p. 15, 31 Jan. 1842, cx. 149, p. 17, 11 Jan. 1845.

17. APM, SP PP 1/33, cx. 144, ps. 1 and 2, 12 Feb. 1835, p. 6, 16 Mar. 1835, p. 16, 16 June 1835, p. 30, 16 Sept. 1835.

18. APM, SP PP 1/33, cx. 145, p. 67, 4 Sept. 1837.

19. APM, SP PP 1/33, cx. 144, p. 15, 31 Jan. 1842.

20. Resolution 257, 23 Mar. 1844; LM 307, 8 Apr. 1846; LM 511, art. 1, 3 July 1850; APM, SP 483, Justino Andrade Camara to PPMG, 15 Oct. 1853.

21. LM 1844, 12 Oct. 1871; LM 2037, 1 Dec. 1873; LM 2164, 11 Nov. 1875; LM 2227, 14 June 1876; LM 2390, 13 Oct. 1877; LM 2395, 13 Oct. 1877.

22. LM 1844, 12 Oct. 1871; LM 1876, 15 July 1872; LM 1925, 19 July 1872; LM 2064, 17 Dec. 1874; LM 2227, 14 June 1876; LM 2163, 19 Nov. 1875; LM 2430, 13 Nov. 1877.

23. Januária first got a chair in Latin and French in 1858. It became vacant and was reinstated in 1876 and again in 1878 (LM 920, 9 June 1858; LM 1638, 13 Sept. 1870; LM 2331, 12 July 1876; LM 2478, 9 Nov. 1878).

24. LM 2228, 15 June 1876; LM 2618, 7 Jan. 1880; LM 2922, 4 Oct. 1882; LM 3115, 6 Oct.

1883; LM 3217, 11 Oct. 1884; *Anais, 1876,* 94, 116–20, 200–210; *Anais, 1879,* 569; *Anais, 1882,* 468.

25. APM, SP PP 1/33, cx. 104, p. 11, 5 Mar. 1836, p. 38, 12 Dec. 1836.

26. APM, SP PP 1/33, cx. 105, p. 20, 8 Feb. 1838, cx. 106, p. 6, 27 Feb. 1840, SP 221, CMJ to PPMG, 31 Jan. 1839, SP 224, CMJ to PPMG, 26 July 1839, and SP PP 1/40, cx. 52, 2 Nov. 1843.

27. APM, SP PP 1/33, cx. 107, p. 11, 28 Aug. 1843, cx. 109, p. 28, 12 Aug. 1851, p. 38, 27 Jan. 1852, p. 52, 28 Jan. 1854, p. 57, 25 Aug. 1862; LM 2972, 7 Oct. 1882; LM 1895, 19 July 1872; LM 3218, 11 Oct. 1884; LM 3463, 4 Oct. 1887.

28. APM, SP PP 1/33, cx. 144, p. 53, 26 Jan. 1836, and SP PP 1/46, cx. 3, p. 47, 15 July 1837.

29. APM, SP PP 1/33, cx. 149, p. 31, 27 July 1845, p. 50, 31 Oct. 1845, p. 101, 13 July 1846, cx. 150, p. 1, 13 Jan. 1847, p. 18, 13 July 1847, p. 36, 18 Dec. 1847, p. 25, 13 Oct. 1847, cx. 151, p. 1, 21 Oct. 1848; LM 538, art. 6, 9 Oct. 1851; LM 581, art. 1, 8 May 1852; LM 619, art. 1, 13 May 1853; LM 953, art. 5, 6 June 1858; LM 1058, 25 Sept. 1860; LM 1060, 9 Sept. 1860; LM 1068, 5 Oct. 1860.

30. LM 1268, 2 Jan. 1866; LM 1715, 5 Oct. 1870; LM 1895, 19 July 1872; LM 1919, 19 July 1872; LM 2094, 2 Jan. 1874; LM 2236, 15 June 1876; LM 2949, 7 Oct. 1882.

31. APM, SP 570, Teófilo de Sales Peixoto to PPMG, 2 Jan. 1855.

32. LM 2972, 7 Oct. 1882; LM 2997, 19 Oct. 1882; LM 3218, 11 Oct. 1884; LM 3262, 30 Oct. 1884.

33. Argollo, *Informação.*

34. For example, Halfield, *Atlas;* Araujo, "Relatório."

35. Halfield maintained some perspective despite the mishaps that he experienced in the comarca of Rio São Francisco. Several members of his crew caught malaria, and, in Pedras de Maria da Cruz, he was set on by an angry mob that mistook him for the assassin of the police subdelegate's wife. (APM, SP PP 1/41, cx. 1, ps. 32, 34, 52); *Rel. PPMG, 1869,* 34.

36. APM, SP PP 1/45, cx. 1, p. 17, n.d.

37. LM 2438, Nov. 1877; LM 2451, 13 May 1878; APM, SG 1173, fazenda provincial de Minas Gerais, ofício 168, 4 Nov. 1881; Diamantina, Aurelio Pires de Figueiredo Camargo to diretoria da fazenda de Minas Gerais, 21 Oct. 1880; Aurelio Pires to diretoria da fazenda de Minas Gerais, 28 Oct. 1880; diretoria da fazenda to Aurelio Pires, 29 Apr. 1882; secretaria da polícia to PPMG, 19 Dec. 1883; diretoria geral das obras públicas de Minas Gerais, 12 Dec. 1883; diretoria de Morro Velho to diretoria geral das obras públicas, 25 Oct. 1883.

38. Mesquita, *Problema econômico.*

39. LM 1058, 25 Sept. 1860; LM 1060, 9 Sept. 1860; LM 1068, 5 Oct. 1860; LM 1104, 16 Oct. 1861; LM 1268, 2 Jan. 1866; LM 1715, 5 Oct. 1870; LM 1895, 19 July 1872; LM 1919, 19 July 1872; LM 2974, 7 Oct. 1882.

40. APM, SP PP 133, cx. 104, p. 37, 1 Dec. 1836, cx. 106, p. 63, 28 Feb. 1842, cx. 107, p. 26, 12 Apr. 1844, p. 36, 4 Apr. 1844, p. 60, 1 Oct. 1844.

41. APM, SP PP 1/33, cx. 145, p. 36, 14 Jan. 1837, cx. 148, p. 44, 26 Feb. 1844, p. 83, 12 July 1844, cx. 149, p. 44, 3 Oct. 1845, cx. 150, p. 40, 7 Jan. 1848, p. 71, 25 Sept. 1848, cx. 151, p. 2, 21 Oct. 1848, p. 60, 7 Jan. 1851.

42. APM, SP PP 1/33, cx. 287, p. 29, 30 May 1833, p. 33, 4 June 1833, cx. 288, p. 50, 20 Apr. 1837, p. 53, 13 May 1837.

43. See, for example, material pertaining to the disputes between Barra do Rio das

Velhas and SR (APM, SP PP 1/33, cx. 290, p. 17, 2 Sept. 1848, p. 26, 26 Feb. 1851, SP 483, CMSR to PPMG, 15 July 1853, and SP 776, CMSR to PPMG, 1 Jan. 1859) and between São Francisco and Januária (Braz, *São Francisco*, 507; APM, SG 541, petition from the citizens of Januária, 11 Nov. 1881, SG 545, CM of São Francisco to PPMG, 13 Dec. 1881, JD of Rio São Francisco to PPMG, 14 Dec. 1881, petition from the inhabitants of São Francisco to PPMG, 9 Jan. 1882, CMJ to PPMG, 31 Mar. 1882). The rapid turnaround of this exchange in the latter case suggests that the post was indeed getting through and that Januária's complaints were based on sour grapes.

44. The juiz de direito barred the enforcement of this law, and it was eventually overturned by the provincial assembly.

45. APM, SP 227, CMSR to PPMG, 24 Dec. 1839, and SP PP 1/33, cx. 6, p. 13, 13 Jan. 1840.

46. Chalhoub, *A cidade febril.*

47. APM, SP PP 1/26, cx. 1, p. 80, 27 Apr. 1845, p. 81, 30 Aug. 1845, SP PP 1/33, cx. 107, p. 8, 28 Aug. 1843, p. 15, 9 Jan. 1844, p. 60, 10 Jan. 1844, p. 68, 26 Sept. 1845.

48. APM, SP 1157, CMJ to PPMG, 10 Feb., 20 Nov. 1866, SP PP 1/26, cx. 9, p. 23, 29 Aug. 1887, p. 64, 21 Oct. 1887, and SP PP 1/26, cx. 11, p. 14, 11 May 1888.

49. APM, SP PP 1/33, cx. 289, p. 23, 30 June 1840, p. 59, 28 July 1843, cx. 290, p. 5, 26 Aug. 1845; *Anais, 1872*, 52–53.

50. APM, SP PP 1/33, cx. 149, p. 105, 9 Sept. 1846, and SP 612, 28 Dec. 1855.

51. APM, SP PP 1/26, cx. 9, p. 23, 29 Oct. 1887.

52. Curtin, "Epidemiology of the Slave Trade"; APM, SP 482, CMJ to PPMG, 26 Feb. 1853, SP PP 1/33, cx. 149, p. 105, 9 Sept. 1846, SP 612, CMMC to PPMG, 28 Dec. 1855. In the case of malaria, such observations were true for people of color who carried one sickle cell gene.

53. APM, SP PP 1/33, cx. 288, p. 40, 6 Dec. 1836, p. 63, 31 Oct. 1837, cx. 289, p. 10, 19 May 1838, p. 11, 23 Aug. 1838, p. 13, 23 Aug. 1838, p. 19, 2 July 1840, p. 43, 21 Feb. 1842, p. 74, 28 Feb. 1844, cx. 290, p. 2, 21 Mar. 1845, SP 221, CMSR to PPMG, 9 Jan. 1839, and SP 223, CMSR to PPMG, 6 May 1839; LM 3114, 6 Oct. 1883; *Anais, 1883*, 102.

54. APM, SP PP 1/33, cx. 149, p. 31, 27 July 1845, p. 50, 31 Oct. 1845, p. 101, 13 July 1846, cx. 151, p. 3, 11 Nov. 1848; LM 1698, 3 Oct. 1870; LM 1713, 15 Oct. 1870; LM 2112, art. 12, 8 Jan. 1875.

55. Paula, *Montes Claros*, 1:34–38.

56. APM, SP 832, exchequer (*fiscal*) of Januária to PPMG, 9 Oct. 1860, Dr. Francisco Fogaça de Bittencourt to PPMG, 15 Oct. 1860.

57. APM, SP PP 1/33, cx. 143, p. 5, 1833, p. 48, 28 Apr. 1834, cx. 144, p. 50, 3 Jan. 1836, SP 767, CM of Grão Mogol to PPMG, 16 Sept. 1859, district of São José de Gorutuba to CM of Grão Mogol, 3 Sept. 1859, CM of Ouro Preto to PPMG, 21 Mar. 1859, SP 877, CM of Rio Pardo, 7 Feb. 1861, CM of Minas Novas, 11 Apr. 1861, and SP 893, CM of São José do Gorutuba, 30 Apr. 1861.

58. APM, SP PP 1/33, cx. 143, p. 5, 1833.

59. APM, SP PP 1/33, cx. 144, p. 50, 3 Jan. 1836, cx. 145, p. 19, 25 Oct. 1836, cx. 287, p. 63, CMSR to PPMG, 15 July 1834. The tax was passed under LM 49.

60. APM, SP 832, atas da câmara municipal, 2 Apr. 1860, CMJ to PPMG, 31 May 1860.

61. APM, SG 536, secretaria do Gabinete Cearense to PPMG, 8 July 1877, SG 556, 22 Oct. 1878, 14 Dec. 1878, 31 Dec. 1878, and SP PP 1/33, cx. 152, p. 35, n.d. (but refers to LM 2438).

62. APM, SP 714, CMMC to PPMG, 21 Sept. 1858; attached petition from the inhabitants of Montes Claros to the president of the municipal council.

63. In 1843, the council received permission to open a subscription for a charity hospital but received no donations (APM, SP PP 1/33, CX. 147, p. 47, 7 Jan. 1843). Camara lobbied the provincial assembly in 1871, securing an initial five contos and additional subsidies thereafter (LM 1776, 21 Sept. 1871; LM 2396, 13 Oct. 1877; LM 2438, 14 Nov. 1877). On the rivalry between Diamantina and Montes Claros, see *Anais, 1876*, 75, 109, 424; *Anais, 1878*, suplemento, 14.

9. Continuity of Political Violence

1. Paula, *Montes Claros*, 1:32–34, 160.
2. Vianna, *Monographia*, 151–59.
3. Wirth, *Minas Gerais in the Brazilian Federation*, 138–81.
4. Wirth, *Minas Gerais in the Brazilian Federation*, 9–13.
5. Vianna, *Efemérides montesclarenses*, passim.
6. A comprehensive study of the São Francisco region during the republic does not exist, making quantitative judgments about the level of violence inadvisable.
7. Wirth, *Minas Gerais in the Brazilian Federation*, 161.
8. Souza ("The Politics of Violence," 122), for example, has argued that the new republic lacked adequate mechanisms to balance power between rival political groups, giving regional oligarchies expanded opportunities to distort the system. They did not distort it but worked within its prescribed rules at the level of state politics. Della Cava (*Miracle at Joaseiro*) offers a different interpretation, maintaining that municipal elites in republican Ceará acted in concert with state officials, not in isolation.
9. Graham, "Political Power and Landownership"; Wirth, *Minas Gerais in the Brazilian Federation*, 22–23.
10. APM, SP PP 1/33, CX. 108, p. 16, Couto Moreno to PPMG, 3 Apr. 1848.
11. Paula, *Montes Claros*, 1:153–56.
12. APM, SP PP 1/18, CX. 302, p. 1, juiz ordinário of Sao Romão to PPMG, 9 Jan. 1826.
13. Freitas, "Marginal Elites," passim, esp. chap. 8.
14. APM, SP PP 1/15, CX. 13, p. 2, 31 May 1831.
15. APM, SP 925, JMOC to PPMG, 13 Mar. 1862.
16. Freitas, "Marginal Elites," chaps. 5–6.
17. Self-presentation was a crucial element in the process of political legitimation of emerging elites in many newly formed states (see Seligman, "Elite Recruitment").
18. Bieber, "Postmodern Ethnographer."
19. APM, SP PP 1/10, CX. 15, p. 3, household census of 1838.
20. Cunha, *Rebellion in the Backlands*, 15.

Bibliography

Archives

Arquivo do Museu Imperial. Petropolis, Rio de Janeiro.
Arquivo Nacional. Rio de Janeiro.
Arquivo da Prefeitura de Montes Claros. Montes Claros, Minas Gerais.
Arquivo Público Mineiro. Belo Horizonte, Minas Gerais.
Biblioteca da Assembléia Legislativa do Estado de Minas Gerais. Belo Horizonte, Minas Gerais.
Biblioteca Municipal de Belo Horizonte. Belo Horizonte, Minas Gerais.
Biblioteca Nacional. Rio de Janeiro, Rio de Janeiro.
Instituto Histórico Geográfico Brasileiro. Rio de Janeiro.

Published Primary Sources

Anais da Assembléia Legislativa da Província de Minas Gerais, 1868–1889.
Coleção das Decisões do Governo do Império do Brasil, 1808–1889.
Coleção das Leis do Império do Brasil, 1808–1889.
Coleção das Leis Mineiras, 1834–1889.
Constituição política do Império do Brasil, 1824.
Recenseamento Geral do Império, 1872.
Relatórios de Presidentes da Província de Minas Gerais, 1834–1889.
Relatórios do Ministério do Império, 1836–1889.

Secondary Sources

Abreu, J. Capistrano de. *Capítulos de história colonial e os caminhos antigos e povoamento do Brasil*. Brasília: Editora da Universidade de Brasília, 1982.
Adorno, Sérgio. *Os aprendizes do poder: O bacharelismo liberal na política Brasileira*. Rio de Janeiro: Paz e Terra, 1988.

Almeida, Tito Franco de. *Estudo e comentários da reforma eleitoral.* Rio de Janeiro: A. M. Fernandes e Silva, 1876.

Alonso, Ana Maria. *Thread of Blood: Colonialism, Revolution, and Gender on Mexico's Northern Frontier.* Tucson: Univ. of Arizona Press, 1995.

Amado, Janaina. "The Frontier in Comparative Perspective: The United States and Brazil." In "Frontiers in Comparative Perspective: The United States and Brazil." Latin American Program Working Papers, no. 188. Washington DC: Wilson Center, 1990.

Anastacia, Carla Maria Junho. "Potentados e bandidos: Os motins do São Francisco." *Revista do departamento de história* 9 (1989): 74–85.

Anderson, Benedict. *Imagined Communities: Reflections on the Origin and Spread of Nationalism.* London: Verso, 1985.

Andrade, Manoel Correia de. *The Land and People of Northeast Brazil.* Trans. Dennis V. Johnson. Albuquerque: Univ. of New Mexico Press, 1980.

Araujo, Francisco Manoel Alvares de. "Relatório da viagem de exploração dos Rios das Velhas e São Francisco feita no vapor Saldanha Marinho." *RIHGB* 39 (1876): 77–155, 211–75.

Argollo, Miguel de Teive e. *Informação prestada ao Exmo. Sr. Dr. Antonio Olyntho dos Santos Pires, ministro e secretario d'estado dos negocios da indústria, viação e obras públicas do Brasil sobre o arrendamento das estradas de ferro, pertencentes a união.* Salvador, 1896.

Aufderheide, Patricia Ann. "Order and Violence: Social Deviance and Social Control in Brazil, 1780–1840." Ph.D. diss., Univ. of Minnesota, 1976.

Barbosa, Waldemar de Almeida. *Dicionário histórico-geográfico de Minas Gerais.* Belo Horizonte: Arquivo Público Mineiro, 1971.

Barman, Roderick J. *Brazil: The Forging of a Nation, 1798–1852.* Stanford: Stanford Univ. Press, 1988.

Barman, Roderick J., and Jean Barman. "The Prosopography of the Brazilian Empire." *Latin American Research Review* 13, no. 2 (1978): 78–97.

Barman, Roderick J., and Jean Barman. "The Role of the Law Graduate in the Political Elite of Imperial Brazil." *Journal of Inter-American Studies and World Affairs* 18 (November 1976): 423–50.

Bastos, Aureliano Candido Tavares. *A província: Estudo sobre a decentralização no Brasil.* 2d ed. São Paulo: Editora Nacional, 1937.

————. *Os males do presente e as esperanças do futuro.* São Paulo: Editora Nacional, 1939.

Beattie, Peter M. "Transforming Enlisted Army Service in Brazil, 1864–1940: Penal Servitude versus Conscription and Changing Conceptions of Honor, Race and Nation." Ph.D. diss, Univ. of Miami, 1994.

Bieber, Judy. "Postmodern Ethnographer in the Backlands: An Imperial Bureaucrat's Perceptions of Post-Independence Brazil." *Latin American Research Review* 33, no. 2 (1998): 37–72.

Blasenheim, Peter. "A Regional History of the Zona da Mata in Minas Gerais, Brazil, 1870–1906." Ph.D. diss., Stanford Univ., 1982.

Botelho, Tarcísio Rodrigues. "Demografia da escravidão Norte-Mineira no século XIX." B.A. monograph, Faculdade de Ciêcias Humanas, Belo Horizonte, 1990.

————. "Famílias e escravarias: Demografia e família escrava no norte de Minas Gerais no século XIX." M.A. thesis, Universidade de São Paulo, 1994.

Boxer, Charles. *The Golden Age of Brazil, 1695–1750: Growing Pains of a Colonial Society*. Berkeley: Univ. of California Press, 1969.

————. *Portuguese Society in the Tropics*. Madison: Univ. of Wisconsin Press, 1965.

Brandão, Berenice Cavalcante, Ilmar Rohloff de Mattos, and Maria Alice Rezende de Carvalho. *A polícia e a força policial no Rio de Janeiro*. Rio de Janeiro: Pontifical Universidade Católica, Divisão de Intercambio e Edições, 1981.

Brasil, Henrique de Oliva. *De Contendas a Brasília de Minas; Monografia*. Belo Horizonte: São Vicente, 1978.

————. *História e desenvolvimento de Montes Claros*. Belo Horizonte: n.p., 1983.

Braz, Brasiliano. *São Francisco nos caminhos da história*. São Francisco and Belo Horizonte, 1977.

Burns, E. Bradford. *The Poverty of Progress: Latin America in the Nineteenth Century*. Berkeley: Univ. of California Press, 1983.

Burton, Richard. *Explorations of the Highlands of Brazil*. 2 vols. New York: Greenwood, 1969.

Cardoso, Vicente Licínio. *A margem da história do Brasil*. 3d ed. São Paulo: Editora Nacional, 1979.

Carneiro, Otavio Barboza. *De Pirapora a Joazeiro pelo Rio São Francisco, conferência lida na Sociedade Nacional de Agricultura, no dia 23 de agosto de 1921*. Belo Horizonte: Imprensa Oficial, 1921.

Carvalho, Daniel de. *Notícia historica sobre o algodão em Minas: Memoria apresentada a conferência algodoeira, como representante da Sociedade Mineira de Agricultura*. Rio de Janeiro: Typ. do *Jornal do Comercio*, 1916.

Carvalho, José Murilo de. *A construção da ordem: A elite política imperial*. Rio de Janeiro: Campus, 1980.

————. "Elite and State Building in Imperial Brazil." Ph.D. diss., Stanford Univ., 1975.

————. "Political Elites and State Building: The case of Nineteenth Century Brazil." *Comparative Studies in Society and History* 24 (July 1982): 378–99.

Carvalho, Marcus Joaquim Maciel de. "Hegemony and Rebellion in Pernambuco (Brazil), 1821–1835." Ph.D. diss., Univ. of Illinois at Urbana-Champaign, 1989.

Carvalho, Orlando M. "Os partidos políticos em Minas Gerais." In *Segundo seminário de estudos mineiros*. Belo Horizonte, 1956.

Castro, Hebe Maria Mattos de. *Ao sul da história: Lavradores pobres na crise do trabalho escravo*. São Paulo: Brasiliense, 1987.

Castro, Jean Berrance de. "As milícias nacionais." *Revista da Historia* 74 (April–June 1968): 377–89.

Celso, Afonso. *Oito anos de parlamento*. Brasília: Editora Universidade de Brasília, 1981.

Chalhoub, Sidney. *A cidade febril*. São Paulo: Companhia das Letras, 1997.
———. *Visões da liberdade*. São Paulo: Companhia das Letras, 1990.
Chandler, Billy Jaymes. *The Bandit King: Lampião of Brazil*. College Station: Texas A&M Univ. Press, 1978.
———. *The Feitosas and the Sertão dos Inhumans*. Gainesville: Univ. of Florida Press, 1972.
Chasteen, John Charles. "Cabanos and Farrapos: Brazilian Nativism in Regional Perspective, 1822–1850." *Locus* 7, no. 1 (fall 1994): 31–46.
———. *Heroes on Horseback: A Life and Times of the Last Gaucho Caudillo*. Albuquerque: Univ. of New Mexico Press, 1995.
———. "Violence for Show: Knife Dueling on a Nineteenth-Century Cattle Frontier." In *The Problem of Order in Changing Societies: Essays on Crime and Policing in Argentina and Uruguay, 1750–1940*. Ed. Lyman L. Johnson. Albuquerque: Univ. of New Mexico Press, 1990.
Colson, Roger Frank. "The Destruction of a Revolution: Polity, Economy and Society in Brazil, 1750–1895." Ph.D. diss., Princeton Univ., 1979.
Conrad, Robert. *World of Sorrow: The African Slave Trade to Brazil*. Baton Rouge: Louisiana State Univ. Press, 1986.
Costa, Emilia Viotti da. *The Brazilian Empire: Myths and Histories*. Chicago: Univ. of Chicago Press, 1985.
———. *Da monarquia à república: Momentos decisivos*. São Paulo: Grijalbo, 1977.
———. "Introdução ao estudo da emancipação política do Brasil." In *Brasil em perpectiva*. Ed. Carlos Guilherme Mota. São Paulo: Bertrand Brasil, 1988.
Costa, Miguel, Filho. *A cana-de-açucar em Minas Gerais*. Rio de Janeiro: Instituto de Açucar e do Alcool, 1963.
Cunha, Euclides da. *Rebellion in the Backlands*. Trans. Samuel Putnam. Chicago: Univ. of Chicago Press, 1944.
Curtin, Philip D. "Epidemiology of the Slave Trade." *Political Science Quarterly* 83 (June 1968): 190–216.
Dean, Warren. "The Frontier in Brazil." In "Frontiers in Comparative Perspective: The United States and Brazil." Latin American Program Working Papers, no. 188. Washington DC: Wilson Center, 1990.
———. "Latifundia and Land Policy in Nineteenth Century Brazil." *Hispanic American Historical Review* 51 (1971): 606–25.
———. *Rio Claro: A Brazilian Plantation System, 1820–1920*. Stanford: Stanford Univ. Press, 1976.
Della Cava, Ralph. *Miracle at Joaseiro*. New York: Columbia Univ. Press, 1970.
Dias, Maria Odila Silva. "The Establishment of the Royal Court in Brazil." In *From Colony to Nation: Essays on the Independence of Brazil*. Ed. A. J. R. Russell-Wood. Baltimore: Johns Hopkins Univ. Press, 1975.
———. *Power and Everyday Life: The Lives of Working Women in Nineteenth-Century Brazil*. New Brunswick: Rutgers Univ. Press, 1995.

Eakin, Marshall C. *British Enterprise in Brazil: The St. John d'el Rey Company and the Morro Velho Mine, 1830–1960*. Durham NC: Duke Univ. Press, 1989.

Evanson, Philip Norman, "The Liberal Party and Reform in Brazil, 1860–1889." Ph.D. diss., Univ. of Virginia, 1969.

Faoro, Raymundo. *Os donos do poder: Formação do patronato político brasileiro*. 2d ed. Porto Alegre and São Paulo: Editora Globo, 1975.

Faria, Maria Auxiliadora. "A guarda nacional em Minas, 1831–1873." M.A. thesis, Federal Univ. of Paraná, Curitiba, 1977.

Filler, Victor Morris. "Liberalism in Imperial Brazil: The Regional Rebellions of 1842." Ph.D. diss., Stanford Univ., 1975.

Fleiuss, Max. *História administrativa do Brasil*. 2d ed. São Paulo: Ed. Melhoramentos, 1925.

Flory, Thomas. *Judge and Jury in Imperial Brazil, 1808–1871*. Austin: Univ. of Texas Press, 1981.

Franco, Maria Sylvia de Carvalho. *Homens livres na ordem escravocrata*. São Paulo: Atica, 1972.

Freitas, Judy Bieber. "Marginal Elites: Power, Politics and Patronage in the Backlands of Minas Gerais, Brazil, 1830–1889." Ph.D. diss., Johns Hopkins Univ., 1994.

———. "Slavery and Social Life Attempts to Reduce Free People to Slavery in the Sertão Mineiro, 1850–1870." *Journal of Latin American Studies* 26, no. 3 (1994): 597–619.

Fundação João Pinheiro. *O vale do São Francisco: Bibliografia*. Belo Horizonte, 1985.

Galvão, Eneas. "Poder judiciária no império." RIHGB, special volume, pt. 3 (1916): 321–39.

Galvão, Miguel Arcanjo. *Relação dos cidadãos que tomaram parte no governo do Brasil no periodo de março de 1808 a 15 de novembro de 1889*. Rio de Janeiro: Arquivo Nacional, 1969.

Gardner, George. *Travels in the Interior of Brasil, Principally through the Northern Provinces and the Gold and Diamond Districts during the Years 1836–1841* (1846). New York: AMS, 1970.

Garner, Lydia Magalhães Nunes. "In Pursuit of Order: A Study in Brazilian Centralization: The Section of Empire of the Council of State, 1842–1889." Ph.D. diss, Johns Hopkins Univ., 1987.

Godoy, Marcelo Magalhães. "Reconstruindo o movimento no tempo de uma estrutura da posse de escravos (Bomfim, 1832–1839)." CEDEPLAR, Universidade Federal de Minas Gerais, 1992. Typescript.

"Governo de Minas Gerais." *Revista do Arquivo Público Mineiro* 1 (1896): 3–96.

Graham, Richard. *Britain and the Onset of Modernization in Brazil, 1850–1914*. London: Cambridge Univ. Press, 1968.

———. "Comparing Regional Elites: A Review Article." *Comparative Studies in Society and History* 25 (April 1983): 396–400.

———. "Joaquim Nabuco, Conservative Historian." *Luso-Brazilian Review* 17 (summer 1980): 1–16.

———. "Landowners and the Overthrow of the Empire." *Luso-Brazilian Review* 7 (1970): 44–56.

———. *Patronage and Politics in Nineteenth-Century Brazil*. Stanford: Stanford Univ. Press, 1990.

———. "Political Power and Landownership in Nineteenth-Century Latin America." In *New Approaches to Latin American History*. Ed. Richard Graham and Peter H. Smith. Austin: Univ. of Texas Press, 1974.

Graham, Sandra Lauderdale. *House and Street: The Domestic World of Servants and Masters in Nineteenth-Century Rio de Janeiro*. Cambridge: Cambridge Univ. Press, 1988.

Greenberg, Kenneth S. *Honor and Slavery: Lies, Duels, Noses, Masks, Dressing as a Woman, Gifts, Strangers, Humanitarianism, Death, Slave Rebellions, the Proslavery Argument, Baseball, Hunting, and Gambling in the Old South*. Princeton: Princeton Univ. Press, 1996.

Guardino, Peter F. *Peasants, Politics and the Formation of Mexico's National State, Guerrero, 1800–1857*. Stanford: Stanford Univ. Press, 1996.

Guha, Ranajit. "Methodology." In *Selected Subaltern Studies*. Ed. Ranajit Guha and Gayatri Chakravorty Spivak. New York and Oxford: Oxford Univ. Press, 1988.

———. "The Prose of Counterinsurgency." In *Selected Subaltern Studies*. Ed. Ranajit Guha and Gayatri Chakravorty Spivak. New York and Oxford: Oxford Univ. Press, 1988.

Gutiérrez, Ramon. *When Jesus Came, the Corn Mothers Went Away: Marriage, Sexuality, and Power in New Mexico, 1500–1846*. Stanford: Stanford Univ. Press, 1992.

Halfield, Henrique Guilherme Fernando. *Atlas e relatório concernente a exploração do Rio São Francisco desde a cachoeira de Pirapora ao Oceano Atlantico*. Rio de Janeiro: Eduardo Rensberg, 1860.

Hall, Anthony. *Drought and Irrigation in Northeastern Brazil*. Cambridge: Cambridge Univ. Press, 1978.

Haring, Clarence H. *Empire in Brasil: A New World Experiment with Monarchy*. Cambridge: Cambridge Univ. Press, 1958.

Hobsbawm, E. J. *Bandits*. London: Weidenfeld & Nicolson, 1969.

———. *Primitive Rebels: Studies in Archaic Forms of Social Movements in the Nineteenth and Twentieth Centuries*. New York: Norton, 1965.

Holanda, Sérgio Buarque de, ed. *História geral da civilização brasileira*. Vol. 2, pts. 1–5. São Paulo: Difusão Européia de Livro, 1963–1972.

Holloway, Thomas H. "The Brazilian 'Judicial Police' in Florianópolis, Santa Catarina, 1841–1871." *Journal of Social History* 20 (1987): 733–56.

———. *Policing Rio de Janeiro: Repression and Resistence in a Nineteenth Century City*. Stanford: Stanford Univ. Press, 1993.

Holub, Norman. "The Liberal Movement in Brazil, 1808–1854." Ph.D. diss., New York Univ., 1968.

Horta, Cid Rebelo. "Famílias governamentáis de Minas Gerais." In *Segundo seminário de estudos mineiros*. Belo Horizonte, 1956.

Huggins, Martha Knisely. *From Slavery to Vagrancy in Brazil: Crime and Social Control in the Third World*. New Brunswick: Rutgers Univ. Press, 1985.

Iglesias, Francisco. *Política econômica do governo provincial mineiro*. Rio de Janeiro: Instituto Nacional do Livro, 1958.

"A imprensa em Minas Gerais—1807–1897." *Revista do Arquivo Público Mineiro* 3 (1898): 169–240.

Jacob, Rodolpho. *Minas Gerais no XXo. seculo*. Rio de Janeiro: Gomes e Irmãos, 1911.

Joseph, Gilbert M. "On the Trail of Latin American Bandits: A Reexamination of Peasant Resistance." *Latin American Research Review* 25, no. 3 (1990): 7–53.

Joseph, Gilbert M., and Daniel Nugent, eds. *Everyday Forms of State Formation: Revolution and the Negotiation of Rule in Modern Mexico*. Durham: Duke Univ. Press, 1994.

Kraay, Hendrik. "As Terrifying as Unexpected: The Bahian Sabinada, 1837–1838." *Hispanic American Historical Review* 72, no. 4 (1992): 501–27.

Latin American Subaltern Studies Group. "Founding Statement." *boundary* 2 20, no. 3 (1993): 110–21.

Leal, Aurelino. "O ato adicional: Reação conservadora: Bernardo Pereira de Vasconcelos: A lei de interpretação: O golpe de estado da maioridade: O ministério das nove horas." *RIHGB*, special volume, pt. 3 (1916): 105–94.

Leal, Victor Nunes. *Coronelismo, enxada e voto, o município e o regime representativo no Brasil*. 2d ed. São Paulo: Editora Alfa-Omega, 1975.

Leff, Nathaniel H. "Economic Retardation in Nineteenth Century Brazil." *Economic Historical Review* 25 (August 1972): 489–507.

Lenharo, Alcir. *As tropas de moderação: O abastecimento da Côrte na formação política do Brasil (1808–1842)*. São Paulo: Símbolo, 1979.

Levine, Robert M. *Pernambuco in the Brazilian Federation, 1889–1937*. Stanford: Stanford Univ. Press, 1978.

Lewin, Linda. "The Oligarchical Limitations of Social Banditry in Brazil: The Case of the 'Good' Thief, Antonio Silvino." *Past and Present* 82 (February 1979): 116–46.

———. *Politics and Parentela in Paraiba: A Case Study of Family-Based Oligarchy in Brazil*. Princeton: Princeton Univ. Press, 1987.

Libby, Douglas Cole. "Proto-Industrialisation in a Slave Society: The Case of Minas Gerais." *Journal of Latin American Studies* 23, no. 1 (February 1991): 1–36.

———. "Reconsidering Textile Production in Late Colonial Brazil: New Evidence from Minas Gerais." *Latin American Research Review* 32, no. 1 (1997): 88–108.

———. *Trabalho escravo e capital estrangeiro no Brasil: O caso de Morro Velho*. Belo Horizonte: Itataia, 1984.

———. *Transformação e trabalho em uma economia escravsta: Minas Gerais no século XIX*. São Paulo: Brasilense, 1988.

Lima, Augusto de, Jr. *A capitania das Minas Gerais (origens e formação)*. Belo Horizonte: Instituto de História, Letras, e Arte, 1965.

Lombardi, Mary. "The Frontier in Brazilian History: An Historiographical Essay." *Pacific Historical Review* 44 (November 1975): 434–46.

Love, Joseph L. *Rio Grande do Sul and Brazilian Regionalism, 1882–1930*. Stanford: Stanford Univ. Press, 1971.

————. *São Paulo in the Brazilian Federation*. Stanford: Stanford Univ. Press, 1980.

Maia, João de Azevedo Carnerio. *O município: Estudos sobre administração local*. Rio de Janeiro: G. Leuzinger e Filhos, 1883.

Mallon, Florencia E. *Peasant and Nation: The Making of Post-Colonial Mexico and Peru*. Berkeley: Univ. of California Press, 1995.

————. "The Promise and Dilemma of Subaltern Studies: Perspectives from Latin American History." *American Historical Review* 100 (December 1994): 1491–1515.

Manchester, Alan K. *British Preeminence in Brazil: Its Rise and Fall*. Chapel Hill: Univ. of North Carolina Press, 1933.

Marinho, José Antonio. *História do movimento político de 1842 em Minas Gerais*. Belo Horizonte: Itataia, 1977.

Martin, Percy Alvin. "Federalism in Brazil." *Hispanic American Historical Review* 18 (May 1938): 143–63.

Martins, Antonio de Assis. *Almanack administrativo, civil e industrial da província de Minas Gerais do ano de 1874 para servir no de 1875*. Rio de Janeiro: Typ. Diario do Rio de Janeiro, 1874.

Martins, Maria do Carmo Salazar. "Anotações sobre a organização administrativa da província de Minas Gerais." In *Sexto seminário sobre a economia mineira*. Belo Horizonte: CEDEPLAR, Universidade Federal de Minas Gerais, 1992.

————. "Revistando a província: Comarcas, termos, distritos e população de Minas Gerais em 1833–35." In *Quinto seminário sobre a economia mineira*. Belo Horizonte: CEDEPLAR, Universidade Federal de Minas Gerais, 1990.

Martins, Roberto B., and Amilcar Martins Filho. "Notes and Comments: 'Slavery in a Non-Export Economy': A Reply." *Hispanic American Historical Review* 64, no. 1 (1984): 135–46.

————. "Slavery in a Non-Export Economy: Nineteenth-Century Minas Gerais Revisited." *Hispanic American Historical Review* 63 (August 1983): 537–68.

Martins, Roberto B., and Maria do Carmo Salazar Martins. "As exportações de Minas Gerais no século XIX." *Revista brasileira de estudos políticos* 58 (January 1984): 105–20.

Mata-Machado, Bernardo. *História do sertão noroeste de Minas Gerais— 1690–1930*. Belo Horizonte: Impresa Oficial, 1990.

Matos, Raymundo José da Cunha. *Corografia histórica da provincia de Minas Gerais*. Vol. 1. Belo Horizonte: APM, 1979.

Mattos, Ilmar Rohloff de. *O tempo saquarema: A formação do estado imperial*. 2d ed. São Paulo: Editora Hucitec, 1990.

Mattoso, Katia M. de Queiros. *Bahia século XIX: Uma província no império*. Rio de Janeiro: Editora Nova Fronteira, 1992.

McBeth, Michael. "The Brazilian Recruit during the First Empire: Slave or Soldier?" In *Essays concerning the Socioeconomic History of Brazil and Portuguese India*. Ed. Dauril Alden and Warren Dean. Gainesville: Univ. of Florida Press, 1977.

Mello, Alfredo Pinto Vieira de. "O poder judiciário no Brasil, 1532–1871." *RIHGB*, special volume, pt. 3 (1916): 97–149.

Melo, Americo Brasiliense de Almeida e. *Os programas dos partidos do segundo império*. Brasília and Rio de Janeiro: Senado Federal, 1979.

Mesquita, Elpidio de. *Aspectos de um problema econômico*. Rio de Janeiro: Typ. Leuzinger, 1909.

Metcalf, Alida. *Family and Frontier in Colonial Brazil: Santana de Parnaiba, 1500–1822*. Berkeley: Univ. of California Press, 1992.

Mignolo, Walter D. "Colonial and Post-Colonial Discourse: Cultural Critique or Academic Colonialism?" *Latin American Research Review* 28, no. 3 (1993): 120–34.

Mourão, João Martins de Carvalho. "Os municípios, sua importância política no Brasil-Colonial e no Brasil-Reino." *RIHGB*, special volume, pt. 3 (1916): 299–318.

Nazarri, Muriel. *The Disappearance of the Dowry: Women, Family and Social Change in São Paulo, Brazil (1600–1900)*. Stanford: Stanford Univ. Press, 1991.

Neves, Antonio da Silva. "Chorographia do município de Boa Vista do Tremendal, estado de Minas Gerais." *Revista do Arquivo Público Mineiro* 13 (1908): 219–354.

———. "Chorographia do município do Rio Pardo." *Revista do Arquivo Público Mineiro* 13 (1908): 355–486.

"Notes and Comments: Comments on 'Slavery in a Non-Export Economy.'" *Hispanic American Historical Review* 63 (August 1983): 569–590.

Novais, Fernando A. *Portugal e Brasil na crise do antigo sistema colonial (1777–1808)*. 2d ed. São Paulo: Editora Hucitec, 1981.

Nugent, David. *Modernity at the Edge of Empire: State, Individual, and Nation in the Northern Peruvian Andes, 1885–1935*. Stanford: Stanford Univ. Press, 1997.

Ottoni, Carlos. "Da Diamantina a São Francisco, impressões de viagem." *Revista do Arquivo Público Mineiro* II (1906): 671–81.

Paiva, Clotilde Andrade. "Engenhos e casas de negócios em Minas oitocentista." In *Anais do sexto seminário sobre a economia mineira*. Belo Horizonte: CEDEPLAR, Universidade Federal de Minas Gerais, 1992.

Paiva, Clotilde Andrade, and Maria do Carmo S. Martins. "Minas Gerais em 1831: Notas sobre a estrutura ocupacional de alguns municípios." In *Anais do terceiro seminário sobre a economia mineira*. Belo Horizonte: CEDEPLAR, Universidade Federal de Minas Gerais, 1986.

Palmer, Thomas W., Jr. "A Momentous Decade in Brazilian Administrative History, 1831–1840." *Hispanic American Historical Review* 30 (May 1950): 209–17.

Pang, Eul-Soo. *Bahia in the First Brazilian Republic: Coronelismo and Oligarchies, 1889–1934*. Gainesville: Univ. of Florida Press, 1979.

Paula, Hermes de. *Montes Claros: Sua história, sua gente, seus costumes*. 3 vols. 2d ed. Montes Claros, 1979.

Pinto, Antônio Pereira, ed. *Reforma eleitoral*. Brasília: Editora da Universidade de Brasília, 1983.

Pitt-Rivers, Julian. "Honour and Social Status." In *Honour and Shame: The Values of Mediterranean Society*. Ed. J. G. Peristiany. Chicago: Univ. of Chicago Press, 1966.

Pohl, Johan Emanuel. *Viagem no interior do Brasil*. Trans. Milton Amado and Eugênio Amado. Belo Horizonte: Itataia, 1976.

Prado, Caio, Jr. *The Colonial Roots of Modern Brazil*. Trans. Suzette Macedo. Berkeley: Univ. of California Press, 1967.

Pratt, Mary Louise. *Imperial Eyes: Travel Writing and Transculturation*. London and New York: Routledge, 1992.

Prefeitura Municipal de Januária. *Álbum comemorativo do primeiro centenário*. Januária, 1960.

Queiroz, Maria Isaura Pereira de. *O mandonismo local na vida política brasileira e outros ensaios*. São Paulo: Instituto de Estudos Brasileiros da Universidade de São Paulo, 1976.

———. *Os cangaceiros: La epopeya bandolera del nordeste de Brasil*. Bogota: El Áncora, 1992.

Ramos, Donald. "Marriage and the Family in Colonial Vila Rica." *Hispanic American Historical Review* 54 (May 1974): 200–225.

———. "City and Country: The Family in Minas Gerais, 1804–1838." *Journal of Family History* 3 (1978): 361–75.

Reis, João Jose. *Slave Rebellion in Brazil: The Muslim Uprising of 1835 in Bahia*. Baltimore: Johns Hopkins Univ. Press, 1993.

Rezende, Astolfo de. "Polícia administrativa: Polícia judiciária: O código do processo de 1832: A lei de 3 de dezembro de 1841: A lei de 20 de setembro de 1871." *RIHGB*, special volume, pt. 3 (1916): 400–422.

Rippy, Fred J. "A Century and a Quarter of British Investment in Brazil." *Inter-American Economic Affairs* 6 (summer 1952): 83–92.

Rosa, João Guimarães. *Grandes sertões: Veredas*. Rio de Janeiro, 1956. Trans. James L. Taylor and Harriet de Onís as *The Devil to Pay in the Backlands* (New York, 1971).

Russell-Wood, A. J. R. "Frontiers in Colonial Brazil: Reality, Myth and Metaphor." In *Society and Government in Colonial Brazil, 1500–1822*. Ed. A. J. R. Russell-Wood. Variorum Collected Studies Series. Hampshire, 1992.

———. "Local Government in Portuguese America: A Study in Cultural Divergence." *Comparative Studies in Society and History* 16 (March 1974): 187–231.

Saint-Hilaire, Auguste de. *Viagem pelas províncias do Rio de Janeiro e Minas Gerais*. Trans. Vivaldi Moreira. São Paulo: Itataia, 1975.

Sampaio, Teodoro. *O Rio São Francisco e a chapada Diamantina*. Salvador: Editora Cruzeiro, 1939.

Santos, Joaquim Felício dos. *Memórias do distrito diamantino*. Belo Horizonte: Itataia, 1976.

Schwartz, Stuart B. "Magistracy and Society in Colonial Brazil." *Hispanic American Historical Review* 50, no. 4 (1970): 715–730.

———. *Sovereignty and Society in Colonial Brazil: The High Court of Bahia, 1609–1752*. Berkeley: Univ. of California Press, 1973.

Seed, Patricia. "Colonial and Postcolonial Discourse." *Latin American Research Review* 26, no. 3 (1991): 181–200.

———. *To Love, Honor and Obey in Colonial Mexico: Conflicts over Marriage Choice, 1574–1821*. Stanford: Stanford Univ. Press, 1988.

Seligman, Lester G. "Elite Recruitment and Political Development." In *Political Development and Social Change*, eds. Jason L. Finkle and Richard W. Gable. New York: Wiley, 1971.

Serviço de inspecção e defesa agricola: Questionários sobre as condições da agricultura dos 176 municípios do estado de Minas Gerais. Rio de Janeiro: Typ. do Serviço de Estatistica, 1913.

Silveira, Alvaro Astolpho da. *O algodoeiro em Minas Gerais*. Belo Horizonte: Imprensa Oficial do Estado, 1916.

Simonsen, Roberto C. *História econômica do Brasil, 1500–1820*. 8th ed. São Paulo: Editora Nacional, 1978.

Slenes, Robert W. "Os múltiplos de porcos e diamantes: A economia escrava de Minas Gerais no século XIX." *Estudos econômicos* 18, no. 3 (1988): 449–96.

Socolow, Susan. "Acceptable Partners: Marriage Choice in Colonial Argentina, 1778–1810." In *Sexuality and Marriage in Colonial Latin America*. Ed. Asunción Lavrin. Lincoln: Univ. of Nebraska Press, 1989.

Souza, Amaury de, "The Cangaço and the Politics of Violence in Northeast Brazil." In *Protest and Resistance in Angola and Brazil: Comparative Studies*. Ed. Ronald H. Chilcote. Berkeley: Univ. of California Press, 1972.

Souza, Francisco Belisário Soares de. *O sistema eleitoral no império*. Brasília: Senado Federal, 1979.

Souza, Laura de Mello e. *Desclassificados do ouro: A pobreza mineira no século XVIII*. 3d ed. Rio de Janeiro: Graal, 1990.

Souza, Paulino Jose Soares de. *Reforma eleitoral: Discursos proferidos nas sessões de 18 de junho, 20 e 22 de julho pelo Conselheiro Paulino José Soares de Souza*. Rio de Janeiro: Typ. Imp. e Const. de Villeneuve & Cia., 1874.

Spivak, Gayatri Chakravorty. "Subaltern Studies; Deconstructing Historiography." In *Selected Subaltern Studies*. Ed. Ranajit Guha and Gayatri Chakravorty Spivak. New York and Oxford: Oxford Univ. Press, 1988.

Spix, J. B., and S. F. P. Martius. *Viagem pelo Brasil*. Trans. Luica Furquim Lahmeyer. 2 vols. Rio de Janeiro: Imprensa Nacional, 1938.

Stein, Stanley J. "The Historiography of Brazil, 1808–1889." *Hispanic American Historical Review* 40 (May 1960): 234–78.

———. *Vassouras: A Brazilian Coffee County, 1850–1900*. Cambridge: Cambridge Univ. Press, 1957.

Stein, Stanley J., and Barbara H. Stein. *The Colonial Heritage of Latin America*. New York: Oxford Univ. Press, 1970.

Stern, Steve J. *The Secret History of Gender: Women, Men, and Power in Late Colonial Mexico*. Chapel Hill: Univ. of North Carolina Press, 1995.

Thurner, Mark. *From Two Republics to One Divided: Contradictions of Postcolonial Nationmaking in Andean Peru*. Durham: Duke Univ. Press, 1997.

Torres, João Camilo de Oliveira. *A democracia coroada: Teoria política do imperio do Brasil*. Petropolis: Editora Vozes, 1964.

———. *História de Minas Gerais*. 5 vols. Belo Horizonte: Difusão Pan-Americana do Livro, 1961.

Uricoechea, Fernando. *The Patrimonial Foundations of the Brazilian Bureaucratic State*. Berkeley: Univ. of California Press, 1980.

Vasconcelos, Diogo L. Á. P. de. *Historia antiga das Minas Gerais*. 2 vols. Rio de Janeiro: Imprensa Nacional, 1948.

———. *História média das Minas Gerais*. Belo Horizonte: Imprensa Oficial, 1918.

Velloso, Antonio Augusto. "Chorographia mineira: O município de Montes Claros." *Revista do Arquivo Público Mineiro* 2 (1897): 561–98.

Vianna, Nelson. *Efemérides montesclarenses*. Rio de Janeiro: Irmãos Pongetti, 1964.

Vianna, Oliveira. *O ocaso do império*. 3d ed. Rio de Janeiro: José Olympio, 1959.

Vianna, Urbino de Sousa. *Monographia do município de Montes Claros, breves apontamentos históricos, geographicos e descriptivos*. Belo Horizonte: Imprensa Oficial do Estado de Minas Gerais, 1916.

Vidal, Hernán. "The Concept of Colonial and Postcolonial Discourse: A Perspective from Literary Criticism." *Latin American Research Review* 28, no. 3 (1993): 113–19.

Wells, James. *Exploring and Travelling Three Thousand Miles through Brazil: From Rio de Janeiro to Maranhão*. 2 vols. London: S. Low, Marston, Searle & Rivington, 1887.

Wirth, John D. *Minas Gerais in the Brazilian Federation, 1889–1937*. Stanford: Stanford Univ. Press, 1977.

Zemella, Mafalda P. *O abastecimento da capitania das Minas Gerais no século XVIII*. São Paulo: Editora Hucitec, 1990.

Zenha, Edmundo. *O município no Brasil, 1532–1700*. São Paulo: Instituto Progresso, 1948.

Index